Applied Power
Analysis for
the Behavioral
Sciences

Applied Power Analysis for the Behavioral Sciences

Christopher L. Aberson
Humboldt State University

Routledge
Taylor & Francis Group
New York   London

Routledge
Taylor & Francis Group
270 Madison Avenue
New York, NY 10016

Routledge
Taylor & Francis Group
27 Church Road
Hove, East Sussex BN3 2FA

Printed in the United States of America on acid-free paper
10 9 8 7 6 5 4 3 2

International Standard Book Number: 978-1-84872-834-9 (Hardback) 978-1-84872-835-6 (Paperback)

Library of Congress Cataloging-in-Publication Data

Aberson, Christopher L.
   Applied power analysis for the behavioral sciences / Christopher L. Aberson.
     p. cm.
   Includes bibliographical references and indexes.
   ISBN 978-1-84872-834-9 (alk. paper) -- ISBN 978-1-84872-835-6 (alk. paper)
     1. Social sciences--Statistical methods. 2. SPSS (Computer file) 3. Statistical power analysis. I. Title.

HA29.A265 2010
300.285'555--dc22   2009034407

Visit the Taylor & Francis Web site at
http://www.taylorandfrancis.com

and the Psychology Press Web site at
http://www.psypress.com

CONTENTS

Preface   ix

Chapter 1   What Is Power? Why Is Power Important?   1

Introduction   1
Review of Null Hypothesis Significance Testing   1
Effect Sizes and Their Interpretation   2
What Has an Impact on Power?   3
Central and Noncentral Distributions   6
Misconceptions About Power   8
Empirical Reviews of Power   9
Overview of Approaches to Determining
    Effect Size for Power Analysis   10
Post Hoc Power   13
How Much Power?   15
Summary   16
Notes   16

Chapter 2   Chi Square and Tests for Proportions   17

Introduction   17
Necessary Information   17
Factors Affecting Power   18
Key Statistics   18
Tests for Single Samples and Independent
    Proportions   29
Summary   35
Notes   36

Chapter 3   Independent Samples and Paired *t*-Tests   37

Introduction   37
Necessary Information   37
Factors Affecting Power   38
Key Statistics   39
A Note About Effect Size for Two-Group
   Comparisons   41
Dealing With Unequal Variances, Unequal
   Sample Sizes, and Violation of Assumptions   51
Additional Issues   62
Summary   65
Note   65

Chapter 4   Correlations and Differences Between
   Correlations   67

Introduction   67
Necessary Information   67
Factors Affecting Power   67
Zero-Order Correlation   68
Comparing Two Independent Correlations   71
Comparing Two Dependent Correlations
   (One Variable in Common)   75
Comparing Two Dependent Correlations
   (No Variables in Common)   77
Note on Effect Sizes for Comparing Correlations   83
Additional Issues   85
Summary   85
Note   85

Chapter 5   Between-Subjects ANOVA (One Factor,
   Two or More Factors)   87

Introduction   87
Necessary Information   87
Factors Affecting Power   87
Omnibus Versus Contrast Power   88
Key Statistics   88
SPSS Syntax for the One-Factor ANOVA   94
Other Contrast Options for One-Factor ANOVA   95
ANOVA With Two Factors   101
Additional Issues   108
Summary   111
Note   112

Chapter 6	Within-Subjects Designs	113
	Introduction	113
	Necessary Information	113
	Factors Affecting Power	113
	Key Statistics	114
	Multivariate Approach to Repeated Measures	121
	Trend Analysis	124
	Additional Issues	130
	Summary	130
	Notes	130
Chapter 7	Mixed-Model ANOVA and Multivariate ANOVA	133
	Introduction	133
	Necessary Information	133
	Factors Affecting Power	133
	Key Statistics	134
	Mixed-Model Designs	134
	Multivariate ANOVA	140
	Additional Issues	148
	Summary	149
Chapter 8	Multiple Regression	151
	Introduction	151
	Necessary Information	151
	Factors Affecting Power	152
	Key Statistics	153
	Power for Detecting Differences Between Two Dependent Coefficients	166
	Power for Detecting Differences Between Two Independent Coefficients	169
	Power for Comparing Two Independent R^2 Values	172
	Additional Issues	175
	Summary	178
	Note	179
Chapter 9	Covariate Analyses and Regression Interactions	181
	Introduction	181
	Analysis of Covariance	181
	Moderated Regression Analysis (Regression With Interactions)	185
	Multivariate Analysis of Covariance	197

	Additional Issues	198
	Summary	201
Chapter 10	Precision Analysis for Confidence Intervals	203
	Introduction	203
	Necessary Information	204
	Confidence Intervals	204
	Types of Confidence Intervals	205
	Confidence Limits Around Differences Between Means	206
	Determining Levels of Precision	210
	Confidence Intervals Around Effect Sizes	210
	Precision for a Correlation	213
	Precision for R^2 Change	214
	Precision for the R^2 Model	216
	Supporting Null Hypotheses	216
	Additional Issues	221
	Summary	223
Chapter 11	Additional Issues and Resources	225
	Introduction	225
	How to Report Power Analyses	225
	Statistical Test Assumptions	226
	Effect Size Conversion Formulae	227
	Probability of Replication	228
	General (Free) Resources for Power and Related Topics	230
	Resources for Additional Analyses	231
	Comparison of Power Programs	232
	SPSS Warnings and How to Deal With Them	234
	Improving Power Without Increasing Sample Size or Cost	235
References		239
Author Index		245
Subject Index		249

PREFACE

Power analyses differ in important ways from other statistical approaches. Most statistical analyses begin with existing data, subject the data to analysis, and then focus on interpretation of the results. Power analysis is different. Power analysis does not involve existing data. In fact, power analyses are only meaningful when conducted prior to data collection. In this manner, it is useful to think of power analysis as part of the hypothesis statement process. When stating a hypothesis, it is usually of the form of "Group X differs from Group Y" on our dependent measure. The statistical core of this statement is Group X and Group Y will differ. For power analysis, we go beyond this basic statement and specify how large a difference would be meaningful to detect between the two groups.

Another way power analysis differs from other statistical analyses is in term of interpretation. For most statistical procedures, texts devote considerable time to interpretation of result or computer output. In contrast, the output for power analysis is simple and requires little interpretation or discussion. Generally, output provides a single value, the power for the test of interest. The interpretation of output for such analyses does not involve much interpretation aside from an evaluation of whether our study is sensitive enough to detect our effects of interest given a particular sample size.

This book also differs considerably from earlier texts on the topic (e.g., Cohen, 1988) in that I do not present power tables or formula for extrapolating between tabled values. Instead, most chapters present hand calculations to facilitate conceptual understanding but rely heavily on computer-generated analyses as the primary approaches for analyses. Given the computational tools available through SPSS's base package, approaches that involve reference to lengthy tables are no longer necessary.

This book is intended as a supplementary text for graduate-level and advanced undergraduate research methods, experimental design, quasi-experimental methods, psychometrics, statistics, advanced statistics, and/or multivariate statistics courses taught in the behavioral, social, biological, and medical sciences. I expect researchers in these fields will appreciate the book's practical emphasis and be able to make use of the materials in their research. Additionally, the present text would work well in a short course dedicated to statistical power. Readers will need only a statistical background consistent with an introductory statistics course to understand fully most of the material in the book.

OVERVIEW OF THE BOOK

Chapter 1 reviews significance testing, introduces power, and presents issues impacting power. Chapters 2 through 9 cover power analysis strategies for a variety of common designs. Chapter 2 (Chi-Square and proportions) and Chapter 3 (*t*-tests) also introduce issues such as non-central distributions and provide examples of the types of decisions and considerations important to power analyses. Regardless of the technique of interest for your design, read Chapters 1–3 first. Chapter 4 covers power for correlations and for tests comparing correlations. Chapters 5 through 7 address ANOVA designs for between, within, and mixed models as well as multivariate ANOVA. Chapter 8 covers multiple regression and comparisons of regression coefficients. Chapter 9 addresses covariate designs and regression interactions. Chapter 10 focuses on precision analysis for confidence intervals around mean difference, correlations, and effect sizes. Chapter 11 addresses a number of smaller topics such as how to report power analyses, freeware and commercial software for power analyses, and how to increase power without increasing sample size. Chapters focusing on simpler analyses (e.g., t-test, between subjects ANOVA) present detailed formulae and calculation examples. However, chapters focusing on more complex topics (e.g., within subjects ANOVA, ANCOVA) present only computer-based analyses as calculation examples would extend several pages and do little to advance understanding.

FORMULAE AND CALCULATIONS

A major focus of this text is conducting analyses using SPSS. However, understanding the basics of the calculations surrounding analyses is very important. To that end, whenever it is possible and not too complicated, I provide detailed calculations for sample analyses. Often these calculations involve several steps and multiple formulae. One of my points of contention with many statistical resources is that calculations are often not clearly detailed. That is, authors present formulae and then jump to the result without demonstrating the steps of the calculation. When I encounter this approach, it often takes some time to figure out what goes where and how the authors derived values. For this reason, I provide detailed calculations, comment on what goes where, and how it got there. This approach is likely a bit more like an introductory than an advanced statistics text. However, the added detail makes the calculations easier to follow.

In many places throughout the text, I present formulae for population values. In practice, we rarely perform such calculations. I present population values to serve as a reminder that the calculations involved in power analyses generally involve a priori estimates of what the population looks like (e.g., estimates of the population effect size).

APPROACHES TO POWER

Several chapters provide three different approaches to the calculation of power. The first involves estimation of power. Estimation involves use of central rather than non-central distributions. I debated inclusion of estimation techniques. On the one hand, estimation approaches enhance understanding of constructs through direct calculation of values. On the other hand, estimation does not always yield accurate power because it uses the wrong distribution. Ultimately, I included estimation procedures, as these techniques are excellent teaching tools. The values may not be completely accurate, but the conceptual piece is clearer with estimation demonstrations.

The next approach involves hand calculations with SPSS to calculate power. Hand calculations provide accurate values for every estimate required for power analyses, except the power value itself. Hand calculations end at the non-centrality parameter. We then take that value to SPSS for calculation of power. This is because power calculations require the use of non-central distributions. Calculations based on non-central distributions are not practical to complete by hand, as they involve numerous iterations. When completing hand calculations in several chapters, I include a single line of SPSS Syntax that handles the final step of the calculation.

The final approach involves use of SPSS syntax for all calculations (described in more detail below). I present these approaches in Chapters 2–10. This approach requires input of descriptive statistics and few calculations. For this approach, syntax files include considerable annotation (more on this approach below).

THE SPSS SYNTAX APPROACH TO POWER ANALYSIS

SPSS contains all the tools for conducting a number of power analyses. These procedures appear throughout the text. SPSS pull-down menus cannot accomplish these analyses. You must use SPSS syntax for these analyses. Although there are some options to obtain power using pull-down menus, these functions require a data file. The power analyses described in this book are a priori, meaning we do not have data yet.

The textbook website includes the SPSS files used in the text and some additional materials that extend analyses (e.g., multiple regression with four predictors). The web site address is www.psypress.com/applied-power-analysis.

I wrote the SPSS syntax included in the text from scratch but several resources informed much of the programming. Articles by D'Amico, Neilands, and Zambarano (2001) and Osborn (2006) first suggested the possibility of using SPSS for power analyses. In several cases, after writing syntax procedures, discovery of protocols written by others helped polish the approaches presented in the text. In particular, several files written by Marta Garcia-Granero indexed on the incredibly useful SPSS Tools website (spsstools.net) were of great value. Syntax written for other techniques (e.g., Lipsey & Wilson, 2001; Preacher & Hayes, 2004) provided great how-to examples for many of the procedures in the book as well.

I have tested all the syntax files in SPSS 17.0 (also known as PASW Statistics 17.0) as well as several earlier versions. I tested the syntax presented in this book against results produced by commercial and freeware programs such as SamplePower, G*Power, PiFace, SAS, and MMRPower. The approaches match with minor differences found across programs, primarily based on whether approaches employ degrees of freedom or sample size in calculations. When a choice exists, I use degrees of freedom as this produces a slightly more conservative test. Note that if you find minor differences between my approaches and others this is likely the source of the difference.

If you are unfamiliar with SPSS syntax files, the following instructions will get you started. First, open SPSS. Next, choose 'File' then 'Open' then 'Syntax.' Choose the file from the CD you want to run (each file is designated by chapter and analysis). Once this file is open, use the notes presented in the book regarding which lines to modify to make any desired changes. After making the changes, choose 'Run' then 'All.' An output window will open with your analysis represented (just as if you had run an analysis using pull-down options). Readers new to SPSS syntax may reasonably be intimidated by the command language structure. For more guidance on the use of SPSS syntax, the tutorial included in the SPSS program provides a nice overview of the process (choose 'Help' then 'Tutorial'). Keep in mind that using the materials provided in this text does not require you to write your own syntax, only to modify the files provided.

In using SPSS for power analysis, I encountered a handful of bugs and error messages. Most of these errors are inconsistent (e.g., try the same syntax again and it works fine). Examples of errors found when running analyses and solutions to the problem appear in Chapter 11.

ACKNOWLEDGMENTS

The idea for this text came about following preparation for a workshop presentation on power. Jodie Ullman of California State University, San Bernardino, invited me to teach the workshop (and to teach several subsequent workshops) and was helpful and supportive throughout. Without her invitation, I would never have written this book. Dale Berger from Claremont Graduate University provided detailed and incisive comments on drafts of most of these chapters that helped improve the text considerably. Thank you, Dale, for the extraordinary time you spent helping me with this project. Michael Smithson graciously allowed me use of several of the protocols found in the precision analysis chapter that are included on the CD. Geoff Cumming allowed use of figures produced by his ESCI software as well as helpful comments on using the software. Stewart I. Donaldson, Claremont Graduate University; Shlomo Sawilowsky, Wayne State University; Allen Huffcutt, Bradley University; and Wesley Schultz, California State University, San Marcos, all provided excellent comments on drafts of the manuscript that improved the book substantially. SPSS, PASS, and nQuery generously provided free copies of their commercial software for power analysis. Finally, thank you to my wife, Nanda, and son, Ernesto, who remind me every day that there are things in life far more important than statistics.

ERRATA AND WEBPAGE

Although I took great care in editing this text, I expect some errors exist and some material remains less than clear. Please do not hesitate to contact me at chris.aberson@humboldt.edu with questions. As a supplement to the book website (www.psypress.com/applied-power-analysis), I plan to maintain a page with errata and syntax updates at www.humboldt.edu/~psych/fs/aberson/power.

1

WHAT IS POWER? WHY IS POWER IMPORTANT?

INTRODUCTION

This chapter reviews null hypothesis significance testing (NHST), introduces effect sizes and factors that influence power, discusses the importance of power in design, presents an introduction to noncentral distributions, addresses misconceptions about power, discusses typical levels of power in published work, examines strategies for determining an appropriate effect size for power analysis, critiques post hoc power analyses, and discusses typical levels of power used for design.

REVIEW OF NULL HYPOTHESIS SIGNIFICANCE TESTING

Null hypothesis significance testing focuses on conditional probabilities. The conditional probabilities used in NHST procedures address how likely it is to obtain an observed (i.e., sample) result given a specific assumption about the population. Formally, the assumption about the population is called the *null hypothesis* (e.g., the population mean is 0), and the *observed result* is what the sample produces (e.g., a sample mean of 10). Statistical tests such as z, χ^2, t, and analysis of variance (ANOVA) determine how likely the sample result or any result more distant from the null hypothesis would be if the null hypothesis were true. This probability is then compared to a set criterion. For example, if a result this far or farther from the null hypothesis would occur less than 5% of the time when the null is true, then we will reject the null. More formally, the criterion is termed a Type I or α error rate (5% corresponds to $\alpha = .05$).

Table 1.1, common to most introductory statistical texts, summarizes decisions about null hypotheses and compares them to what is true for

Table 1.1 Reality versus Statistical Decisions

		Reality	
		Null Hypothesis True	**Null Hypothesis False**
Research decision	Fail to reject null	Correct failure to reject null $1 - \alpha$	Type II or β error
	Reject null	Type I or α error	Correct rejection of null $1 - \beta$

the data ("reality"). Two errors exist. A Type I or α error reflects rejecting a true null hypothesis. Researchers control this probability by setting a value for it (e.g., use a two-tailed test with $\alpha = .05$). Type II or β errors reflect failure to reject a false null hypothesis. Controlling this probability is at the core of this book. However, Type II errors are far more difficult to control than Type I errors. Table 1.1 also represents correct decisions, either failing to reject a true null hypothesis or rejecting a false null. The probability of rejecting a false null hypothesis is power. Of course, this topic receives considerable coverage throughout the text.

For power analysis, the focus is on situations for which the expectation is that the null hypothesis is false (see Chapter 10 for more comments on this). Power analysis addresses the ability to reject the null hypothesis when it is false.

EFFECT SIZES AND THEIR INTERPRETATION

One of the most important statistics for power analysis is the effect size. Significance tests tell us only whether an effect is present. Effect sizes tell us how strong or weak that effect is.

Although researchers increasingly present effect size alongside NHST results, it is important to recognize that the term *effect size* refers to many different measures. The interpretation of an effect size is dependent on the specific effect size statistic presented. For example, a value of 0.14 would be relatively small in discussing the d statistic but large when discussing η^2. For this reason, it is important to be explicit when presenting effect sizes. Always reference the value (d, r, η^2, etc.) rather than just noting "effect size."

Table 1.2 provides a brief summary of common effect size measures and definitions of small, medium, and large values for each (Cohen, 1992). Please note that the small, medium, and large labels facilitate comparison across effects, but these values do not indicate the practical importance of effects.

Table 1.2 Measures of Effect Size, Their Use, and a Rough Guide to Interpretation

Effect Size	Common Use/Presentation	Small	Medium	Large
Φ (also known as V or w)	Omnibus effect for χ^2	0.10	0.30	0.50
h	Comparing proportions	0.20	0.50	0.80
d	Comparing two means	0.20	0.50	0.80
r	Correlation	0.10	0.30	0.50
q	Comparing two correlations	0.10	0.30	0.50
f	Omnibus effect for ANOVA/regression	0.10	0.25	0.40
η^2	Omnibus effect for ANOVA	0.01	0.06	0.14
f^2	Omnibus effect for ANOVA/regression	0.02	0.15	0.35
R^2	Omnibus effect for regression	0.02	0.13	0.26

WHAT HAS AN IMPACT ON POWER?

I learned an acronym in graduate school that I use to teach about influences on power. That acronym is BEAN, standing for beta (β), effect size (E), alpha (α), and sample size (N). We can specify any three of these values and calculate the fourth. Power analysis typically involves specifying α, effect size, and β to find sample size.

Power is $1 - \beta$. As α becomes more liberal (e.g., moving from .01 to .05), power increases. As effect sizes increase (e.g., the mean is further from the null value relative to the standard deviation, SD), power increases. As sample size rises, power increases.

Several figures represent the influence of effect size, α, and sample size on power. Figure 1.1 presents two distributions: the null and the alternative. The null distribution is the distribution specified in the null hypothesis and represented on the left-hand side of the graph. For this example, the null hypothesis is that the population mean is zero. The null sampling distribution of the mean is centered on zero, reflecting this null hypothesis. The alternative sampling distribution, found on the right-hand side of each graph, reflects the distribution of means from which we are actually sampling. Several additional figures follow and are useful for comparison with Figure 1.1. For simplicity, the population standard deviation and the null hypothesis remain constant for each figure. For each of the figures, the lines represent the z-critical values.

A sample mean allows for rejection of the null hypothesis if it falls outside the critical values that we set based on the null distribution. The vertical lines in Figure 1.1 represent the critical values that cut off

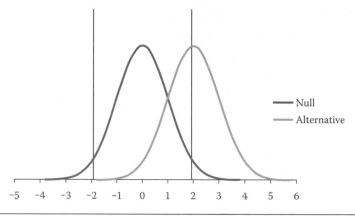

Figure 1.1 Null and alternative distributions for a two-tailed test and $\alpha = .05$.

2.5% in each tail of the null distribution (i.e., a two-tailed test with $\alpha = .05$). A little more than half of samples drawn from the alternative distribution fall above the upper critical value (the area to the right of the line near +2.0). Sample means that fall above the critical value allow for rejection of the null hypothesis. That area reflects the power of the test, about .50 in this example.

Now compare the power in Figure 1.1 to power in Figure 1.2. The difference between the situations represented in these two figures is that the effect size, represented in terms of the difference between the null and alternative means, is larger for Figure 1.2 than Figure 1.1 (recall that standard deviation is constant for both situations). The second figure shows that as the effect size increases, the distributions are further

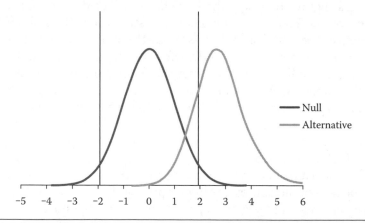

Figure 1.2 Null and alternative distributions for a two-tailed test with increased effect size and $\alpha = .05$.

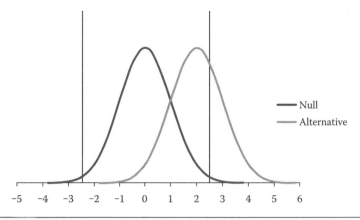

Figure 1.3 Null and alternative distributions for a two-tailed test with $\alpha = .01$.

apart, and power increases because more of the alternative distribution falls in the rejection region.

Next, we consider the impact of α on power. Figures 1.1 and 1.2 presented a two-tailed test with $\alpha = .05$. Figure 1.3 reduces α to .01. Notice the change in the location of the vertical lines representing the critical values for rejection of the null hypothesis. Comparing Figures 1.1 and 1.3 shows that reducing α decreases power. The area in the alternative distribution that falls within the rejection region is smaller for Figure 1.3 than 1.1. Smaller values for α make it more difficult to reject the null hypothesis. When it is more difficult to reject the null hypothesis, power decreases.

Figure 1.4 demonstrates the impact of a larger sample size on power. This figure presents distributions that are less dispersed than those in

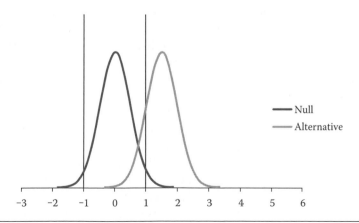

Figure 1.4 Null and alternative distributions for a two-tailed test and $\alpha = .05$ with a large sample.

Figure 1.1. For this figure, the x-axis represents raw scores rather than z-values. Recall from the central limit theorem that the dispersion of a distribution of sample means (standard error of the mean) is a function of the standard deviation in the population and the sample size. Specifically, this is the standard deviation divided by the square root of sample size. As sample size rises, dispersion decreases. As seen in Figure 1.4 (assuming that the difference between the means of the distributions are the same for Figures 1.1 and 1.4), the reduced dispersion that results from larger samples increases power.

For an interactive tutorial on the topic, see the WISE (Web Interface for Statistics Education) home page at http://wise.cgu.edu. The Web page includes a detailed interactive applet and tutorial on power analysis (see Aberson, Berger, Healy, & Romero, 2002, for a description and evaluation of the tutorial assignment). Chapters 2 and 3, particularly the material relevant to Figures 2.1 and 3.1, provide descriptions useful for power calculations.

CENTRAL AND NONCENTRAL DISTRIBUTIONS

The examples presented in the preceding section use the normal distribution. In practice, these tests are less common in most fields than those conducted using t, F, or χ^2. Power analyses become more complex when using these distributions. Power calculations are based on the alternative distribution. When we use a z-test with a normally distributed null distribution, the alternative distribution is also normally distributed no matter how large the effect size is. Distributions of this type are termed *central distributions*. However, when we deal with other tests, the alternative distribution takes on different shapes that vary with effect size. These are termed *noncentral distributions*. When conducting tests such as t, F, or χ^2, we actually deal with both central and noncentral distributions. The null distribution is a central distribution, and the alternative distribution is a noncentral distribution.

Central and noncentral distributions differ in important ways. Degrees of freedom are the only influence on the shape of central distributions. The null distribution when using t, F, or χ^2 is a central distribution. Since the null hypothesis specifies no effect, these distributions correspond to situations for which the effect size is zero (i.e., effect size is constant). Thus, the shape of the null distribution varies only with degrees of freedom. For any specific value for degrees of freedom, there is just one distribution used to compute probabilities. For example, if we have a t-distribution with $df = 50$, we can calculate the area at or above $t = 2.9$ (or any other value).

Degrees of freedom and effect size define the shape of noncentral distributions. For any specific value for degrees of freedom, there are infinite possible effect sizes. Since there are infinite possible values for effect size for each of the infinite possibilities for degrees of freedom, there are simply too many possible combinations for construction of tables that allow simple calculation of probabilities. In fact, probability calculations require iterative techniques that until recently were beyond the scope of most desktop computer resources. Suffice it to say, calculations of probabilities associated with these distributions are far more complicated than for central distributions. The text provides several SPSS protocols for performing these calculations.

Figure 1.5[1] demonstrates differences between central and noncentral distributions using an example of a t-distribution with 10 degrees of freedom. The null distribution, on the left, is symmetrical. Recall that the null distribution is a central distribution. The distribution on the right, however, is nonsymmetrical. This is the noncentral t-distribution. This is the distribution used to calculate power. The noncentral t represents the actual population distribution for t from which we are sampling. As in previous examples, the critical value is defined in relation to the null distribution, but calculation of power focuses on where the critical value falls in relation to the alternative distribution (on the right). On this figure, the vertical line slightly to the left of 2.30 on the x-axis represents the t-critical value. Because the shape of the noncentral t-distribution depends on both the degrees of freedom and the effect size, there is no

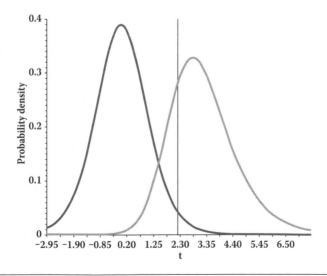

Figure 1.5 Central versus noncentral t-distributions ($df = 10$).

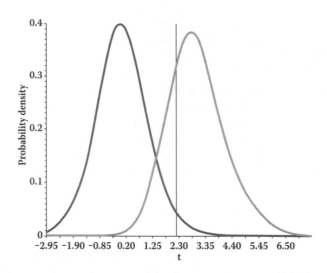

Figure 1.6 Central versus noncentral t-distributions ($df = 100$).

simple table such as we find in the back of statistics texts for the central t-distribution. Calculation of area based on the noncentral distribution is much more difficult.

Noncentral distributions sometimes look similar to central distributions. Figure 1.6[2] demonstrates a situation with 100 degrees of freedom. Again, the vertical line slightly to the left of 2.30 on the x-axis represents the t-critical value. Here, the central and noncentral distributions are similar. As sample size increases, central and noncentral distribution shapes begin to converge. In situations like this, approximations of power using central distributions produce reasonably accurate estimates. However, given the availability of computer protocols that are presented in this book, approximation is a poor strategy for analysis (but see the discussion of the value of approximation in this chapter).

MISCONCEPTIONS ABOUT POWER

Students and researchers often misunderstand factors relating to statistical power. One common misunderstanding is the relationship between Type II and Type I errors. Given a design with a 5% Type I error rate, researchers often predict the rate of Type II errors also to be 5% (Hunter, 1997; Nickerson, 2000). The probability of a Type II error is generally much greater than 5%, and in a given study, the probability of a Type II error is inversely related to the Type I error rate. In practice, a 5% Type II error rate is extraordinarily small. A commonly recommended goal for power is 80%. This corresponds to a Type II error rate of 20%.

Another misconception is the belief that failure to reject the null hypothesis is sufficient evidence that the null hypothesis is true (Nickerson, 2000). Even when power is 80%, there still exists a 20% chance of making a Type II error. Compare this rate to the commonly used Type I error rate of 5%. The Type I rate suggests that falsely rejecting a true hypothesis occurs 1 time out of 20. The Type II rate suggests that failing to reject a false null hypothesis happens one time out of every five samples. Thus, when researchers make claims about supporting the null hypothesis based on failing to reject the null hypothesis, these claims usually provide little statistical evidence.

EMPIRICAL REVIEWS OF POWER

Surveys of power in published work in the behavioral sciences indicate that samples generally do not provide adequate power for detecting small- and medium-size effects. Power surveys across fields such as abnormal psychology (e.g., Cohen, 1962; Sedlmeier & Gigerenzer, 1989); management (Cashen & Geiger, 2004; Mone, Mueller, & Mauland, 1996); rehabilitation counseling (Kosciulek & Szymanski, 1993); psychiatry (Brown & Hale, 1992); behavioral ecology and animal behavior (Jennions & Møller, 2003); adult education (West, 1985); and consulting, clinical, and social psychology (Rossi, 1990) all suggest that low power is common. For small effects, these surveys report typical power levels of .15 to .26, indicating that power to detect small effects is generally low. Power to detect medium effects was higher, with reported ranges from .39 to .66. Not surprisingly, power for detecting large effects was best, ranging from .77 to .90.

Notably, in a review of articles published over a 1-year period in major health psychology outlets, power was consistently higher than reported in the reviews just mentioned (Maddock & Rossi, 2001). This finding existed across small (power = .36), medium (.77), and large (.92) effect sizes. For small and medium effects, studies reporting federal funding were more powerful (.41 for funded vs. .28 for not funded for small effects and .80 for funded vs. .71 for not funded for medium effects). Federally funded projects often require power analyses as part of the grant submission, so requiring power analyses appears to promote designs that are more sensitive.

The relatively poor statistical power observed in published work suggests that either researchers do not conduct power analyses or if they do conduct power analyses, they assume large effects. However, the Maddock and Rossi (2001) study found that when required to conduct power analyses, researchers designed studies with more power. Broadly speaking, this suggests that when left to their own devices, researchers tend to design underpowered studies.

Another possible reason for low power in published work reflects a fundamental misunderstanding of how to address issues of effect size for sample size planning. Most power analyses begin, in one form or another, with an effect size estimate. The researcher determines sample size based on effect size, the desired level of power, and Type I error. In my experience, estimation of the effect size is problematic to the point of being arbitrary (see also Lipscy, 1990). There are several reasons for this. Researchers often use standard effect size estimates (i.e., small, medium, and large) without reference to the size of an effect that would be practically important. In consulting on power analyses, it is my sense that many researchers think that they are being conservative if they choose a medium effect size. Compounding these problems are failures to understand typical effect sizes in the field of inquiry. Many fields in the behavioral sciences deal with small effects, clearly calling into question the approach of "medium effect size as conservative."

Another issue is that researchers sometimes begin with a conservative effect size estimate but then, discouraged by large sample size requirements for adequate power, increase their effect size to reduce sample size. A related problem occurs when researchers begin with an idea of the sample size they want and design backward to find the effect size they plan to detect.

In short, there are many ways to do a bad job in estimating effect size for power analysis. The approaches recommended in this book involve a focus on designing to detect meaningful effects. Of course, this question can be problematic as well. The following section on determining effect size will be used for power analysis expands on this discussion.

OVERVIEW OF APPROACHES TO DETERMINING EFFECT SIZE FOR POWER ANALYSIS

Perhaps the most difficult requirement of power analysis is estimation of effect size. Designing for too small an effect wastes resources through collection of more data than needed. Designing for too large an effect does not achieve the desired level of power. Unfortunately, determining an effect size for power analysis is not always easy. Good estimates of effect size require careful consideration. This section reviews strategies for determining effect size for power analyses and presents critiques of each approach.

Perhaps the most important point in this section is that the effect size you choose impacts the outcome of the power analysis more than any other decision. Do not take this choice lightly. Good power analyses start with informed choices about effects. The more time, effort, and most importantly, thought put into this estimate, the better the analysis.

Determination of Expectations for Small, Medium, or Large Effects

Use of arbitrary effect size estimates (e.g., small, medium, large) is a bad approach. Sometimes, this approach is the most effective or useful approach available, but premature use takes consideration away from important issues such as whether effects are meaningful (discussed in greater detail in the next section), the raw differences we wish to detect, and the precision of measurement. Lenth (2000) gives a useful demonstration of these issues in a test for a medium effect. One example involves a between-subjects test that detects relatively a roughly 1-mm difference between groups using an instrument with a relatively large standard deviation (1.9 mm). The second test involves a paired test using a more precise instrument ($SD = 0.7$ mm). This test allows for detection of mean differences that are nearly six times smaller than in the first example. Although the same effect sizes exist for both tests, the second test is far more sensitive to the construct of interest.

Another issue is that use of "shirt size" effects often does not correspond to careful thought about the specific problem of interest. Whenever students consult with me on power analysis, I ask what sort of effect size they plan for their design. Most say medium. When questioned, few can justify why they chose that level of effect other than to say that it sounded like a reasonable compromise between small and large.

Effects Based on Previous Work

Often, researchers look to previous work as a guide to estimating effect sizes. Certainly, having some information about effects is better than arbitrarily specifying effects. However, this approach does not address whether the effect sizes presented in previous work reflect a meaningful result. Also, it is important to recognize that the effect observed in any single study reflects a sample. This sample effect size may or may not be a good estimate of the population effect size. For effect sizes based on previous work, the sample effect is more likely to be an overestimation of the population effect than an underestimation. Published work tends to favor significant results. Studies with larger effects are more likely to produce significant results, so the published literature often overrepresents larger effects.

Effect size estimates derived from a body of literature (e.g., 10 studies examining similar effects found d ranging from 0.10 to 0.30) temper concerns about getting a reasonable estimate of the effect as there is a larger sample of effect sizes used in estimation. In situations like this, representation of significant (and therefore larger) effects remains an issue, so choosing from the lower end of estimates rather than the upper end (e.g., 0.10ish rather than 0.30ish) is a conservative decision that sometimes offsets overrepresentation. Carefully conducted meta-analyses that include unpublished literature reduce sampling concerns and may provide accurate effect size estimates.

Examination of previous work is a good reality check when used in conjunction with the "meaningful effect" strategy discussed in the next section. What others found provides information regarding typical effect sizes for the area of inquiry and helps provide context for interpretation of effect sizes. For example, if effects in your field typically hover around $d = 0.20$, then designing a study to find a similarly small effect is reasonable only if that size of effect is practically meaningful for your research.

Meaningful or Practically Important Effects

The approach that I recommend involves designing for the minimum effect that is practically meaningful. The idea of meaningfulness is slippery and often not entirely obvious, particularly for basic areas of research. In thinking about meaningful effects, there are a number of questions to ask, but not all the questions may be relevant to every project.

A good beginning question when designing an intervention or similar study is how much impact the intervention needs to make to justify the cost. For example, McCartney and Rosenthal (2000) showed that the impact of an active learning program that produced a small effect of $r = .14$ on improving student learning related to a return of over $7 for every $1 spent on the program. In this case, what appears to be a small effect offers considerable gains. Now, consider another situation in which a similar program costing 10 times as much produced a similar effect size. For this program, the return is $0.70 for every $1 spent. Both programs produce the same effect size, but the first yields greater benefits based on the cost. Continuing the educational program example, another question is how this effect compares to those found for similar programs. If a typical educational program produces only a $0.25 return on each dollar, then the program with the $0.70 return would be a bargain.

Unfortunately, for many basic research topics, cost–benefit analyses are less relevant. For this type of work, it is important to become familiar with the published literature in your area. A good approach is to start with a search of the literature to get a sense of typical effects for research in your area, then use those effect sizes to construct an initial effect size estimate. After deriving this initial estimate, it can be useful to translate the standardized effect size to the actual units of interest to get a better understanding of the effect size in practical terms. For example, if examining whether an experimental manipulation reduces anxiety and the literature shows that this form of anxiety reduction produces effects of $d = 0.20$, translating this information into units on the anxiety scale may be easier to interpret than the effect size. If scores on the scale of interest ranged from 1 to 10, with higher scores meaning greater anxiety, and the scale had a standard deviation of 2.0, an effect size of $d = 0.20$ would reflect a raw score difference of less than 1 point. A reasonable question is whether such a small difference is enough to support use of the technique or if the practical value of a difference smaller than 1 point is too small to be of interest.

Effects Based on Pilot Work

Another strategy is the use of pilot work to estimate effect sizes. Pilot studies offer many advantages. Pilot studies establish whether measures make sense to participants and if participants experience manipulations as intended. Pilot work informs decisions about the precision of instruments by allowing more accuracy in estimation of standard deviation for measures. In addition, effect sizes derived from pilot work provide another useful estimate of effect size that, when used in conjunction with the techniques described, helps to provide an informed effect size target for power calculations.

POST HOC POWER

This book focuses on power analyses as an a priori venture. The value of power analyses is highest before data collection. There are, however, some arguments for providing power analyses for completed work. These approaches, sometimes termed *post hoc*, *observed*, or *retrospective power*, provide a power estimate based on the effect size observed in the sample and the sample size. Post hoc power analysis therefore tells how much power we had (given our sample size and α) to attain statistical significance if the effect size in our sample is the true population effect. Proponents of post hoc power analysis argue that for nonsignificant results, post hoc power provides useful information about the need for replication, with low power suggesting replication is necessary to draw conclusions about whether a Type II error existed (e.g., Onwuegbuzie & Leech, 2004). This perspective suggests that high post hoc power supports the veracity of the failure to reject the null hypothesis conclusions (i.e., provides support for the null hypothesis). That is, we had relatively high post hoc power but still could not reject the null hypothesis.

My view is that post hoc power is not particularly useful. First, power is inversely related to both significance test probabilities and effect sizes. Failing to reject the null hypothesis generally means that post hoc power was low, and a larger sample size is needed to obtain statistical significance for the observed effect size (e.g., Lenth, 2001; Nakagawa & Foster, 2004). Thus, post hoc power tells us nothing new. Another flaw in the logic of post hoc power proponents is that power increases as significance test probabilities decrease, meaning that higher levels of post hoc power occur when tests approach significance. Use of power to support null hypotheses therefore employs a procedure by which results that almost met criteria for rejection of the null hypothesis correspond to more support for null effects (Hoenig & Heisey, 2001). For example, given two analyses with the same sample size, a comparison of two groups that produces $p = .70$ would return an estimate of low power (e.g., .10), whereas a sample producing $p = .08$ (i.e., just missing the criteria for rejecting the null at $\alpha = .05$) would yield substantially more power (e.g., .70). Under the flawed view, the second result would suggest stronger evidence that the null hypothesis was in fact true as power was higher in this situation.

Most uses of post hoc power estimates likely occur for two reasons. First, programs such as SPSS provide post hoc power estimates (called "observed" power). Second, reviewers sometimes request these values, and authors lack the knowledge to argue against such presentation. In short, I do not believe post hoc power estimates provide useful information and, along with others (e.g., Maxwell, Kelley, & Rausch, 2008), call for strategies such as confidence intervals drawn around effect sizes when focusing on "support" for null hypotheses.

Post hoc power analysis is perhaps best characterized by this quotation: "To call in the statistician after the experiment is done may be no more than asking him [or her] to perform a post-mortem examination: he [or she] may be able to say what the experiment died of" (Fisher, 1938, p. 17). That is, if we find that post hoc power is low, all we know is that the observed effect size was too small to be detected with the design we used.

HOW MUCH POWER?

One remaining question for this chapter is how much power to target. Power of .80 for tests aiming to reject the null hypothesis seems a de facto standard. Many examples in the text design around this 80% value; however, that is not an endorsement of 80% as a meaningful level of power in all circumstances. Whereas 80% is a reasonable level of power for most situations, there are times when exceeding 80% power is recommended. For example, if the cost of a Type II error were high (e.g., for a treatment that was expensive to develop), then designing for more power would be desirable.

The 80% standard is interesting to investigate. Figure 1.7 shows power for small, medium, and large effect sizes. One thing to note on the graph is that the relationship between power and sample size is roughly linear when moving from power of .20 to .80. However, moving from power of .80 to higher values corresponds to a sharp upturn in required sample size (the small effect shows this relationship most clearly). Table 1.3 shows this in terms of the percentage increase in sample size required to increase power.

As shown in Table 1.3, increasing power reflects consistent jumps of about one quarter of the sample size for moving from .5 to .6, .6 to .7, and .7 to .8. However, moving from .8 to .9 requires an increase of around one third of the sample size. Moving from .9 to .95 requires another one quarter increase. This suggests that power of .80 combines the best sample–power balance. However, if you can afford more power,

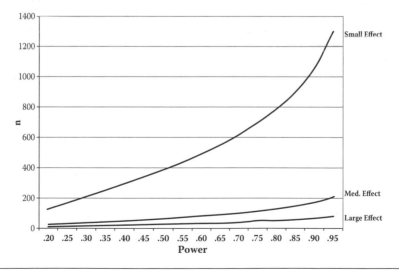

Figure 1.7 Sample size and power for small, medium, and large effects.

Table 1.3 Percentage and Sample Size Increases for Small, Medium, and Large Effects

Power Increases From	Small	Medium	Large
.50 to .60	26.8% (104)	28.1% (18)	21.4% (6)
.60 to .70	26.0% (128)	24.4% (20)	23.5% (8)
.70 to .80	27.1% (168)	25.5% (26)	23.8% (10)
.80 to .90	33.8% (266)	34.4% (44)	30.8% (16)
.90 to .95	23.5% (248)	22.1% (38)	23.5% (16)

by all means, design for more power. For example, if designing for a large effect and additional participants would not increase costs considerably, then a design with power of .90 or even .95 would be advantageous.

SUMMARY

This introductory chapter examined NHST, effect sizes, and basic issues in power analysis. Many of the issues in the present chapter receive extended coverage in other chapters. For example, throughout the text, there are formulae and examples addressing calculation of effect size estimates and noncentrality parameters. Similarly, issues relevant to determining effect size estimates receive coverage throughout the book.

NOTES

1. Figure 1.5 was created using the Exploratory Software for Confidence Intervals (ESCI) software program. ESCI provides an outstanding visualization tool for exploring distribution shapes (see Chapter 11 for information on obtaining the software).
2. Figure 1.6 was produced using ESCI.

2

CHI SQUARE AND TESTS FOR PROPORTIONS

INTRODUCTION

Chi-square (χ^2) tests for independence (also known as multicategory, contingency) and goodness of fit (GoF; also known as one-way classification) address questions regarding distribution of scores into categories. The GoF test involves distributions for categories of a single variable, whereas the test for independence examines whether membership in one category relates to membership in another (i.e., an interaction between variables). This chapter provides a detailed example using the test of independence and brief examples for GoF and 3×2 independence tests. This chapter also addresses tests involving comparing a proportion to a hypothesized proportion (one-sample test) and tests comparing two independent proportions.

As this is the first chapter focusing on specific techniques, I highlight some general considerations for power analyses and discuss specific tests. In particular, discussions of noncentrality parameters (NCPs), determination of meaningful effects, and an introduction to the use of SPSS syntax for power analysis are relevant to the material in this chapter and many of the designs presented in other chapters.

NECESSARY INFORMATION

The tests covered in this chapter focus on frequencies or proportions. Both forms of χ^2 are concerned with frequencies, those expected based on the null hypotheses and observed values. Estimating power for χ^2 requires construction of the proportions reflecting the alternative distribution and proportions reflecting the null hypothesis. The two tests of proportions (one sample and independent) involve the same type of information but generally for fewer groups. In either case, the alternative distribution should reflect a population that deviates from the null hypothesis in a manner that would be practically meaningful or interesting.

FACTORS AFFECTING POWER

Larger deviations between observed and expected values produce larger effect sizes, as do larger differences between group proportions. Differences between more extreme proportions (those closer to 0 or 1.0) produce larger effect sizes. For example, the difference between proportions of .8 and 1.0 corresponds to a larger effect size than the difference between .4 and .6. As with any analysis, larger effect sizes, larger samples, and more liberal α levels yield more power.

KEY STATISTICS

This section presents formulae for χ^2 tests. Information for other tests of proportions is presented in other sections of the chapter. One value that deserves special mention is the NCP. NCPs measure the distance between the distribution from which we are sampling (also known as the alternative distribution) and the distribution specified in the null hypothesis. The shape of the alternative distribution reflects the effects we wish to detect and sample size employed so the NCP calculation is driven by the effect size and sample size.

For our purposes, the NCP is an intermediate step to determining power. The NCP value has little immediately interpretable meaning aside from bigger meaning more power. NCPs are available for the t, F, and χ^2 distributions. F and χ^2 use a value called λ (Lambda); t uses δ (Delta).

Pearson's Chi Square (χ^2)

The fit of observed frequency data to a model of expected frequencies is commonly assessed with Pearson's χ^2 statistic. This statistic, shown in Formula 2.1, focuses on two frequency values, observed (f_o) and expected (f_e). The more deviant the observation is from the expectation, the larger the χ^2 value is. In short, the approach sums the squared difference between the observed and expected frequencies of each cell over the expected frequency. The term *expected* reflects what we would observe if no effect were present. In the context of power analysis, observed takes on a slightly different meaning. Since power analysis is a priori, we do not have data at this point, so the term *observed* is a bit of a misnomer. Observed reflects what our populations of interest look like. As discussed in the next section, we are interested in what sort of observed difference would be meaningful. A key question to ask is how large the deviation between observed and expected would have to be for the result to be interesting or practically important. When conducting power analysis for χ^2, we establish the proportions (or frequencies) we would observe if there were practically meaningful differences between groups. The expected frequency (f_e) is then calculated based on these "observed" values.

$$\chi^2 = \sqrt{\sum_{i=1}^{m} \frac{(f_{oi} - f_{ei})^2}{f_{ei}}} \tag{2.1}$$

Phi (Φ)

Phi (also known as Cramer's *V* or *w*) is the most common measure of effect size for frequency data. When applied to a 2 × 2 test of independence, the value is equivalent to Pearson's correlation coefficient (*r*). It focuses on observed and expected proportions rather than frequencies. In comparing the χ^2 and Φ formulae, we see that Φ is simply χ^2 expressed proportionally rather than based on frequencies (technically, the square root of those values). That is, it is the significance test statistic (χ^2) with all of the elements relevant to sample size removed. The second version of the formula (Formula 2.3) demonstrates this concept more directly.

$$\Phi = \sqrt{\sum_{i=1}^{m} \frac{(p_{oi} - p_{ei})^2}{p_{ei}}} \tag{2.2}$$

$$\Phi = \sqrt{\frac{\chi^2}{n}} \tag{2.3}$$

Lambda (λ)

The NCP for χ^2 is λ (lambda). This is a function of Φ and sample size. For power analyses, λ reflects the χ^2 we would obtain if a sample result reflected the expected values exactly.

$$\lambda = n\Phi^2 \tag{2.4}$$

Example 2.1: 2 × 2 Test of Independence

In this example, I present power analysis for a replication study addressing effects of a prospective tenant's reference to HIV/AIDS on responses to inquiries about the availability of rooms or apartments for rent (Page, 1999). In the original study, callers inquired about the availability of rentals and either mentioned or did not mention undergoing treatment for HIV/AIDS. The outcome measure was whether the rental was reported as still available or not. The study found that 40% of applicants who mentioned HIV/AIDS were told the rental was available compared to 76% of applicants who did not mention HIV/AIDS.

In replicating this study, we address how large a sample size is necessary to produce a power of .80. The first step in this process is to determine what size of effect our design will employ. There are two approaches to determining effect size detailed next.

EFFECT SIZES BASED ON PREVIOUS RESEARCH

Determining effect sizes based on previous research asks the question of how large a sample is needed to find an effect size equivalent to that in the previous study. This is a common approach to power analysis but not one that I can endorse without consider-able qualification. Estimates based on a single sample may not accurately represent the population effect size. Searches for other studies that focus on similar hypotheses may ameliorate this problem. In general, the more studies used to estimate effect sizes, the better. Keep in mind that published research tends to favor statistically significant find-ings (Rosenthal, 1979). Significant findings tend to have larger effect sizes, so reliance on previously published work often overestimates the population effect size.

When designing a study based on effect sizes from similar studies, it is important to recognize that what someone else found may not be relevant to whether the size of effect you want to detect is meaningful or practically valuable. Of course, this does not mean that the approach is useless. What others found may represent a meaningfully sized effect or the smallest effect that you are interested in detecting. Do not accept mindlessly what other researchers found as a reflection of the size of effect you want to detect. Instead, focus on meaningful effects.

EFFECT SIZES BASED ON DETECTING MEANINGFUL EFFECTS

This approach that determines effect sizes based on detecting meaningful effects begins with the question of how large a sample is necessary to detect the smallest effect we would term meaningful. This approach requires important decisions about what we consider a meaningful difference. This is not always an easy question to answer. Addressing this question adequately involves serious thought and can promote large sample requirements, especially if the researcher believes small differences are important to detect.

Designing for meaningful effects is a process for which it is difficult to provide sys-tematic guidance. Every research study is different, with unique concerns and outcomes. Questions about what is or what is not a meaningful result must be answered in the context of that project. I provide a rationale for the choices made for the determination of meaningful results and general strategies for answering questions of meaningfulness but ultimately only the researcher can answer this question about his or her study.

In thinking about what is a meaningful result, it is sometimes useful to first think about data in terms of raw scores (e.g., frequencies, means) rather than as standardized effect sizes. This differs from classic approaches to power analysis that focus first on effect size (e.g., Cohen, 1988; Kraemer & Thiemann, 1987). Thinking about standardized effect sizes often removes the context of effects, making it difficult to determine what is meaningful. In discussing statistical reporting of effects, in 1999 Wilkinson and the Task Force on Statistical Inference noted that "if the units of measurement are meaningful on a practical level … then we usually prefer an unstandardized measure to a standardized measure" (p. 599). Unstandardized measures generally are easier to think about and understand than are standardized measures. This does not mean that standardized effect sizes are not useful, only that it can be easier to begin by examining raw statistics.

DETERMINING EFFECT SIZE FOR ANALYSIS

Going back to the rental study, a good place to start is by examining differences in rental availability between HIV/AIDS-positive applicants and a control group. A good beginning question is how much discrimination would be meaningful. Consideration of the level of discrimination found in the earlier study is a good starting point. Page (1999) found a 36% difference in rental availability between HIV/AIDS-positive applicants and the control group (40% vs. 76%). It would be reasonable to term this level of bias "meaningful." A large difference in availability reflects clear discrimination. However, if we designed for power of .80 to detect this much bias (36% difference), we would have considerably less power to detect smaller differences in bias. Unless the 36% difference was the smallest meaningful difference we were interested in detecting, designing around this value would not be a good approach.

Given the issues discussed, an important question regards how large a difference is meaningful. Certainly, any amount of discrimination is troubling, so we could design a study that allowed for detection of very small differences (e.g., 5%). However, this small a difference does not seem particularly large when compared to the previous finding of 36%. As a compromise, I am going to define a 20% difference as the smallest difference I am interested in having power to detect.

For χ^2, the effect size is a function of the proportions. Differences between more extreme proportions produce larger effect sizes than differences between proportions closer to .50. For that reason, it is important to establish proportions based on reasonable estimates for each group rather than simply choosing two proportions that create specific levels of difference. A good starting point is the information from the study about the control group. In the previous study, 76% of the rentals in the control group were available. This value serves as a good baseline as there does not appear to be any reason to believe availability for this group would change substantially. Table 2.1 shows how the 20% difference is applied to construct proportions corresponding to these values.

Table 2.1 Proportions Reflecting a Meaningful Difference (Null in Parentheses)

	HIV/AIDS Mentioned (Treatment) $p_o\,(p_e)$	% of Condition	No HIV/AIDS Mentioned (Control) $p_o\,(p_e)$	% of Condition
Rental available	.28 (.33)	56	.38 (.33)	76
Rental not available	.22 (.17)	44	.12 (.17)	24

A few notes on the values in Table 2.1 are necessary. The proportions reflect the overall proportions of the sample, with half of the participants assigned to the control group and half assigned to the treatment group. The original study found 76% of rentals available to those who did not mention HIV/AIDS. These cells are set at .38 and .12. The value of .38 is the proportion of the total that corresponds to 76% of the control group (recall the control group is only half of the entire sample). The value of .12 is the proportion corresponding to the 24% of the control group for whom the rental was not available. Treatment group proportions are set as deviations from those values. Thus, a 20% difference here would reflect a .10 difference in proportions across columns. The 20% difference discussed reflects a difference in terms of how many people in each condition were told the rental was available. The proportional values are out of the total sample, with an equal division of participants between treatment and control groups. The expected proportions reflect the average of the two proportions in the row or, more simply, what the proportions would look like if there were no differences between treatment and control. These proportions are especially important as these are the values used for p_e in calculations. Based on the proportions in Table 2.1, Φ is calculated using Formula 2.2.

$$\Phi = \sqrt{\sum_{i=1}^{m} \frac{(p_{oi} - p_{ei})^2}{p_{ei}}} = \sqrt{\frac{(.28 - .33)^2}{.33} + \frac{(.38 - .33)^2}{.33} + \frac{(.22 - .17)^2}{.17} + \frac{(.12 - .17)^2}{.17}} = .21$$

The effect size is then used to calculate the NCP. For this calculation, we need to choose a sample size as a starting point. The calculations (using Formula 2.4) show that with $n = 100$, λ is equal to 4.41.

$$\lambda = n\Phi^2 = 100(.21)^2 = 4.41$$

As a short aside, it appears that thinking about these differences in terms of percentages makes a bit more sense than beginning with an effect size. For example, a study designed to detect a minimum of a 20% difference in availability (56% vs. 76% for HIV and control, respectively) would produce $\Phi = .21$. In this case, the percentage result is more intuitive to most than the effect size. Please note that my focus on proportions instead of effect sizes is not a criticism of the utility of effect size measures. Effect sizes are indispensable measures but are not always an easily interpretable starting point for determining meaningful effects for power analysis. One note of caution is that the percentage difference expressed here (20%) may correspond to different effect sizes. Percentage difference and effect size do give different information. For example, if the proportions of interest were .80 and 1.0, respectively, the effect size would be considerably larger ($\Phi = .33$).

USING THE NONCENTRALITY PARAMETER TO CALCULATE POWER

Given an effect size of $\Phi = .21$, we are ready to compute power. There are two questions addressed in this section. First, how much power does $n = 100$ yield? Second, what sample size produces power $= .80$?

For the first question, we need λ (Formula 4.41) and a critical value for χ^2 with our desired α. Using $\alpha = .05$ corresponds to a critical value of $\chi^2 = 3.84$ for $df = 1$. The degrees of freedom are Rows $- 1 \times$ Columns $- 1$ for this test. Since power calculations for χ^2 distributions require use of a noncentral distribution, this calculation requires a computer protocol (see discussion of this issue in Chapter 1).

Using SPSS, the following command computes power:

```
COMPUTE power = 1-NCDF.CHISQ(Chi_Table,df,Lambda).
```

The value called Chi_Table reflects the critical value for χ^2 (3.84). With $df = 1$ and $\lambda = 4.41$, the command looks like this:

```
COMPUTE power = 1-NCDF.CHISQ(3.84,1,4.41).
```

The NCDF (noncentral distribution function) command in SPSS performs calculations based on noncentral distributions; the value it gives is the area below λ. Because SPSS gives the area below λ, the syntax takes 1 minus the result as this corresponds to the area above λ that gives power. Using this calculation, SPSS yields power $= .56$.[1]

Approximating Power Calculations

Although it is not possible to calculate correct power estimates for χ^2 by hand, good approximations are possible. I include this section as my experience teaching about power suggests that approximation, albeit not always accurate, facilitates theoretical understanding of power. The approach demonstrated here works only when $df = 1$. This approach works for the current example but does not work particularly well for small samples or small effect sizes. As discussed in Chapter 1, with large samples, central and noncentral distributions look similar.

Calculating approximate power directly from λ is relatively simple when $df = 1$. With $df = 1$, the χ^2 distribution is simply the normal distribution squared (z^2). Converting λ and the critical value of χ^2 to z involves taking the square root of each value. Then, take these values to Formula 2.5, which yields a z-statistic that can be used to approximate power.

$$z_{power} = z_{critical} - z_\lambda \qquad (2.5)$$

For this example, the critical value for χ^2 with $df=1$ and $\alpha = .05$ is 3.84. Converted to z, we get $z_{critical} = 1.96$. Then, λ converts to $z_\lambda = 2.10$. Inserting these values into Formula 2.5 yields $z_{power} = -0.14$. This value reflects the point on the alternative (or true) z-distribution that corresponds to the critical value of the null distribution. The area below z_{power} reflects samples that do not allow for rejection of the null hypothesis. This corresponds to β or Type II error. The area above z_{power} reflects samples that allow for rejection of the null. This is $1 - \beta$ or power.

$$z_{power} = 1.96 - 2.10 = -0.14$$

Taking z_{power} to a normal distribution table shows that 56% of the distribution falls at or above $z = -0.14$. Figure 2.1 shows these calculated values. In this figure, power is the area of the alternative distribution that falls to the right $z_{critical}$. This area is a little above 50% (56% for this example). The value for z_λ represents the center of the alternative distribution (Formula 2.6).

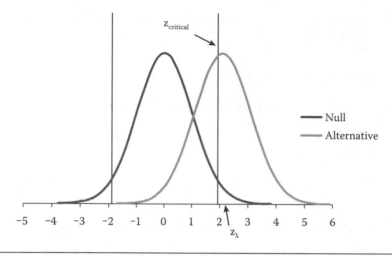

Figure 2.1 Graph of power area using normal distribution approximation.

The approximation technique also allows for the determination of a sample size corresponding to a particular level of power. For example, if we want to find power = .80 (or some other value), we can work backward and rearrange the formulae. First, find the z-value above which you find 80% of the distribution. This corresponds to $z = -0.85$. Plug that value into Formula 2.6 with the critical value for z_λ and solve for z_λ. Square z_λ to get λ. Finally, take λ to Formula 2.7 and solve for n. In this case, for power = .80, a sample of 179 is necessary. To facilitate assignment of equal numbers of participants to the two groups round up to $n = 180$.

$$z_\lambda = z_{critical} - z_{power} \tag{2.6}$$

$$z_\lambda = 1.96 - (-.85) = 2.81$$

$$(z_\lambda)^2 = (2.81)^2 = 7.90$$

$$n = \frac{\lambda}{\Phi^2} \tag{2.7}$$

$$n = \frac{7.90}{.21^2} = 179$$

USING SPSS SYNTAX FOR POWER ANALYSIS

The calculations detailed in this chapter are effective but impractical for complex designs. The SPSS syntax files in this book run analyses and require minimal modification for new analyses. Each of the syntax examples also is available on the companion Web site. A limitation to using SPSS syntax is that for some analyses, SPSS will not solve for a desired power level in a single step. This necessitates running analyses several times and trying out new sample size values to hone in on the solution.

The syntax presented in Table 2.2 calculates power for a sample of $n = 100$ using the proportions in Table 2.1 and $\alpha = .05$. The first lines of the table show the portion of the SPSS command syntax that the user can modify to calculate power for a specified sample size, proportions, and α. The left panel of Table 2.3 shows the output for an initial analysis based on 100 participants, yielding power of .56 (just as calculated earlier).

To determine the sample size needed to achieve a desired level of power (.80) with the specified effect size, change the value for n in the command compute $n = 100$ to another value. The basic approach to using this syntax file is to run the analysis with a specific sample size and then to run it again with a new sample until achieving the desired level of power. For the first analysis, power was .56 with $n = 100$, so we try a larger sample size and then adjust the sample size upward or downward as necessary until the reported power reaches the desired level. The right panel in Table 2.3 shows that $n = 180$ yields power $= .8085$. Table 2.4 shows the modified part of the syntax for this analysis in bold.

Notes on the Syntax Files

For each of the χ^2 syntax files, the syntax places files in a temporary folder (d:\temp). If this folder does not exist on your computer, you can either create the folder or change the directory to one where you would prefer the temporary files to go.

Other χ^2 Tests

Brief examples of GoF tests and independence tests with more than two categories appear in Table 2.5. Complete syntax files for these analyses are available from the companion Web site with only the portions requiring user modification presented for both analyses in the text.

Goodness of Fit   The syntax in the left-hand side of Table 2.5 addresses power for the GoF test. In this example, there is a single variable with four categories. For more or few categories, simply add or delete as needed. The GoF test requires that you provide expected proportions p_e as well as the observed proportions p_o. For example, the line reading 3 .20 .25 reflects the group (3), the observed proportion (.20), and the expected proportion (.25). The proportions can be set to any value as long as they sum to 1.0. In this example, the analysis compares a population for which meaningful differences between

Table 2.2 SPSS Syntax with Annotation for χ^2 Independence Test

Syntax	Comments

`DATA LIST LIST / x1 x2 po.`
`BEGIN DATA`
`1 1 .28`
`1 2 .38`
`2 1 .22`
`2 2 .12`
`END DATA.`
`Compute alpha = .05.`
`Compute n = 100.`
	x1, x2, and *po* are variable names; do not change
	
	1 1 .28 = First category of x1, first category of x2, .28 is the proportion of the entire sample in that cell
	Change the *po* values for a different effect size
	Enter your desired alpha value here
	Enter your desired sample size here

	**** Modifications end here******
`Compute fo = n * po.` `Weight by fo.`	Calculates observed frequencies

`If (x1=1) sumx1_1 = sum(fo).`
`If (x1=2) sumx1_2 = sum(fo).`
`If (x2=1) sumx2_1 = sum(fo).`
`If (x2=2) sumx2_2 = sum(fo).`
`execute.`
`SORT CASES BY x1.`
`Compute nobreak=1.`
	Assigns observed frequencies to categories

`AGGREGATE OUTFILE='d:\temp\` `  temp.sav'`	Creates a new file that creates various values for calculation

`    /PRESORTED`
`    /BREAK=nobreak`
`    /cat1=MAX(x1)`
`    /cat2=MAX(x2)`
	Calculates number of categories

`    /N = n(fo)`
`    /Row1 = n(sumx1_1)`
`    /Row2 = n(sumx1_2)`
`    /Col1 = n(sumx2_1)`
`    /Col2 = n(sumx2_2).`
	Row and column values

`MATCH FILES FILE=*`
`    /TABLE='d:\temp\temp.sav'`
`    /BY=nobreak.`
`Execute.`
	Matches original and new aggregated file

`Compute df = (cat1-1)*(cat2-1).`	Computes values for χ^2 calculation

`If (x1=1 and x2=1) fe =`
`(row1*col1) / n.`
`If (x1=1 and x2=2) fe =`
`(row1*col2) / n.`	

Syntax	Comments
| ```
If (x1=2 and x2=1) fe =
 (row2*col1) / n.
If (x1=2 and x2=2) fe =
 (row2*col2) / n.
Compute chiwork =
 ((fo-fe)**2) / fe.
``` | This is the calculation for each category |
| ```
execute.
SAVE OUTFILE='d:\temp\
 chipower.sav'
/COMPRESSED.
WEIGHT OFF.
SORT CASES BY x1.
AGGREGATE OUTFILE='d:\temp\
 temp2.sav'
``` | Puts the values together |
| ```
    /PRESORTED
    /BREAK=nobreak
``` | The sum of the values here gives $\chi^2$ |
| ```
    /Chi = SUM(chiwork).

MATCH FILES FILE=*
    /TABLE='d:\temp\temp2.sav'
    /BY=nobreak.
Execute.

SAVE OUTFILE='d:\temp\
 chipower.sav'
/COMPRESSED.
WEIGHT by FO.
Compute fail = 1-alpha.
``` | Calculations for critical value and power |
| ```
Compute Phi = sqrt(chi/n).
Compute lambda = N*(Phi*Phi).
Compute Chi_Table = IDF.
 CHISQ(fail,df).
``` | |
| ```
Compute power = 1-NCDF.
 CHISQ(Chi_Table,df,Lambda).
EXECUTE.
``` | Uses the NCDF command to calculate power |
| ```
SUMMARIZE
    /TABLES=N power
``` | This outputs the calculated values |
| ```
    /FORMAT=NOLIST NOTOTAL
    /TITLE='Case Summaries'
    /MISSING=VARIABLE
    /CELLS=MEAN.
EXECUTE.
``` | |

Table 2.3 Output for Power Analyses ($n = 100$ and $n = 180$)

N	Power
100.0000	.5601

N	Power
180.0000	.8085

Table 2.4 Syntax Modification for $n = 180$ (Modification in Bold)

```
DATA LIST LIST / x1 x2 po.
BEGIN DATA
1 1 28
1 2 38
2 1 22
2 2 12
END DATA.
compute alpha = .05.
compute n = 180.
```

Table 2.5 Syntax (Partial) for Goodness of Fit and 3×2 Independence Test

Goodness of Fit	3 X 2 Independence
| ```
DATA LIST LIST / x1 po pe.
BEGIN DATA
1 .25 .25
2 .20 .25
3 .20 .25
4 .35 .25
END DATA.

Compute n = 100.
Compute alpha = .05.
``` | ```
DATA LIST LIST / x1 x2 po.
BEGIN DATA
1 1 .25
1 2 .25
2 1 .10
2 2 .10
3 1 .25
3 2 .05
END DATA.

Compute n = 100.
Compute alpha = .05.
``` |

categories reflect proportions of .25, .20, .20, and .35 to a null distribution that represents equal proportions across the groups (.25 for each).

Test of Independence With More Than Two Categories For the test of independence with more than two categories, the only change from the 2×2 format is the addition of a third category for the first variable. For example, the line that reads 3 1 .25 set the proportion at .25 for the third category of x1 and first category of x2.

TESTS FOR SINGLE SAMPLES AND
INDEPENDENT PROPORTIONS

In addition to χ^2 approaches to testing for differences in proportions, several other techniques compare proportions. This section presents power analysis for tests comparing a sample to a hypothesized value for the population (single-sample test) and comparing proportions between two independent populations. Calculations for both approaches are similar, so I present general formulae first then address application to each design.

Formulae for Differences in Proportion Tests

The effect size for tests involving differences in proportions is termed h. The value h is like d and can be thought of (at least intuitively) in the same manner (i.e., units of standard deviation). The calculation of h involves what is commonly termed the *arcsine transformation*. This transformation deserves some special mention. The name *arcsine transformation* is imprecise, sometimes leading to incorrect use of the transformation, likely because of confusion over the proper calculation. Both SPSS and MS Excel provide an arcsine function that does not correspond to the transformation in Formula 2.8. SPSS and MS Excel correctly calculate the arcsine portion of the formula but do not include the 2 or square root of p parts.

Formula 2.8 notes the arcsine-transformed proportion as p′. Others (e.g., Cohen, 1992) note this value as Φ. I avoid this notation as Φ is also the effect size for χ^2 in previous parts of the chapter. The calculation is applied to two proportions of interest, either the alternative and null proportions or two independent proportions.

$$p' - 2\arcsin\sqrt{p} \tag{2.8}$$

After converting both proportions and the effect size, calculate h by subtracting one transformed proportion from the other.

$$h = p'_1 - p'_2 \tag{2.9}$$

The NCP does not exist for this test as the difference between proportions is tested against the normal distribution, and such tests use a central distribution. Formulae 2.10 and 2.11 use z_λ to note the value that is analogous to the NCP used in the previous parts of the chapter. The choice between Formulae 2.10 and 2.11, depends on the test. For a one-sample test, use Formula 2.10. For a test of independent samples, use Formula 2.11. For unequal sample sizes among independent groups, use the harmonic sample size defined by Formula 2.12. Once z_{power} is calculated, we apply Formula 2.5. Since this test uses the normal distribution (rather than χ^2 as seen in the previous examples), accurate hand calculation of power is possible.

$$z_\lambda = h\sqrt{n} \qquad (2.10)$$

$$z_\lambda = h\sqrt{n/2} \qquad (2.11)$$

$$n_{\text{harmonic}} = \frac{2n_1 n_2}{n_1 + n_2} \qquad (2.12)$$

Example 2.2: Single-Sample Comparison

As a graduate student, I worked coding studies for a large-scale meta-analysis involving drug abuse treatment programs. One of the outcomes of interest was the proportion of program participants who remained abstinent for a certain period (e.g., 6 months). This was one of several possible outcomes, often with so many categories that the data were not appropriate for χ^2. For example, categories might include abstinent 1 year, mostly abstinent for a year (one or two slipups), abstinent 6 months, abstinent 3 months, abstinent 1 month, dropped out of treatment, and not abstinent. Two designs for examining effectiveness of programs involved comparing a sample from the program to a program goal for abstinence or comparing two samples of participants who received different forms of treatment. For example, a program might compare its abstinent rates to (a) a benchmark for abstinence (single-sample comparisons) or (b) abstinence rates of a sample drawn for a comparison program (independent samples comparisons).

Imagine that a program would qualify for extended funding if it demonstrated substantial improvement over a 42% success rate for routine treatments as reported in previous meta-analysis of similar programs.[2] The program believed that, at minimum, they had a 60% success rate. How large a sample of program participants is necessary to provide power of .90 to detect this difference? This approach involves a one-sample proportion test as there is a sample proportion compared against a hypothesized value.

Calculating the effect size involves transforming both proportions (.60 and .42), then taking the difference between the two transformed proportions. Next, the effect size can be used to calculate z_λ, which is then used to obtain power. The examples that follow use an arbitrary sample size of 20 and a one-tailed $\alpha = .05$ test:

$$p_1 = 2\arcsin\sqrt{p} = 2\arcsin\sqrt{.60} = 1.77$$

$$p_1 = 2\arcsin\sqrt{p} = 2\arcsin\sqrt{.42} = 1.41$$

$$h = p'_1 - p'_2 = 1.77 - 1.41 = 0.36$$

$$z_\lambda = h\sqrt{n} = 0.36\sqrt{20} = 1.61$$

$$z_{\text{power}} = 1.645 - 1.61 = 0.035$$

The area above z_{power} of 0.035 is .49, indicating that we have power = .49, well below our desired level. Using the syntax in Table 2.6, we can do this calculation as well as calculations for a range of sample sizes. Simply set the alternative (prop_alt) and null (prop_null) proportions as .60 and .42, respectively. The syntax returns power for a range of sample sizes.

Table 2.6 Syntax for One-Sample Proportion Tests

Syntax	Comments
INPUT PROGRAM. LOOP n=20 TO 100 by 20. END CASE. END LOOP. END FILE. END INPUT PROGRAM. EXECUTE.	These values run analyses for a set of sample sizes. $n = 20$ to 100 by 20 means the analysis is run for samples 20, 40, etc., until it reaches 100
Compute prop_alt = .60. Compute prop_null = .42. Compute alpha = .050. Compute tails = 1. Compute ars_1 = 2*(ARSIN(prop_alt**.5)). Compute ars_2 = 2*(ARSIN(prop_null**.5)). Compute h = ars_1-ars_2. Compute z = h*(n**.5). Compute alpha_tails = alpha/tails. Compute prob = 1-alpha_tails. Compute z_tabled =IDF. NORMAL(prob,0,1). Compute z_power = z_tabled - z. Compute Power = 1-CDF. NORMAL(z_power,0,1). execute.	60% for treatment 42% as the benchmark (null) ****Do not modify here or below*** Arcsine transformation is ars_1 and ars_2
matrix. GET M /VARIABLES=N Power. print M/title = "Power for Differences Single Sample Proportion"/clabels = "N" "N" "Power"/format f10.4. End Matrix.	

Table 2.7 Output for Single-Sample Proportion Power

Power for Differences Single-Sample Proportion	
N	Power
20.0000	.4897
30.0000	.6324
40.0000	.7405
50.0000	.8200
60.0000	.8769
70.0000	.9169
80.0000	.9445
90.0000	.9633
100.0000	.9759

As shown in Table 2.7, a sample of around 70 participants yields the desired power. The output gives sample size and power; other calculated values (e.g., h) appear on the SPSS data screen.

Example 2.3: Independent Proportions Comparison

Imagine that instead of comparing against a benchmark, another program wanted to compare the effectiveness of its current program to a value-added version of the program that included new therapeutic components. The current program reports a success rate of 55%. Given the increased costs associated with the new program, they would consider the value-added program worthwhile if it were to, at minimum, increase success to 62%. By *worthwhile*, this would mean that the level of improvement would be enough to justify a full-scale change in the program. As the new program is experimental, only a proportion of program participants (20%) are scheduled to participate in the value-added program.

Comparisons of independent samples for proportions proceed in the same fashion as the single-sample test with some additional considerations. The effect size statistic h is calculated the same way. The calculation of z differs slightly, and groups have different sample sizes. With unequal sample sizes, the harmonic sample size replaces n in the calculation of z. The following example uses a sample of 200 participants (20% assigned to the new treatment):

$$p_1 = 2\arcsin\sqrt{p} = 2\arcsin\sqrt{.62} = 1.813$$
$$p_1 = 2\arcsin\sqrt{p} = 2\arcsin\sqrt{.55} = 1.671$$

$$h = p_1' - p_2' = 1.813 - 1.671 = 0.142$$

$$n_{\text{harmonic}} = \frac{2n_1 n_2}{n_1 + n_2} = \frac{2 * 40 * 160}{40 + 160} = 64$$

$$z_\lambda = h\sqrt{\frac{n}{2}} = 0.142\sqrt{\frac{64}{2}} = 0.80$$

$$z_{\text{power}} = 1.96 - 0.80 = 1.16$$

Taking the value of 1.16 to a normal distribution table shows that power is .12 for a sample of 200 program participants (.12 is the area at or above $z = 1.16$).

The syntax in Table 2.8 is for a two-sample case with independent groups. This syntax requires modification of proportions for each group and the proportion of the total sample in the first group (set at .50 for equal samples, .75 for three quarters of the total sample in the first group, etc.).

Based on the results in Table 2.9, detecting this effect with power = .80 requires a sample of between 2400 and 2500 participants. Although this is a large sample, the result should not be surprising as the h statistic is very small.

Additional Issues

The χ^2 test for independence is for nominal categories. If categories are ordinal (e.g., class rank), other measures such as γ (gamma) may be more appropriate. Siegel and Castellan (1988) provide a good discussion of power for nonparametric tests, but certainly more work is necessary in this area.

Violations of χ^2 assumptions occur when cells have very small expected frequencies (e.g., less than 5). For tests of independence, small expected frequencies are a product of low observed frequencies across a category level. For example, a 2 (Condition: Treatment vs. Control) × 3 (Response: Yes vs. Maybe vs. No) design might produce a very small proportion of "No" responses across both conditions, leading the expected frequencies for "no" cell to be very low. One solution is to collapse categories to address this problem (e.g., combine no and maybe responses into a single category). Collapsing this way will turn a 2 × 3 design into a 2 × 2. The simpler 2 × 2 design often will have more power. However, if you expect a problem of this nature, it is a good practice to evaluate power for both the 2 × 2 and 2 × 3 designs, using whichever yields a larger sample size requirement (provided that assumptions are met in both cases).

Table 2.8 Syntax for Independent Samples Proportion Tests

```
INPUT PROGRAM.
LOOP n=200 TO 2500 by 100.
END CASE.
END LOOP.
END FILE.
END INPUT PROGRAM.
EXECUTE.
```

Modify the five lines below

```
Compute prop1 = .62.
```
First group's proportion
```
Compute prop2 = .55.
```
Second group's proportion
```
Compute Prop_N1 = 0.2.
```
Proportion of cases in first group
```
Compute alpha = .05.
Compute tails = 2.
```

End modification area

```
Compute N1 = N * Prop_N1.
Compute N2 = N * (1-Prop_N1).
Compute n_harm = ((2*n1*n2)/(n1+n2)).
```
Calculation of harmonic *n*
```
Compute ars_1 =
 2*(ARSIN(prop1**.5)).
Compute ars_2 =
 2*(ARSIN(prop2**.5)).
Compute h = ars_1-ars_2.

Compute z = h*((n_harm/2)**.5).
Compute alpha_tails = alpha/tails.
Compute prob = 1-alpha_tails.
Compute z_tabled
 =IDF.NORMAL(prob,0,1).
Compute z_power = z_tabled - z.
Compute Power = 1-CDF.
 NORMAL(z_power,0,1).
execute.

matrix.
GET M /VARIABLES=n1 n2 Power.
print M/title = "Power for
 Differences Between Proportions"/
 clabels = "N1" "N2" "Power"/
 format f10.4.
End Matrix.
```

Table 2.9 Output for Independent Samples Proportion Tests

Power for Differences Between Proportions		
N1	N2	Power
40.0000	160.0000	.1239
60.0000	240.0000	.1648
80.0000	320.0000	.2054
100.0000	400.0000	.2457
120.0000	480.0000	.2855
140.0000	560.0000	.3245
160.0000	640.0000	.3627
180.0000	720.0000	.3999
200.0000	800.0000	.4359
220.0000	880.0000	.4707
240.0000	960.0000	.5041
260.0000	1040.0000	.5362
280.0000	1120.0000	.5668
300.0000	1200.0000	.5960
320.0000	1280.0000	.6237
340.0000	1360.0000	.6500
360.0000	1440.0000	.6748
380.0000	1520.0000	.6982
400.0000	1600.0000	.7203
420.0000	1680.0000	.7410
440.0000	1760.0000	.7605
460.0000	1840.0000	.7787
480.0000	1920.0000	.7958
500.0000	2000.0000	.8117

SUMMARY

This chapter addressed power for χ^2 tests of independence and GoF, tests involving a single proportion compared to a hypothesized value, and comparisons of two independent proportions. For each design, power analysis involves specifying the null and alternative distributions. The null distribution reflects the proportions specified in the null hypothesis (e.g., equal proportions across groups). The alternative distribution establishes the proportional differences we wish to test relative to the null distribution (e.g., a 10% difference between two groups). Ideally, proportions reflect the smallest difference the researcher defines as meaningful. Relevant to these analyses, this chapter includes formulae and SPSS syntax for calculating power. The chapter also includes a discussion of determining effect sizes for design through consideration of the size of a meaningful difference as well as the examination of previous research findings.

NOTES

1. The full syntax here should read:

```
COMPUTE power = 1-NCDF.CHISQ(3.84,1,4.41).

Execute.
```

   SPSS does not accept commands of this nature without an active data file, so you will need to create a dummy variable to activate the data file (I usually just enter a 1 in the first cell). This value serves no computational purpose. Power will appear in the SPSS data file under the column "Power."

2. This success rate came from Prendergast et al. (2002) but represents a considerable simplification of the factors contributing to success rate.

3

INDEPENDENT SAMPLES AND PAIRED *t*-TESTS

INTRODUCTION

This chapter focuses on power for designs traditionally addressed using *t*-tests (either independent or paired). These procedures often examine treatment–control group comparisons and pre–post designs. I present power analyses for independent and paired designs with SPSS syntax provided for primary analyses and for tests addressing violation of homogeneity of variances assumptions and unequal sample sizes.

NECESSARY INFORMATION

For designs using independent sample *t*-tests, the initial step is determining means (μs) representing meaningful differences between groups and making a reasonable estimate of standard deviation (σ) for both groups. For paired *t*-test designs, means representing meaningful differences, standard deviation, and the expected correlation (ρ) between dependent measures are required. For the paired *t*-test, the standard deviation of the difference may be substituted for σ and ρ; however, it is usually easier to focus on the standard deviation and the correlation.

For both tests, you may alternatively start with an estimate of the effect size and work backward to create μ and σ for your groups. The effect size estimate most commonly used for two-group designs is Cohen's *d*. Technically, power analysis involves a population effect size, which is usually noted as δ or Δ (lower- and upper-case delta, respectively). This text uses *d* to designate the population effect size. This is because δ

represents the noncentrality parameter (discussed in the next section), and it is confusing to use the same symbol for two different values.

Estimation of the standard deviation deserves special mention. Estimating the population standard deviation (σ) is sometimes tricky. One approach is to pretest. In general, a pretest with even as few as 20 participants helps to establish a reasonable estimate of variability for the dependent measure. Of course, there are other benefits to pretesting, such as establishing whether manipulations actually work and if measures make sense to participants. Another strategy is estimating the standard deviation of the dependent measure from previous uses of the measure. This can be accurate when dealing with established measures. However, this approach requires close attention to the study populations used. For example, a standard deviation based on college students might not represent an accurate estimate of the standard deviation for office workers.

Finally, when estimating standard deviations, it is important to consider potential differences between treatment and control group variability. For example, if group assignment is nonrandom (e.g., samples from existing groups), groups may differ in terms of standard deviations. Unequal variances across groups impact power and complicate estimates of necessary sample sizes. Anticipating these issues in the design stage produces more accurate power analyses.

FACTORS AFFECTING POWER

For between-subjects designs addressed using the independent samples *t*-test, the mean difference and standard deviations impact power. The mean difference and the pooled standard deviation comprise the effect size. For within-subjects designs addressed using the paired *t*-test, the correlation between the two administrations of the dependent measure also affects the effect size, with correlations of greater than .50 increasing power and correlations of less than .50 decreasing power.

As noted in Chapter 1, sample size, desired α error, and the directionality of the test (i.e., one or two tailed) affect power. Use of one-tailed (directional) or two-tailed (nondirectional) tests deserves some special mention. A one-tailed approach yields a more powerful test when outcomes are in the predicted direction. For example, a directional test in which the expectation is that the treatment group outperforms the control group has more power than a nondirectional test if the actual study results find the treatment group outperformed the control. If it were the case that the control outperformed the treatment group, the directional test would have no power to detect this effect, but the nondirectional test retains some power.

The choice of a one- or two-tailed test is an a priori decision. You cannot peek at the data to see which test allows the best conclusion. Often, the decision between one- or two-tailed tests hinges on one key question: "Do I care if the results are opposite what I expect?" In many situations, researchers want to be able to discuss findings in either direction. I rarely see the use of one-tailed tests in the literature in psychology, likely because SPSS output produces two-tailed probabilities for most tests.

KEY STATISTICS

This section presents statistical formulae for the analyses that follow. As discussed further in the chapter, SPSS can do most of these calculations. If possible, I provide general formulae relevant to both independent and paired-samples tests.

Independent Samples t

The *t*-statistic (Formula 3.1) reflects the difference between the sample means minus the hypothesized difference over the standard error of the differences (Formula 3.2). The hypothesized difference between means is set at zero (this is the default in SPSS and other statistical packages). Tests of the nonnil hypothesis (e.g., Thompson, 1998) are not discussed in this chapter but are easily accommodated by simply changing the hypothesized difference (represented in Formula 3.1 as 0) to the nonnil value of interest. The nonnil approach is especially useful for analyses that seek a particular effect size/statistical significance combination (e.g., conclude with a reasonable degree of certainty that our samples do not come from a population for which the true difference between means is 2.5).

The standard error of the differences focuses on the standard error of each group and the correlation between measures. For independent samples, $r = .00$ in Formula 3.2:

$$t = \frac{(\bar{x}_1 - \bar{x}_2) - 0}{s_{\bar{x}_1 - \bar{x}_2}} \text{ (for samples)} \tag{3.1}$$

$$s_{\bar{x}_1 - \bar{x}_2} = \sqrt{s_{\bar{x}_1}^2 + s_{\bar{x}_2}^2 - 2rs_{\bar{x}_1}s_{\bar{x}_2}} \text{ (for samples)} \tag{3.2}$$

Formulae 3.1 and 3.2 use sample notation for calculations of *t* and the standard error of the differences between means. The formulae that follow reflect population values. The use of population values serves as a reminder that the values used for calculations are not based on data collection. Power analysis focuses on expected or meaningful values for a population determined before data collection. The effect size, Cohen's d, as noted in Formula 3.3 is the mean difference over the pooled standard deviation (Formula 3.4).

$$d = \frac{\mu_1 - \mu_2}{\sigma_p} \tag{3.3}$$

$$\sigma_p = \sqrt{\frac{\sigma_1^2(n_1 - 1) + \sigma_2^2(n_2 - 1)}{n_1 + n_2 - 2}} \tag{3.4}$$

Formula 3.5 details calculation of the noncentrality parameter. The value noted as n_j reflects the number of people per group. The section on unequal variances and sample sizes presents formulae addressing designs in which group sizes differ.

$$\delta = d\sqrt{\frac{n_j}{2}} \tag{3.5}$$

Paired Samples t

The paired-samples t approach uses the same values as the independent samples approach with the exception of the effect size and noncentrality parameter. For the effect size, shown in Formula 3.6, the denominator is the standard deviation of the differences (sometimes written as σ_D). Note that the standard deviation of the differences ($\sigma_{x_1-x_2}$) is not the same value as the standard error of the differences ($s_{\bar{x}_1-\bar{x}_2}$); one has xs and the other has means as the subscript (x-bars).

$$d = \frac{\mu_1 - \mu_2}{\sigma_{x_1-x_2}} \tag{3.6}$$

$$\sigma_{x_1-x_2} = \sigma_p\sqrt{2(1-\rho)} \tag{3.7}$$

Formula 3.8 is the noncentrality parameter for the paired t-test.

$$\delta = d\sqrt{n} \tag{3.8}$$

Approximating Power

Following calculation of the noncentrality parameter, that value, along with the critical value of *t*, goes into Formula 3.9 to produce a value that I term t_{power}. The t_{power} value allows for calculation of approximate power. As noted in Chapter 1, estimation is a good way to get a conceptual understanding of power. However, estimation does not always yield accurate power values. The approach detailed here is an excellent teaching tool, but I recommend the computer-based approaches detailed in the sections that follow for formal analyses.

The value called t_{power} reflects the area on the alternative distribution above which we can reject the null hypothesis. This means that negative values of t_{power} produce more power than positive ones.

$$t_{power} = t_{critical} - \delta \qquad (3.9)$$

Exact Power

Obtaining exact power calculations requires a computer protocol. The following SPSS syntax performs this calculation (see Chapter 2 notes on using the syntax):

```
Compute Power = 1-NCDF.T(t-critical, df, δ).
```

Other sections in this chapter present formulae for additional topics, such as unequal variances and solving for desired sample size, as well as SPSS syntax files for completing all of the calculations presented in the chapter.

A NOTE ABOUT EFFECT SIZE FOR TWO-GROUP COMPARISONS

Many resources on power analysis begin with an estimate of effect size (e.g., Cohen, 1988). The application of these procedures in conjunction with the publication of shortcut guides (e.g., Cohen, 1992) sometimes focuses researchers on thinking in terms of small, medium, or large effects (corresponding to $d = 0.20$, 0.50, and 0.80, respectively) and addressing power based on these estimates. It is not always useful to focus on effect size at the outset of the research design stage. Although others criticize this "shirt size" approach (e.g., Lenth, 2001) for theoretical reasons, my objection is practical. It is often easier for researchers to think in term of units that have meaning to their work rather than a standardized measure of effect.

In many chapters of the text, the preferred approach is to begin with an estimate of raw measures. For the designs in this chapter, that would be mean differences. For example, if designing a smoking cessation program and comparing smokers who participated with those placed on a waiting list for the program, determining a meaningful level of effectiveness for the program would be easier to accomplish when focusing on mean differences (e.g., Wilkinson and Task Force on Statistical Inference, 1999). In this case, we might determine that a difference of 10 cigarettes per day (half a pack) would be the minimal level of effectiveness required to term the approach successful. This approach does not preclude use of effect sizes; rather, it encourages a focus on units relevant to the particular study.

This does not suggest that effect size estimates are not useful. Effect sizes are, of course, vitally important for understanding the context of differences. A difference of 10 cigarettes means less if your sample averages 50 cigarettes a day compared to a sample that averages 10 cigarettes a day. Similarly, a 10-cigarette difference is more meaningful if your samples produced a smaller standard deviation (e.g., 10 cigarettes) rather than a larger standard deviation (e.g., 40 cigarettes). Effect sizes are an important aspect of the context of power analysis, just not a great starting point for understanding meaningful differences between groups unless some standard is already established (e.g., effective smoking cessation programs produce a mean $d = 0.50$).

For those interested in beginning with effect sizes, employ the techniques in this chapter by starting with an effect size estimate and then creating means and standard deviations that correspond to your effect size.

Example 3.1: Comparing Two Independent Groups

In collaboration with several colleagues, I developed interactive computer-based tutorials for teaching core statistical concepts (see http://wise.cgu.edu for some of our work). An assessment of the effectiveness of one of the tutorials involved a quasi-experiment in which students in the lab sections of one course used a Web-based tutorial and another lab section in the same course completed a standard assignment. Following each assignment, students completed a short exam on the topic.

To estimate the standard deviation, I examined previous grades on a 30-point exam used for several previous semesters in the same course. This allowed for a standard deviation estimate based on data from several hundred students. Scores from previous courses yielded a standard deviation of around 5.0. There was no reason to expect different standard deviations for the two groups, so I estimated σ_p at 5.0.

Determining a meaningful effect involved comparing the work involved in implementing the new tutorial assignment to improved student outcomes. One practical consideration was the time required for instructors to implement the tutorial in courses. Implementation of the tutorial assignment involves several hours of work. Instructors would need to complete the tutorial assignment, work through common mistakes, anticipate student questions, and explore the interactive elements of the assignment to familiarize themselves with the capabilities of the instrument. In addition, because of the unfamiliar tutorial interface, the instructor would likely spend more time on student questions than for other types of assignments.

Given these new challenges, how large an effect would justify using the computer tutorial as a replacement for a more standard assignment? That is, how much improvement would convince instructors that the technique was worth their time? Based on previous experiences with the exam and what most students would accept as a "meaningful" improvement, I judged scores would have to improve performance by at least 2 points on the 30-point exam to justify the extra effort.

CALCULATION EXAMPLES (APPROXIMATE POWER)

Given these criteria, we examine the sample size required to find a mean difference $(\mu_1 - \mu_2)$ of 2 points with a standard deviation (σ_p) of 5. The following calculation shows this reflects $d = 0.40$:

$$d = \frac{\mu_1 - \mu_2}{\sigma_p} = \frac{2}{5} = 0.40$$

The next step is calculation of the approximate power for 80 students per group ($n = 80$ is an arbitrary value used to demonstrate calculations). Calculation of the noncentrality parameter yields $\delta = 2.53$. This approach requires the values for t above which the null is rejected (i.e., the critical value for t). For this example, with $n = 80$ per group, we have $df = 158$ for $\alpha = .05$, two tailed, corresponding to a $t_{critical}$ value of 1.98. The value of $\delta = 2.53$ is then compared to the $t_{critical}$ value of 1.98 using the formula that follows. The approximation approach for this independent samples example is appropriate for paired designs as well.

$$\delta = d\sqrt{\frac{n_j}{2}} = 0.40\sqrt{\frac{80}{2}} = 2.53$$

$$t_{power} = t_{critical} - \delta = 1.98 - 2.53 = -0.55$$

The calculation yields $t_{power} = -0.55$. This value reflects the point on the alternative distribution above which we reject the null hypothesis. This calculation does nothing more than convert a point on the null distribution to a point on the alternative distribution. Figure 3.1 represents these distribution points.[1] In this figure, there are two distributions. The one on the left is the null distribution. The x-axis represents scores on this distribution and range from −2.95 to +6.5. The $t_{critical}$ value of 1.98 is reflected on this axis. The value δ represents the distance between the centers of the distributions, which is 2.53. As seen on the graph, 2.53 is the center of the distribution on the top x-axis. The area on the alternative distribution (the one on the right) that falls above the $t_{critical}$

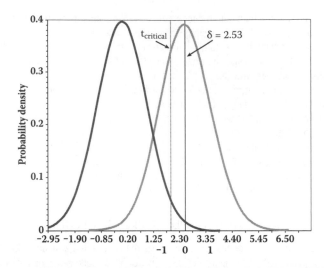

Figure 3.1 Demonstration of noncentrality parameter and power. Distribution on left is null. Distribution on right is the alternative distribution.

value represents power. From these graphs, we can see that this is a good chunk of the area, roughly about three quarters.

The t_{power} value is not particularly meaningful for interpretation, but it is necessary for calculations of power. One way to think of t_{power} is as a value that reflects a translation of the x-axis that represents scores on the null distribution to an axis that represents scores on the alternative distribution. Conceptually, this would involve moving the axis over such that 0 now fell at the center of the alternative distribution. Figure 3.1 represents this with the values below the original x-axis (−1 to +1 in bold). Here the center of the alternative distribution would become zero. The t_{power} value of −0.55 is simply where the $t_{critical}$ value would fall on the new x-axis.

Figure 3.1 also demonstrates an important difference between central and noncentral distributions. The null distribution is a central t-distribution. This distribution is a function of degrees of freedom and is symmetrical. The alternative distribution is a noncentral t-distribution. This distribution is a function of degrees of freedom and effect size. Note that the noncentral distribution is not completely symmetrical. Although it is subtle, if you look closely, you can see a slight positive skew to the distribution.

As in Chapter 2, we can approximate power using $t_{power} = -0.55$, with $df = 158$. MS Excel provides a function that accomplishes this calculation. Using MS Excel with the function 1-TDIST(0.55,158,1), we get power = .708. TDIST is an Excel function for the calculation of t-distribution probabilities, 0.55 is used because Excel cannot handle negative t-values, 158 is degrees of freedom, and 1 is for a one-tailed probability (note that the calculation involves a one-tailed value as we want the area above the critical value; this does not mean we are performing a one-tailed test). For negative values of t, the function 1-TDIST calculates the correct probability. If the t_{power} statistic comes out positive, omit the "1-" part of the equation. Again, this strategy is useful for a conceptual understanding, but accurate calculations of power require computer protocols that address noncentral distributions.

CALCULATION EXAMPLES (EXACT POWER)

SPSS provides an exact calculation of power. The calculation based on noncentral distributions is accomplished using the SPSS syntax that follows. The command requires the $t_{critical}$ value (1.98), df (158), and δ (2.53). The "1-" value remains regardless of the value of t_{power}.

```
Compute Power = 1-NCDF.T(1.98, 158, 2.53).
```

Using this strategy, the calculation yields power = .709. This appears consistent with Figure 3.1, which shows the power region as approximately three quarters of the alternative distribution (the area to the right of $t_{critical}$ = 1.98). Note that in this case, the approximation technique and the exact technique yield similar but not exactly equivalent results. This is because we have a relatively large sample size.

SOLVING FOR SAMPLE SIZE

If we want to find power = .80 (or some other value), we can work backward and rearrange some of the formulae. First, find the *t*-value above which 80% of the distribution falls. The exact value of the *t*-distribution changes depending on degrees of freedom. Practically, however, this value changes very little as degrees of freedom rise above 10. For example, df = 10, t = −0.88 is the point at or above which 80% of the distribution falls. For df = 50 and 1,000, the corresponding *t*-values are −0.85 and −0.84, respectively. Of course, most designs involving two groups have df > 10, but as an approximation strategy, using df = 10 produces a reasonable estimate.

Next, using Formula 3.10, find δ. Then, plug δ and d = 0.40 (from the calculation examples for approximate power) into Formula 3.11. The calculation indicates a sample size of 99 per group (n_j reflects the sample size per group, not the overall sample size). Also, recall that this technique uses an approximate rather than an exact technique.

$$\delta = t_{critical} - t_{power} \tag{3.10}$$

$$\delta = 1.98 - (-0.84) = 2.82$$

$$n_j = 2\left(\frac{\delta}{d}\right)^2 \tag{3.11}$$

$$n_j = 2\left(\frac{2.82}{0.40}\right)^2 = 99$$

Example 3.2 Power for Independent Samples *t* Using SPSS Syntax

The calculations for Example 3.1 are straightforward but can be easily accomplished using SPSS syntax. Tables 3.1 and 3.2 provide SPSS syntax for designs employing independent samples *t*. In the syntax file, the variables are named instruct (type of instruction: computer tutorial or standard lecture) and exam (score on the exam that followed instruction.

This syntax in Table 3.1 and many of the others that follow in this book use matrix data input. This allows us to provide SPSS with descriptive statistics instead of raw data for analysis. Providing raw data for analysis requires a full SPSS data file that includes scores that correspond to our parameters. That is, if we wanted to know power for a study with 100 participants in each group with the means that differed by 2 points, entering raw scores requires that we create data (200 cases) with those characteristics. In contrast, the matrix command allows us to enter only the mean, sample size, and pooled standard deviation.

The second section of the syntax is the MANOVA command (Table 3.2). We are not conducting multivariate analysis of variance (MANOVA). The very flexible SPSS MANOVA command provides a variety of analyses that are presented in several chapters that follow. The MANOVA command is the only syntax option in SPSS that accepts both matrix data input and provides estimates of power. As seen throughout this book, this approach is flexible but often requires multiple runs. Although I present the syntax files separately, to conduct the power analysis, run the files in Tables 3.1 and 3.2 together.

Regarding the descriptive values entered, the general procedure presented involves plugging in sample sizes until we reach our desired power. Means and standard

Table 3.1 SPSS Matrix Syntax for Data Input for Independent Samples *t*-test

Syntax	Comments
MATRIX DATA VARIABLES = Instruct ROWTYPE_ Exam / FACTORS = Instruct.	First line specifies format data; Rowtype_ indicates what is in the row, factors/IVs precede this statement
BEGIN DATA	
1 N 80	1 indicates data for the first group, 2 for the second, N = sample size for that group
2 N 80	For example, 2 N 80 = Second group, n of 80
1 MEAN 22	1 Mean 22 = First group has a mean of 22
2 MEAN 20	
. CORR 1	CORR = correlation between DVs (with 1
. STDEV 1.65	DV it is 1); the period is required for designs with 1 IV. SD = pooled standard deviation
END DATA.	

Table 3.2 SPSS Syntax for Independent Samples *t*-Test Power Analysis

Syntax	Comments
`MANOVA Exam BY Instruct` `(1,2)`	General format is DV by IV (levels). 1, 2 indicates groups 1 through 2 are being analyzed
`/MATRIX=IN(*)`	Tells SPSS to read data from the Matrix above
`/POWER exact t (.05)`	Produces power output (may also use *F*); use .10 for a test examining one-tailed power
`/PRINT = Parameters` `(efsize).`	Prints effect size (in η^2 units)

deviations are also required. Example 3.2 uses means that differ by 2 points. In the syntax, I entered means of 20 and 22 to reflect the two groups. This combined with the standard deviation of 5.0 produces the effect size of $d = 0.40$ used in the previous example.

The initial analysis examined a sample size of 80 per group, reflecting the calculation example. This analysis appears in Table 3.3. Although the tables include the complete output, much of this information is not useful.

For $n = 80$, SPSS reports power as .71. This corresponds to the calculations detailed in the calculation example sections. The noncentrality parameter is reported as 6.4. This is not the same value calculated previously because SPSS reports λ (lambda), the noncentrality parameter associated with analysis of variance (ANOVA) (and χ^2). Just as *t* corresponds to the square root of *F*, δ is the square root of λ ($\sqrt{6.40} = 2.53$).

As seen when calculating power by hand, we need to raise the sample size to obtain power $= .80$. Modifications to the syntax accomplish this analysis. Tables 3.4 and 3.5 provide an analysis with $n = 99$ per group. For most analyses, you will have to plug in values and run the analysis again. The modifications to the previous syntax are bolded in Table 3.4.

Example 3.3 Paired *t*-Test

Instead of examining score improvement with a treatment group, a separate study examined improvement following student use of a technique by which they took exams online and received immediate feedback on answers. Later in the semester, the students answered the same 30 items as part of a larger exam, allowing for a comparison of scores on the items. As the computer-based technique required programming of exams and feedback answers independently, application of the technique to new classes is time consuming, suggesting that a strong justification for the procedure would have to be present to make it worthwhile. Because the procedure is time consuming, it will only be considered effective if participants improve by 5 points on a subsequent exam on the same topics. As before, $\sigma = 5.0$.

Table 3.3 Output for *n* = 99 per Group Power Analysis

The default error term in MANOVA has been changed from WITHIN CELLS to WITHIN+RESIDUAL. Note
that these are the same for all full factorial designs.
* * * * * A n a l y s i s o f V a r i a n c e -- design 1 * * * * * *

Tests of Significance for Exam using UNIQUE sums of squares

Source of Variation	SS	DF	MS	F	Sig of F
WITHIN CELLS	3950.00	158	25.00		
Instruct	160.00	1	160.00	6.40	.012

Estimates for Exam

--- Individual univariate .9500 confidence intervals
--- two-tailed observed power taken at .0500 level

Instruct Parameter	Coeff.	Std. Err.	t-Value	Sig. t	Lower -95%	CL- Upper
2	1.00000000	.39528	2.52982	.01239	.21928	1.78072

Parameter	ETA Sq.	Noncent.	Power
2	.03893	6.40000	.710

Table 3.4 Syntax for *n* = 99 per Group Power Analysis

```
MATRIX DATA VARIABLES = Instruct ROWTYPE_ Exam
/FACTORS = Instruct.

BEGIN DATA
1 N 99
2 N 99
1 MEAN 22
2 MEAN 20
 . CORR 1
 . STDEV 5
END DATA.

MANOVA Exam BY Instruct (1,2)
/MATRIX=IN(*)
/POWER exact t (.05)
/PRINT = Parameters (efsize).
```

This test requires an estimate of the correlation between the two exams. This was not necessary for the independent sample example as participants were not tested twice. Estimating the correlation requires consideration of several factors. Correlations between measures in pre–post designs are often large (e.g., .70 or higher is not surprising). For research using reliable instruments or standardized measures, there is often considerable information on scale reliability that informs this estimate. If there are no data addressing test–retest reliability, it is best to take a conservative approach to estimating the correlation between measures ρ. I recommend using $\rho = .50$ in these situations. Larger correlations increase the effect size through reduction of the standard deviation of the differences, whereas correlations below $\rho = .50$ reduce the effect size.

Table 3.5 Edited Output for *n* = 99 per Group Power Analysis

Source of Variation	SS	DF	MS	F	Sig of F
WITHIN CELLS	4900.00	196	25.00		
Instruct	198.00	1	198.00	7.92	.005

Instruct Parameter	Coeff.	Std. Err.	t-Value	Sig. t	Lower -95%	CL- Upper
2	1.00000000	.35533	2.81425	.00539	.29923	1.70077

Parameter	ETA Sq.	Noncent.	Power
2	.03884	7.92000	.800

CALCULATION EXAMPLES

This example uses $n = 25$. As with most calculation examples, this is an arbitrary sample size used to demonstrate the calculation. In the example, notice that the standard deviation of the differences $\sigma_{x_1-x_2}$ is equal to the pooled standard deviation. That is because $\rho = .50$. Note that with $\rho = .70$, $\sigma_{x_1-x_2} = 3.87$ and $d = 1.29$. With $\rho = .30$, $\sigma_{x_1-x_2} = 5.92$ and $d = 0.84$.

$$\sigma_{x_1-x_2} = \sigma_p \sqrt{2(1-\rho)} = 5.0\sqrt{2(1-.50)} = 5\sqrt{1} = 5$$

$$d = \frac{\mu_1 - \mu_2}{\sigma_{x_1-x_2}} = \frac{5}{5} = 1.0$$

$$\delta = d\sqrt{n} = 1\sqrt{25} = 5$$

The noncentrality parameter uses the overall sample size because the same people are in each group. Starting with an estimate of 25 students participating in the study, we can calculate power.

Taking this value to a computer protocol for calculating noncentral probabilities, a sample of 25 students, $df = 24$, and t-critical value for a two-tailed test with $\alpha = .05$ of 2.06 yields power $= .998$. Thus, a sample of 25 students provides considerable power to find differences of the size of interest if they exist. Alternatively, we could reduce the sample size and retain a decent level of power.

Example 3.4 Power for Paired t-Test Using SPSS Syntax

The syntax for the paired t-test, found in Table 3.6, differs from the independent samples syntax in a few important manners. First, there is no independent variable (IV) or factor specified. The dependent variables define the factor as every person participates in both levels (pre and post). Next, specifications for descriptive statistics note two values, reflecting both measures (pre then post). The correlation between measures must be included (it is .50 for this example). In the MANOVA portion of the syntax, you must name the factor and then include a design statement to make the analysis run.

The output in Table 3.7 shows several analyses and is somewhat confusing. The first test examines the power of the constant. This test is meaningless for most purposes; however, it does produce a measure of power that can easily be misinterpreted. The power for the constant addresses the power of detecting a grand mean that deviates from zero. In most cases, this yields high power. Tests of within-subjects effects include the power estimate for the test of interest. In this example, the intercept power and within-subjects power yield similar estimates, but that will not always be the case (compare to Table 3.8).

Given this result, it is reasonable to reduce the sample size if desired. To accomplish this, run additional analyses to find a balance between power and sample. Table 3.8 shows the syntax and edited output for a sample of 13 students. With roughly half of the initially proposed sample, we retain excellent power (.91). Therefore, in this case, substantially reducing sample size retains adequate power.

Table 3.6 SPSS Matrix Syntax for Data Input for Paired-Samples *t*-Test

Syntax	Comments

`MATRIX DATA VARIABLES =`
`ROWTYPE_ pre post.`
`BEGIN DATA`
	Rowtype_ tells SPSS what will be in the row. There are no between-subject factors, so there is no IV statement. There must be two variables after the rowtype statement

`MEAN 20 25`
`STDEV 5.0 5.0`
`N 25 25`
	Mean, *SD*, and *N* are listed for pre then post (same as the order following rowtype)

`CORR 1` `CORR .50 1`	CORR is correlation between DVs. The ones reflect the pre–pre and post–post correlations. The .50 is the pre–post correlation
`END DATA.`	
`MANOVA pre post`	List the two DVs in order
`/WSFACTOR = time(2)`	Names within subject factor (indicates the number of variables). Time is not a variable described in the Matrix command
`/MATRIX=IN(*)`	Tells SPSS to read data from the Matrix above
`/POWER exact t (.05) F(.05)`	Produces power output
`/PRINT = Parameters` `(efsize)`	Prints effect size (η^2)
`/WSDESIGN = time.`	Calculates a within-subject test based on the factor we named time

DEALING WITH UNEQUAL VARIANCES, UNEQUAL SAMPLE SIZES, AND VIOLATION OF ASSUMPTIONS

The independent samples procedures presented in previous sections of the chapter assumed homogeneity of variances and employed calculations appropriate for homogeneous variances and equal sample sizes. Heterogeneous variances and unequal sample sizes impact power for designs with independent samples, so careful consideration of these issues may help the researcher avoid disappointment after study completion.

Table 3.7 Paired t-Test Output Example for *n* = 25, notes in bold

```
* * * * * A n a l y s i s   o f   V a r i a n c e -- design 1 * * * * * * *

Tests of Between-Subjects Effects.

       Tests of Significance for T1 using UNIQUE sums of squares

Source of Variation       SS          DF        MS          F        Sig of F

WITHIN+RESIDUAL         900.00        24       37.50
CONSTANT              25312.50         1    25312.50     675.00        .000

              Observed Power at the .0500 Level

Source of Variation     Noncentrality      Power

                      Estimates for T1

--- Individual univariate .9500 confidence intervals
--- two-tailed observed power taken at .0500 level
CONSTANT

Parameter           Coeff.     Std. Err.    t-Value    Sig. t   Lower -95%  CI- Upper

1                31.8198052    1.22474     25.98076    .00000    29.29206    34.34755

Parameter         ETA Sq.      Noncent.      Power

1                  .96567    675.00000      1.000 <<<< Meaningless, do not interpret.

* * * * * A n a l y s i s   o f   V a r i a n c e -- design 1 * * * * * *
Tests involving 'TIME' Within-Subject Effect.
```

Tests of Significance for T2 using UNIQUE sums of squares

Source of Variation	SS	DF	MS	F	Sig of F
WITHIN+RESIDUAL	300.00	24	12.50		
TIME	312.50	1	312.50	25.00	.000

Observed Power at the .0500 Level

Source of Variation	Noncentrality	Power
TIME	25.000	.998

Estimates for T2

--- Individual univariate .9500 confidence intervals
--- two-tailed observed power taken at .0500 level

TIME Parameter	Coeff.	Std. Err.	t-Value	Sig. t	Lower -95%	CL- Upper
1	3.53553391	.70711	5.00000	.00004	2.07614	4.99493

Parameter	ETA Sq.	Noncent.	Power	
1	.51020	25.00000	.998	<<<<< Interpret this one

Table 3.8 Modified Syntax and Edited Paired *t*-Test Output Example for $n = 13$, notes in bold

```
MATRIX DATA VARIABLES = ROWTYPE_ pre post.

BEGIN DATA
MEAN 20 25
STDEV 5 5
N 13 13
CORR 1
CORR .5 1
END DATA.
```

(MANOVA syntax omitted, same as in Table 3.6)
Tests involving 'TIME' Within-Subject Effect.

Tests of Significance for T2 using UNIQUE sums of squares

Source of Variation	SS	DF	MS	F	Sig of F
WITHIN+RESIDUAL	150.00	12	12.50		
TIME	162.50	1	162.50	13.00	.004

Observed Power at the .0500 Level

Source of Variation	Noncentrality	Power
TIME	13.000	.911

Estimates for T2

--- Individual univariate .9500 confidence intervals
--- two-tailed observed power taken at .0500 level

TIME Parameter	Coeff.	Std. Err.	t-Value	Sig. t	Lower -95%	CL- Upper
1	3.53553391	.98058	3.60555	.00361	1.39903	5.67204

Parameter	ETA Sq.	Noncent.	Power
1	.52000	13.00000	.911

Homogeneity of Variance

The independent samples t-test assumes that the variances for the two groups are roughly equal. Programs such as SPSS provide output for analyses both assuming and not assuming homogeneity. Some sources suggest that equal variance estimates are fine as long as the sample sizes are relatively equal (no more than a 4:1 ratio between the largest and smallest) and the largest variance is no more than 10 times the smallest variance (Tabachnick & Fidell, 2007b). If the ratio of largest-to-smallest variance exceeds 10:1 or sample sizes exceeded 4:1, then unequal variance estimates are preferred.

Many statistical packages include adjustments to degrees of freedom and standard error that account for violations of the heterogeneity of variance assumption. Formula 3.12 shows this adjustment, with a reduction in the degrees of freedom driven by the level of inequality between variances. I refer to this as df_{unequal}. This adjustment reduces the degrees of freedom to account for Type I error inflation resulting from unequal variances. Since the adjustment involves a reduction in degrees of freedom, the t-test probability for the unequal variances approach will be larger (usually) than the probability obtained using no adjustment. Of course, tests that make rejection criteria more stringent result in a loss of power.

$$df_{\text{unequal}} = \frac{\left(\left(s_1^2/n_1\right)+\left(s_2^2/n_2\right)\right)^2}{\dfrac{\left(s_1^2/n_1\right)^2}{n_1-1}+\dfrac{\left(s_2^2/n_2\right)^2}{n_2-1}} \tag{3.12}$$

Transformation of data addresses many heterogeneity issues effectively. Heterogeneity often occurs because of nonnormality. Transformations that return data to normality often address this problem adequately (see Tabachnick & Fidell, 2007b).

Heterogeneity and nonnormality, in addition to influencing power through the degrees of freedom adjustment, often reduce the size of observed effects. To demonstrate this, Table 3.9 presents data for a treatment and a control group, and Table 3.10 presents the summaries of raw and transformed analyses. The values in the first and second columns of Table 3.9 reflect raw data, and the two rightmost columns reflect data subjected to a logarithmic transformation. In the raw data, the treatment group variance is over 100 times the size of the control group's variance (listed as variance ratio in Table 3.10); the dependent variable shows

Table 3.9 Demonstrating the Impact of Violation of Assumptions on Power

	Raw Scores		Log Transformed	
	Control	Treatment	Control	Treatment
	33	1,811	1.53	3.26
	3,200	441	3.51	2.65
	10	1,081	1.04	3.03
	0	706	0.00	2.85
	0	730	0.00	2.86
	5	444	0.74	2.65
	328	715	2.52	2.85
	10,000	1,968	4.00	3.29
	500	19,898	2.70	4.30
	26	21,331	1.43	4.33
	23	526	1.38	2.72
	656	669	2.82	2.83
	4	684	0.65	2.84
	10	12,503	1.03	4.10
	301	2,685	2.48	3.43
	820	1,632	2.91	3.21
	500	5,986	2.70	3.78
	492	602	2.69	2.78
	3,937	125,600	3.60	5.10
	13	3,734	1.15	3.57
	19	20,121	1.30	4.30
	500	15,212	2.70	4.18
M	972	10,867	1.95	3.40
s	2,260	26,629	1.16	0.70
s^2	5,107,600	709,103,641	1.35	0.49

large values for skew and kurtosis. A general strategy for evaluating the skew and kurtosis is to divide those values by their corresponding standard errors, with ratios of less than 3.0 indicating a roughly normal distribution (again see Tabachnick & Fidell, 2007b). Using these criteria, we see very large ratios (listed as skew ratio and kurtosis ratio in Table 3.10). The raw data do not conform to the assumptions of the *t*-test. A test based on these data reduces power in two manners. First, the effect sizes differ considerably when we failed to meet assumptions ($d = 0.53$) compared to the transformed data analyses ($d = 1.52$). Second,

Table 3.10 Summary Statistics for Raw and Transformed Data

	Raw Data	Transformed
s^2 ratio	138.8	2.8
Skew	5.79	−0.48
SE skew	0.36	0.36
Skew ratio	16.1	1.3
Kurtosis	36.07	−0.16
SE kurtosis	0.70	0.70
Kurtosis ratio	51.5	0.2
d	0.53	1.52
Power	0.40	1.0

if using the adjustment for unequal variances, $df_{unequal}$ would be smaller than the unadjusted df (21.3 vs. 42).

As demonstrated in Table 3.10, violating assumptions often affects power considerably. Techniques to address assumption violations are useful as a data analytic tool; however, it is also useful for power analyses to take homogeneity of variance issues into account when violations are expected. For example, if previous work with a scale regularly produced nonnormal data, then it is a good bet that future uses of the scale will do the same.

One strategy to address violations is to conduct a t-test that uses estimates appropriate for unequal variances. This strategy adjusts the degrees of freedom ($df_{unequal}$), as shown in Formula 3.12, for what is usually a more conservative test. The SPSS syntax in Example 3.5 provides power analysis for adjusted and unadjusted tests. If you expect groups to exhibit even moderately unequal variances, use whichever power analysis suggests a larger sample size.

Unequal Sample Sizes

The formulae examined previously assumed equal sample sizes across groups. Practically, studies that lack random assignment make equal sample size requirements challenging. For most formulae, the harmonic mean of the two sample sizes as expressed in Formula 3.13 provides a good substitute. Simply place the harmonic mean in the formula for the noncentrality parameter (Formula 3.14).

$$n_{harmonic} = \frac{2n_1 n_2}{n_1 + n_2} \tag{3.13}$$

$$\delta = d\sqrt{\frac{n_{\text{harmonic}}}{2}} \qquad (3.14)$$

If sample sizes are not equal, equal and unequal variance approaches use different estimation methods for the standard error of the difference between mean, meaning that the denominator of the *t*-test changes depending on the approach. It is possible for unequal variance adjustments to produce tests that have more power than those with equal variances. However, this only occurs when you have unequal sample sizes and your largest group is the group with the larger variance.

Designing for Unequal Variances or Unequal Sample Sizes

If pretests or previous work suggest that control and treatment groups produce different variances, then it is best to address these issues in the design stage. If information exists from previous work or pretesting, then use those values to inform standard deviation estimates. If that information is not available but you do want to design for unequal variances and have only an estimate of the overall variance (or standard deviation), create two variances that pool to the overall variance with the constraint that one is much larger than the other. For example, to create two variances for which one is 10 times the size of the other with a pooled variance expected to be 22, set the first group's variance as 40 and the second group as 4.

Designs that incorporate unequal sample sizes are a useful strategy for increasing power when one group is involved in an expensive treatment or reflects a hard-to-reach population. In these cases, assigning more participants to the cheaper of your treatments and sampling more from easier-to-obtain groups increases power (Lipsey, 1990; see Chapter 11 for more discussion of this approach).

Example 3.5 Unequal Variances and Unequal Sample Sizes

This example deals with legitimately unequal variances, that is, variances that are unequal because of differences between the groups rather than nonnormal distributions. Difference of this nature do not respond to transformations and may be a product of the research design.

A few years back, I developed a reaction time based on attitudes toward hate crimes. One phase of the study compared the reactions of gay and heterosexual men to the stimulus materials. As no similar measures existed, one approach to establishing validity of the instrument involved comparing the responses of the two groups, with the expectation that the gay men held attitudes that are more negative. On our campus, there is not a large gay male population, so lab members recruited participants from the local community. The control group, heterosexual men, were recruited from traditional sources (e.g., students in introduction to psychology courses).

To start the analysis, I estimated $\sigma = 1.0$ from previous work with the reaction time task with heterosexual men. The initial study designed for an effect size around $d = 0.60$, with the gay men indicating more negative responses to the stimuli than heterosexual men. The choice of $d = 0.60$ was determined by reference to other validity studies and was the smallest effect that allowed for a reasonable argument for the validity of the instrument. Using the procedures outlined in this chapter, these estimates produced a suggested sample size of $n = 45$ per group.

Following data collection, an initial look at the data revealed a mean difference that was larger than expected. There were, however, considerable differences in standard deviations between the groups. I expected both groups to demonstrate variances similar to an earlier group (heterosexual men). This assumption held for the heterosexual male sample, who produced a standard deviation of roughly 1.0. The gay male group showed a standard deviation of 4.0. This produced a variance that was 16 times larger than found for the heterosexual men. The larger-than-expected standard deviation for the comparison group created larger standard errors, a smaller-than-desirable t-statistic, and an effect size well under the desired value ($d \approx 0.30$). In short, the study failed to find differences between gay and heterosexual men, giving no support to claims of the instrument's validity.

In retrospect, some of these issues might have been avoided. The groups differed in obvious manners over and above sexual orientation. In particular, the gay men from the community were often older. During data collection, researcher assistants observed that these participants often took much longer to learn the computer task and sometimes could not respond to stimuli before response deadlines expired. The heterosexual (college-aged) men performed the task consistently, but the gay men (community sample) produced reaction time data that were all over the place.

A major source of error in the design was estimation of the standard deviation. It was a mistake to expect the comparison group to show the same standard deviation as the control group. Although this study represents a unique situation, it may be the case that in true experiments manipulations influence standard deviations as well as means. For example, a manipulation by which one group solved problems while distracted and a control group solved problems without distraction might produce more variability in the distracted conditions. Pretesting seems to be the only way to get a clear estimate of such differences; however, considering potential differences between groups that contribute to difference in variances is an important step in research design.

CALCULATIONS AND SPSS SYNTAX FOR HETEROGENEITY AND UNEQUAL SAMPLE SIZE ADJUSTMENTS

Using this example, I present calculations for a modification to the study that uses unequal sample sizes and addresses heterogeneity of variance. For the control group (heterosexual men), the standard deviation estimate remains $\sigma = 1.0$. For the experimental group (gay men), the new estimate is $\sigma = 4.0$. This design uses a sample of heterosexual men that is three times larger than the sample of gay men.

Initially, I was interested in differences of $d = 0.60$ or larger. However, a focus on effect size is a difficult starting point for analyses based on unequal variances. The effect size uses standard deviation units that undergo an unequal variance adjustment. Following the adjustment, your effect size may differ considerably from your starting size. The strategy I suggest focuses on an effect size without adjusting for unequal variances and then uses the mean differences (i.e., the numerator) associated with that value as the target difference. As will be seen, this value may reflect a substantially smaller adjusted effect size.

The calculations that follow use an arbitrary starting sample size of 30 comparison group participants and 90 control group participants. The first step is to calculate the mean difference based on a pooled standard deviation estimate. Again, this simply provides some descriptive values for future calculations.

$$\sigma_p = \sqrt{\frac{\sigma_1^2(n_1-1)+\sigma_2^2(n_2-1)}{n_1+n_2-2}} = \sqrt{\frac{4^2(30-1)+1^2(90-1)}{30+90-2}} = 2.16$$

$$d = \frac{\mu_1-\mu_2}{\sigma_p}$$

$$0.60 = \frac{\mu_1-\mu_2}{2.16}$$

$$\mu_1-\mu_2 = 1.30$$

Next are calculations of standard deviation, degrees of freedom, and effect sizes that account for unequal variances. The primary issue here is calculation of a denominator for the *d* that does not use a pooled variance estimate. For lack of a better name, Formula 3.15 terms this $\sigma_{unequal}$. The effect size ($d_{unequal}$) is of interest as it is much smaller than the effect size based on a pooled standard deviation.

$$\sigma_{unequal} = \sqrt{\frac{\left(\dfrac{\sigma_1^2}{n_1}+\dfrac{\sigma_2^2}{n_2}\right)}{\left(\dfrac{n_1+n_2}{n_1 n_2}\right)}} \tag{3.15}$$

$$\sigma_{unequal} = \sqrt{\frac{\left(\dfrac{4^2}{30}+\dfrac{1^2}{90}\right)}{\left(\dfrac{30+90}{30*90}\right)}} = 3.5$$

$$df_{unequal} = \frac{((4^2/30)+(1^2/90))^2}{\dfrac{(4^2/30)^2}{30-1}+\dfrac{(1^2/90)^2}{90-1}} = 30.2$$

$$d_{unequal} = \frac{1.30}{3.5} = 0.37$$

Next is the calculation of the harmonic mean of the sample sizes and the noncentrality parameter. Recall that the harmonic mean is used when the sample sizes between groups differ.

$$n_{harmonic} = \frac{2n_1 n_2}{n_1 + n_2} = \frac{2(30)(90)}{30 + 90} = 45$$

$$\delta = d\sqrt{\frac{n_{harmonic}}{2}} = 0.37\sqrt{\frac{45}{2}} = 1.76$$

Calculating power for $\delta = 1.76$ requires the t-critical value for a two-tailed test with $\alpha = .05$ and $df = 30.2$. Recall that $df = 30.2$ reflects the unequal variance adjustment to the degrees of freedom. Using SPSS syntax (the one line provided in the Exact Power section), power is .40, far less than the desired level of .80.

INDEPENDENT SAMPLES SYNTAX FOR UNEQUAL VARIANCES AND UNEQUAL SAMPLE SIZES

The syntax in Table 3.11 carries out calculations for both equal and unequal variance estimates. Modify only those values in bold. Values required for this calculation include the means and standard deviations for each group, a range of sample sizes for sample calculations, and the proportion of the total sample in the first group.

In Table 3.12, d, delta, and power_eq are equal variance assumed values, and d_un, delta_un, and power_un are for unequal variances. Note the differences in power depending on the estimation technique. For equal variances, a sample of 30 in the treatment and 90 in the control group yield power of .807 (power_eq), but the unequal variance power is only .40 (power_un). Unequal variance tests do not achieve power of .80 until a sample of 78 in the treatment and 234 in the control group.

ADDITIONAL ISSUES

There are several alternative approaches to the independent samples t-test for situations when data are nonnormal or do not meet homogeneity assumptions. New developments in the use of bootstrapping techniques (also known as resampling; e.g., Keselman, Othman, Wilcox, & Fradette, 2004) and other robust methods of analysis (e.g., Wilcox & Keselman, 2003) involve promising techniques that usually outperform the traditional t-test when assumptions fail. In general, these techniques do not perform as well when assumptions are met. Although bootstrapping and other procedures are valuable, and often more powerful, alternatives to the procedures discussed in this chapter, there are not well-established conventions for the use of these procedures or power analysis strategies for these techniques.

Table 3.11 SPSS Syntax for Variance and Sample Adjusted Power

Syntax	Comments

`INPUT PROGRAM.`
`LOOP n=20 TO 400 by 2.`
`END CASE.`
`END LOOP.`
`END FILE.`
`END INPUT PROGRAM.`
`EXECUTE .`
 	
`Compute Prop_N1 = 0.25.`
`Compute N1 = N * Prop_N1.`
`Compute N2 = N *`
` (1-Prop_N1).`
`Compute M1 = 1.3.`
`Compute M2 = 0.`
 	
`Compute S1 = 4.`
`Compute S2 = 1.`
`Compute alpha = .05.`
`Compute tails = 2.`
`execute.`
	The Loop command does calculations for a range of values, in this case from 20 to 400 in increments of 2
	
	This is the total sample size ($n1 + n2$)
	
	The Prop_N1 command calculates the proportion of the sample in the first group. For this example, we have 25% in Group 1
	
	M1 and M2 are the means. The difference between M1 and M2 should equal the mean difference
	
	S1 and S2 are the standard deviations. Make sure these match the right group
	Alpha and tails are optional

***** Modifications End Here******

```
Compute df = n-2.
Compute n_harm = ((2*n1*n2)/(n1+n2)).
Compute var1 = s1*s1.
Compute var2 = s2*s2.
Compute nxs1 = (n1-1)*(var1).
Compute nxs2 = (n2-1)*(var2).
Compute s2p = (nxs1+nxs2)/(df).
Compute sp = sqrt(s2p).
Compute d = (M1-M2)/sp.
Compute delta = d*sqrt(n_harm / 2).
Compute alpha_tails = alpha/tails.
Compute fail = 1-alpha_tails.
Compute t_table = IDF.t(fail,df).
Compute sat_num = ((var1/n1)+(var2/n2)) *((var1/n1) +
 (var2/n2)).
Compute sat_denom = ((((var1/n1)**2))/(n1-1)) +((((var2/
 n2)**2))/(n2-1)).
Compute sx1_un = s1/sqrt(n1).
Compute sx2_un = s2/sqrt(n2).
Compute sx1x2_un = sqrt(sx1_un**2+sx2_un**2).
```

Table 3.11 SPSS Syntax for Variance and Sample Adjusted Power (continued)

Syntax	Comments
Compute t_un = (M1-M2)/sx1x2_un.	
Compute d_un = t_un * sqrt((n1+n2)/(n1*n2)).	
Compute df_un = sat_num/sat_denom.	
Compute delta_un = d_un*sqrt(n_harm / 2).	
Compute t_table_un = IDF.t(fail,df_un) .	
Compute Power_Eq = 1-NCDF.t(t_table,df,delta) .	
Compute Power_Un = 1-NCDF.t(t_table_un,df_un,delta_un) .	
execute.	
MATRIX.	
GET M /VARIABLES= n1 n2 d delta d_un delta_un power_eq power_un .	
print M/title = "t test with homogeneity adjusted power"/clabels = "n1" "n2" "d" "delta" "d_un" "delta_un" "power_eq" "power_un"/format f8.3.	
End Matrix.	

Table 3.12 SPSS Output for Variance and Sample Adjusted Power

	t-test with homogeneity adjusted power						
n1	n2	d	delta	d_un	delta_un	power_eq	power_un
30.000	90.000	.601	2.848	.371	1.762	.807	.400
36.000	108.000	.600	3.117	.371	1.930	.872	.468
42.000	126.000	.599	3.364	.371	2.085	.917	.531
48.000	144.000	.599	3.594	.371	2.229	.947	.589
54.000	162.000	.599	3.810	.371	2.364	.967	.642
60.000	180.000	.598	4.015	.371	2.492	.979	.689
66.000	198.000	.598	4.209	.371	2.613	.987	.731
72.000	216.000	.598	4.395	.371	2.729	.992	.768
78.000	234.000	.598	4.574	.371	2.841	.995	.801
84.000	252.000	.598	4.746	.371	2.948	.997	.830
90.000	270.000	.598	4.911	.371	3.052	.998	.855
96.000	288.000	.598	5.072	.371	3.152	.999	.877

SUMMARY

This chapter examined power analysis for designs employing independent and paired *t*-tests. Independent samples designs require estimates of means and standard deviations (or just the effect size) to estimate power. Paired designs require means, standard deviations, and estimates of the correlation between measures. For independent samples, homogeneity of variance and unequal sample sizes influence power. Careful consideration of these issues establishes more accurate power estimates.

NOTE

1. This graph was produced using ESCI (Exploratory Software for Confidence Intervals) software; see Chapter 11 for information on this outstanding visualization tool.

4

CORRELATIONS AND DIFFERENCES
BETWEEN CORRELATIONS

INTRODUCTION

This chapter examines power for tests of zero-order Pearson correlations and for tests of differences involving either independent or dependent correlations. Approaches to comparing dependent correlations are not widely presented in the behavioral sciences literature (i.e., these techniques do not appear in most statistics textbooks), so sections on those topics provide resources for testing hypotheses as well as conducting power analysis.

NECESSARY INFORMATION

The tests covered in this chapter require specification of either a meaningful correlation (ρ) for the population or meaningful differences between population correlations. Procedures involving three or more correlations require specifications of correlations between all variables addressed in the procedure.

FACTORS AFFECTING POWER

Correlations are measures of effect sizes, so larger correlations produce more power. For tests involving differences between correlations, the size of the difference to be detected, and if relevant, the correlation between the variables compared impact power, with larger differences between predictors yielding more power and greater overlap between the predictors being compared yielding less power. In addition, differences between stronger correlations (e.g., .60 and .80) produce more power than tests of differences between smaller correlations (e.g., .20 and .40). For all tests, larger sample sizes and more liberal α increase power.

ZERO-ORDER CORRELATION

Key Statistics

Addressing power for a zero-order correlation involves converting the correlation (ρ) to Cohen's d (Formula 4.1) and then computing a noncentrality parameter (δ) from d (Formula 4.2). After computing these values, the analysis proceeds like the t-test procedures discussed in Chapter 3. Formula 4.2 for the calculation of δ uses $n - 2$ in the numerator (degrees of freedom). There is no strong agreement on whether to use sample size n or degrees of freedom $n - 2$ for noncentrality and power calculations. My recommendation is to use degrees of freedom as this yields a more conservative test as this approach makes for a smaller noncentrality parameter.

$$d = \frac{2\rho}{\sqrt{(1-\rho^2)}} \qquad (4.1)$$

$$\delta = \frac{d\sqrt{n-2}}{2} \qquad (4.2)$$

As discussed in previous chapters, computations of power for several tests in this chapter involve the noncentral t-distribution. Computer protocols allow us to calculate accurate values for power for those tests.

Example 4.1 Zero Order Correlation

An issue of particular interest in social psychology is the correlation between measures of attitudes and behaviors, behavioral intentions, or expectations. The example that follows reflects work in my laboratory examining how implicit and explicit attitudes differentially predict behavioral expectations of aggression. Expectations of aggression are important in that they relate to enactment of aggressive scripts that predict actual acts of aggression (Anderson & Bushman, 2002). One question asked in this example is whether a measure of implicitly held attitudes toward gay men predicts expectations of aggression.

An important starting point is to ask how large a correlation we want to be able to detect. The best question is not how big the expected correlation is but how large the minimum meaningful correlation is. To establish context, one approach is to reference results from similar research. Meta-analytic results focusing on relationships between implicit attitudes and other behavior-relevant measures reported an average correlation of roughly .30 (Greenwald, Poehlman, Uhlmann, & Banaji, 2009). Of course, simply being the average correlation found across similar studies does not mean a correlation of .30 is practically meaningful. At this point, a reasonable question is whether this correlation is large enough to be of practical value. For research of this nature, this can be a slippery question. On the one hand, expectations of aggression do relate to aggressive behavior, and even small reductions in aggressive behavior can be practically important. On the other hand, the research addresses measures potentially related to behavior rather than actual behaviors, so there is a degree of separation between the dependent measure and actual acts of aggression. In addition, there is some evidence that the link between predictors and expectations often produces smaller effects than predictor–behavior relationships do (e.g., Greitemeyer, 2009). Therefore, it is reasonable to expect that the influence of attitudes on behaviors (particularly extreme behaviors like aggression) may be substantially smaller than the attitude–aggressive expectation link. For this reason, we settled on a correlation of .30, believing that this would provide some "cushion" for finding relationships between attitudes and actual behaviors in future research.

It is important to note that even small correlations can be meaningful. For example, as Rosenthal and Rubin (1982) discussed, a correlation of .10 between a treatment and a life-or-death outcome corresponds to saving 10 more people's lives out of 100 than a treatment producing a correlation of .00 between treatment and outcome. Although a correlation of .10 corresponds to a "small" effect size (Cohen, 1988), clearly the treatment demonstrates a meaningful effect. Context is far more important than small, medium, and large labels.

CALCULATIONS

After determining that a meaningful correlation for the population in this example is $\rho = .30$, we can address power analysis. The example that follows begins with a sample size of 66 and a two tailed test with $\alpha = .05$. The degrees of freedom for this test is $n - 2$, yielding a critical value of $t(64) = 2.00$.

$$d = \frac{2\rho}{\sqrt{(1-\rho^2)}} = \frac{2*.30}{\sqrt{1-.30^2}} = .629$$

$$\delta = \frac{d\sqrt{n-2}}{2} = \frac{.629\sqrt{66-2}}{2} = 2.52$$

To find power for 66 participants, we can take the noncentrality parameter to SPSS. Using the following line of syntax, with a critical value of $t(64) = 2.00$ and $\delta = 2.52$, SPSS computes power $= .70$ (see the notes in Chapter 2 about using this approach):

```
SPSS Syntax: Compute Power = 1-NCDF.T(2.00, 64, 2.52).
```

SPSS SYNTAX

The syntax presented in Table 4.1 computes power for a range of sample sizes. We need to specify the desired range of sample sizes, the population correlation, α, and the number of tails on the test.

Table 4.1 Syntax for Zero-Order Correlation Power Analysis

Syntax	Comments (What to Modify)
```INPUT PROGRAM.```	
```LOOP n=60 TO 100 by 2.```	60 to 100 by 2 means that power
```END CASE.```	calculations will be performed for samples
```END LOOP.```	of size 60, 62, 64, ... , 100; change values
```END FILE.```	for different samples (e.g., 100 to 1,000
```END INPUT PROGRAM.```	by 10)
```EXECUTE.```	
```Compute r = 0.3.```	Input correlation here
```Compute alpha = .05.```	Input alpha
```Compute tails = 2.```	Input tails
```Compute r = abs(r).```	***Do not modify here or below
```Compute t = (r*((n-2)**.5))/``` ```((1-(r**2))**.5).```	
```Compute d = 2*r/``` ```((1-(r**2))**.5).```	Formula 4.1 (convert to d)
```Compute delta = (d*sqrt``` ```(n-2))/2.```	Formula 4.2 (noncentrality)
```Compute alpha_tails = alpha/``` ```tails.```	
```Compute fail =``` ```1-alpha_tails.```	
```Compute df = n-2.```	
```Compute t_table =``` ```IDF.t(fail,df).```	Critical value of t
```Compute Power = 1-NCDF.t``` ```(t_table,df,delta).```	Power based on the noncentral t
```Execute.```	
```Matrix.```	
```GET M /VARIABLES=n d delta``` ```Power.```	

```Print M/title = "Power```
```Analysis for Correlation"```
```/clabels = "N" "d" "Delta"```
```"Power"/format f10.4.```	

```End Matrix.```	

Table 4.2 Output for Power Analysis of Single-Sample
Correlation

Power	Analysis	for Correlation	
N	d	Delta	Power
60.0	.6290	2.3950	.6537
62.0	.6290	2.4360	.6689
64.0	.6290	2.4763	.6836
66.0	.6290	2.5159	.6978
68.0	.6290	2.5549	.7114
70.0	.6290	2.5933	.7246
72.0	.6290	2.6312	.7373
74.0	.6290	2.6685	.7495
76.0	.6290	2.7053	.7612
78.0	.6290	2.7416	.7724
80.0	.6290	2.7775	.7832
82.0	.6290	2.8128	.7936
84.0	.6290	2.8478	.8035
86.0	.6290	2.8823	.8131
88.0	.6290	2.9164	.8222
90.0	.6290	2.9501	.8309
92.0	.6290	2.9835	.8393
94.0	.6290	3.0164	.8473
96.0	.6290	3.0490	.8549
98.0	.6290	3.0813	.8622
100.0	.6290	3.1132	.8692

Table 4.2 presents the output for this analysis with the power corresponding to each sample size. As shown in the calculations section, use of 66 participants yields a power of .70. Power of .80 requires a sample of 84 participants.

COMPARING TWO INDEPENDENT CORRELATIONS

This test compares correlations drawn from independent populations. For example, this approach allows for tests involving meaningful differences among correlations between two variables measured for control group participants and the correlation between the same measures among experimental group participants in a between-subjects design.

Key Statistics

The first step in this test is application of Fisher's transformation (Fisher, 1921) to the two expected population correlations. Formula 4.3 notes the converted value as z_ρ. Other sources represent the Fisher's transformed correlation as z_r or r'. Many statistics texts provide a table for this transformation, but it is not difficult to compute with a hand calculator. Microsoft Excel provides a function called FISHER that performs the calculation as well.

$$z_\rho = 0.5 * \ln \frac{1+\rho}{1-\rho} \tag{4.3}$$

After calculating z_ρ for both correlations, take the difference between these values, noted as q and shown in Formula 4.4. This value is the effect size for the differences between the correlations.

$$q = |z_{\rho_1} - z_{\rho_2}| \tag{4.4}$$

Next is the calculation of z_δ. That value serves a role much like the noncentrality parameters discussed in other sections. However, this is not a noncentrality parameter because the normal distribution used for this test is a central rather than noncentral distribution. Calculation of z_δ requires a standard deviation as well. This value, shown in Formula 4.5, is a function of the sample sizes and serves as the denominator for Formula 4.6. The final calculation (Formula 4.7) finds the point on the alternative distribution that corresponds to the decision criteria. After computing z_{power}, take this value to a normal distribution table. The area above z_{power} reflects the proportion of sample results given the population correlations we specified that would allow for rejection of the null hypothesis. Since the normal distribution is a central distribution, it is possible to calculate power by hand accurately (see Chapters 1 and 2 for a discussion of this issue and for examples of the calculation techniques).

$$\sigma_q = \sqrt{\frac{1}{n_1 - 3} + \frac{1}{n_2 - 3}} \tag{4.5}$$

$$z_\delta = \frac{q}{\sigma_q} \tag{4.6}$$

$$z_{power} = z_{critical} - z_\delta \tag{4.7}$$

Example 4.2 Comparing Independent Correlations

Extending Example 4.1, we predicted that participants assigned to different research conditions would show different levels of correlation between implicit attitudes and aggressive expectations. One condition involved priming of participants to think about their evaluations of gay men. In the second condition, there was no priming. We expected that in the first condition priming promoted deliberation over responses, a situation usually linked to very small correlations between implicit attitudes and behaviors.

The second condition promoted spontaneous processing, a situation linked to stronger implicit–behavior correlations. We predicted expectations to follow the same pattern seen for behaviors. For the first condition, we expected little relationship between attitudes and expectations, so we chose a small correlation of .10 for this condition (noted ρ_1). The expected correlation for the second condition was .30 as before (noted as ρ_2).

CALCULATIONS

To determine power for detecting differences of this size, first convert both correlations using the Fisher transformation.

$$z_{\rho 1} = \frac{\ln(1+\rho) - \ln(1-\rho)}{2} = \frac{\ln(1+.10) - \ln(1-.10)}{2} = \frac{.095 - (-.105)}{2} = 0.100$$

$$z_{\rho 2} = \frac{\ln(1+\rho) - \ln(1-\rho)}{2} = \frac{\ln(1+.30) - \ln(1-.30)}{2} = \frac{.262 - (-.357)}{2} = 0.310$$

After calculating z_ρ for both correlations, calculate the effect size q. Note that a difference between correlations of .20 as found produces different effect sizes depending on the correlation values. In this example, $q = 0.21$. However, if the correlations were .60 and .80, then $q = 0.41$.

$$q = |z_{\rho_1} - z_{\rho_2}| = |.100 - .310| = 0.210$$

Following the calculation of the effect size q, calculate the standard deviation and z_δ. The following example computes power for a sample of 100 participants per condition:

$$\sigma_q = \sqrt{\frac{1}{n_1 - 3} + \frac{1}{n_2 - 3}} = \sqrt{\frac{1}{100 - 3} + \frac{1}{100 - 3}} = 0.144$$

$$z_\delta = \frac{q}{\sigma_q} = \frac{.210}{.144} = 1.458$$

To obtain power for a one-tailed test with $\alpha = .05$ ($z = 1.645$), calculate z_{power} using the next formula. Since this test uses the normal distribution, it is not necessary to reference a noncentral distribution. To find power, use the normal distribution to determine the area corresponding to power. A sample of $n = 100$ per group yields power of .43. The value of .43 is simply the area above $z = 0.187$ on the normal distribution (see Chapter 2 for a graphical demonstration of this technique).

$$z_{power} = z_{critical} - z_\delta = 1.645 - 1.458 = 0.187$$

SPSS SYNTAX

The syntax in Table 4.3 performs calculations for a range of sample sizes. The syntax is flexible, allowing for unequal sample sizes. For unequal sample sizes, specify the proportion of the sample in each group (as demonstrated in Chapter 3).

Table 4.3 Syntax for Comparing Two Independent Correlations

Syntax	Comments
```INPUT PROGRAM.```	
```LOOP n=200 TO 1000 by 50.```	Range of sample sizes; keep in mind
```END CASE.```	these are split between two groups
```END LOOP.```	
```END FILE.```	
```END INPUT PROGRAM.```	
```EXECUTE.```	
```Compute r1 = 0.3.```	The two correlations to compare
```Compute r2 = 0.1.```	
```Compute Prop_N1 = 0.5.```	Proportion in Group 1 set to .50 for
```Compute alpha = .05.```	equal ns
```Compute tails = 1.```	
```Compute N2 = N * (1-Prop_N1).```	**** Do not modify here or below ****
```Compute N1 = N * Prop_N1.```	
```Compute z_r1 = 0.5 * (Ln((1 +``` ```r1) / (1 - r1))).```	Formula 4.3 (Fisher transformation for both correlations)
```Compute z_r2 = 0.5 *``` ```(Ln((1 + r2) / (1 - r2))).```	Formula 4.4 (q) Formula 4.5 (standard deviation of z)
```Compute z_diff = abs(z_r1-z_r2).```	
```Compute sdz = Sqrt((1 /``` ```(n1 - 3))+(1 / (n2 - 3))).```	Formula 4.6 (z_δ)
```Compute z = z_diff/sdz.```	
```If tails = 1 prob = 1-alpha.```	
```If tails = 2 prob = 1-(alpha/2).```	
```Compute tabled = IDF.``` ```NORMAL(prob,0,1).```	
```Compute z_power = tabled - z.```	
```Compute power = 1-CDF.Normal``` ```(z_power,0,1).```	Power based on normal distribution
```Compute p = (1-CDF.``` ```Normal(z,0,1))*tails.```	
```execute.```	
```Matrix.```	
```GET M /VARIABLES=n1 n2 Power z p.```	

```print M/title = "Power```
 ```Analysis for Comparing```
 ```Independent Correlations"```
 ```/clabels = "N1" "N2" "Power"```
 ```"z" "p"/format f10.4.```	

```End Matrix.```	

Table 4.4 Output for Comparing Two Independent Correlations

Power Analysis for Comparing Independent Correlations				
N1	N2	Power	z	p
100.0	100.0	.4254	1.4568	.0726
125.0	125.0	.4956	1.6338	.0512
150.0	150.0	.5590	1.7934	.0365
175.0	175.0	.6160	1.9399	.0262
200.0	200.0	.6669	2.0761	.0189
225.0	225.0	.7119	2.2039	.0138
250.0	250.0	.7517	2.3247	.0100
275.0	275.0	.7866	2.4395	.0074
300.0	300.0	.8171	2.5491	.0054
325.0	325.0	.8436	2.6543	.0040
350.0	350.0	.8666	2.7554	.0029
375.0	375.0	.8865	2.8529	.0022
400.0	400.0	.9036	2.9472	.0016
425.0	425.0	.9183	3.0386	.0012
450.0	450.0	.9309	3.1273	.0009
475.0	475.0	.9416	3.2135	.0007
500.0	500.0	.9508	3.2976	.0005

Table 4.4 shows that using a one-tailed test with $\alpha = .05$, power reaches .80 at around $n = 300$ per group. Note that the output also provides z and p statistics. Those values are the significance tests for differences between independent correlations that may be used to perform significance tests for completed research (enter the observed correlations and test for the actual sample size).

COMPARING TWO DEPENDENT CORRELATIONS (ONE VARIABLE IN COMMON)

Dependent correlations are correlations that come from the same sample. For example, a researcher might measure the correlation between two predictors and one outcome variable and ask whether one of the predictors related more strongly to the outcome than the other. This section deals with situations when the correlations to be compared share a single variable in common (e.g., the same outcome variable but different predictors).

Key Statistics

Testing a difference between dependent correlations requires a more complex procedure than testing differences between independent correlations. Power depends on the correlation between the two predictors as well as their correlations with the shared outcome variable. For this test, it is important to establish accurate estimates of the correlations between predictors ρ_{12} as this value impacts calculation of the noncentrality parameter considerably. The first step in these calculations is to average the two correlations of interest using Formula 4.8. Next, Formula 4.9 defines a value noted as $\rho_{\det}$. This is the determinant of the correlation matrix. You can also complete this calculation using a matrix algebra calculator (there are many freely available online). Finally, using Formula 4.10, calculate the noncentrality parameter δ and then address power based on the noncentral t-distribution as in previous sections.

The approach detailed next comes from the work of Williams (1959) and performs better in terms of Type I errors than approaches based on the normal distribution (Hittner, May, & Silver, 2003):

$$\bar{\rho} = \frac{(\rho_{y1} + \rho_{y2})}{2} \tag{4.8}$$

$$\rho_{\det} = 1 - \rho_{y1}^2 - \rho_{y2}^2 - \rho_{12}^2 + 2\rho_{y1}\rho_{y2}\rho_{12} \tag{4.9}$$

$$\delta = |\rho_{y1} - \rho_{y2}| \sqrt{\frac{(n-1)(1+\rho_{12})}{2(n-1)/\rho_{\det}(n-3) + \bar{\rho}^2(1-\rho_{12})^3}} \tag{4.10}$$

Example 4.3 Comparing Dependent Correlations, One Variable in Common

Extending the previous examples, another issue of interest is whether certain measures of attitudes predict expectations better than others do. In particular, do implicitly held attitudes predict aggression better than explicitly stated attitudes?

Tests of this nature require information about how strongly the two variables of interest correlate with the dependent measure and how strongly the predictors correlate with each other (i.e., the information in a correlation matrix with all three variables). In Example 4.1, we determined that a meaningful relationship between implicit attitudes and expectations was .30. Based on previous work, I expected the correlation between explicit attitudes and expectations to be no more than .04. Although this was a very weak relationship, the present test asks specifically if the implicit–expectation relationship is stronger than the explicit–expectation relationship. This is a different question than whether one relationship is statistically significant while the other is not. The final estimate needed is the correlation between the implicit and explicit measures. These values vary widely in the literature and are often context specific. An earlier study in the research lab using both measures found a correlation of .20. This was consistent with the range of correlations found in other studies examining relationships between implicit and explicit attitudes for other socially sensitive topics. These results suggest that .20 is a reasonable estimate of the correlation between predictors.

CALCULATIONS

The three correlations of interest were .30 for the implicit (1)–intention (y) relationship, .04 for explicit (2)–intention (y), and .20 for implicit (1)–explicit (2). Formula 4.8 calculates the average of the two predictor-dv (dependent variable) correlations. Next, Formula 4.9 produces the determinant of the correlation matrix.

$$\bar{\rho} = \frac{(\rho_{y1} + \rho_{y2})}{2} = \frac{.04 + .30}{2} = .17$$

$$\rho_{det} = 1 - \rho_{y1}^2 - \rho_{y2}^2 - \rho_{12}^2 + 2\rho_{y1}\rho_{y2}\rho_{12} = 1 - .30^2 - .04^2 - .20^2 + 2(.30)(.04)(.20) = .8732$$

After calculating the average and determinant, Formula 4.10 yields the noncentrality parameter. This example uses $n = 100$. The degrees of freedom for this test is $n - 3$, and the critical value for a two-tailed test with $\alpha = .05$ is $t = 1.98$. Modifying the single line of SPSS syntax for calculating power given the noncentrality parameter (see the section on zero-order correlation) to read Compute Power = 1-NCDF.T(1.98, 97, 2.11) yields power = .55.

$$\delta = |\rho_{y1} - \rho_{y2}| \sqrt{\frac{(n-1)(1+\rho_{12})}{\left(2(n-1)/(n-3)\right)\rho_{det} + \rho^2(1-\rho_{12})^3}} =$$

$$|.30 - .04| \sqrt{\frac{(100-1)(1+.2)}{\left(2(100-1)/(100-3)\right).8732 + .17^2(1-.2)^3}} = 2.11$$

SPSS SYNTAX

The SPSS syntax in Table 4.5 performs this calculation for a range of values. The aspects of the syntax that require modification are similar to those in Table 4.3 but include three rather than two correlations.

The syntax produces the output in Table 4.6. Consistent with previous calculations, a sample of $n = 100$ produces power of .55. The output shows that power of 80% requires a sample between 170 and 180. The syntax in Table 4.5 may be modified to get an exact sample size corresponding to the desired level of power (e.g., change LOOP $n =$ 100 TO 300 by 10 to LOOP $n = 170$ TO 180 by 1).

COMPARING TWO DEPENDENT CORRELATIONS (NO VARIABLES IN COMMON)

This test compares two correlations based on two separate pairs of variables when all four variables are measured on the same sample. A common application of this technique is for repeated-measures test of correlations. For example, this test is appropriate for determining whether the strength of a correlation between two variables differs

Table 4.5 Syntax for Comparing Two Dependent Correlations (One Variable in Common)

Syntax	Comments
| ```
INPUT PROGRAM.
LOOP n=100 TO 300 by 10.
END CASE.
END LOOP.
END FILE.
END INPUT PROGRAM.
EXECUTE.
``` | |
| ```
Compute r1y = .3.
Compute r2y = .04.
Compute r12 = .2.
Compute alpha = .05.
Compute tails = 2.
Compute df = n-3.
Compute r_diff =abs(r1y-r2y).
Compute r_ave = (r1y+r2y)/2.
Compute r_det = 1-(r1y**2)-
 (r2y**2)-(r12**2)+(2*r1y*r2y*r12).
Compute numer = (n-1)*(1+r12).
Compute denom1 = ((2*(n-1))/(n-3))*r_det.
Compute denom2 = (r_ave**2)*((1-r12)**3).
Compute denom = denom1+denom2.
Compute delta = r_diff*((numer/
 denom)**.5).
Compute alpha_tails = alpha/tails.
Compute fail = 1-alpha_tails.
Compute t_table = IDF.t(fail,df).
Compute Power =
 1-NCDF.t(t_table,df,delta).
Compute t = delta.
Compute p = (1-CDF.t(t,df))*tails.
execute.
Matrix.
GET M /VARIABLES=n Power t p.
print M/title = "Power Analysis for
 Comparing Dependent Correlations
 One Shared Variable"
/clabels = "N" "Power" "t" "p"/
 format f10.4.
End Matrix.
``` | The three correlations go here<br><br><br><br><br>****No modifications below<br> this point<br>Formula 4.8 (average<br> correlations)<br>Formula 4.9 (determinant)<br><br><br><br><br><br>Formula 4.10 (noncentrality<br> parameter) |

Table 4.6 Output for Comparing Two Dependent Correlations
(One Variable in Common)

Power Analysis for Comparing
Dependent Correlations One Shared
Variable

N	Power	t	p
100.0	.5529	2.1139	.0371
110.0	.5949	2.2202	.0285
120.0	.6340	2.3216	.0220
130.0	.6702	2.4187	.0170
140.0	.7035	2.5122	.0132
150.0	.7341	2.6022	.0102
160.0	.7620	2.6893	.0079
170.0	.7875	2.7736	.0062
180.0	.8105	2.8554	.0048
190.0	.8314	2.9349	.0038
200.0	.8503	3.0124	.0029
210.0	.8673	3.0879	.0023
220.0	.8825	3.1616	.0018
230.0	.8962	3.2336	.0014
240.0	.9084	3.3041	.0011
250.0	.9192	3.3731	.0009
260.0	.9289	3.4407	.0007
270.0	.9375	3.5069	.0005
280.0	.9452	3.5720	.0004
290.0	.9519	3.6359	.0003
300.0	.9579	3.6987	.0003

across conditions that included the same participants. Questions of this nature might also examine whether the same variables correlate in the same manner across situations or over time.

Key Statistics

For these tests, the four variables yield six correlations representing all possible pairs. Power calculations use all six of these correlations. Formulae 4.11–4.14 note correlations with the subscripts 1, 2, x, and y. Numbers correspond to the first measurement situation and the letters to the second. The test compares ρ_{12} and ρ_{xy}.

Formula 4.11 averages the correlations of interest. Formula 4.12 derives the covariance for the difference between the Fisher transformed correlations noted here as cov_{ps}. The q statistic found in Formula 4.13 examines the differences between the correlations of interest and requires the Fisher's transformation on each correlation using Formula 4.3.

The z_δ value calls for sample size, covariance between the correlations, and q. This test uses the normal distribution, so we plug z_δ into Formula 4.7. The procedure comes from the work of Steiger (1980) with a modification proposed by Silver and Dunlap (1987). This is one of several procedures recommended by Silver et al. (2004).

$$\bar{\rho} = \frac{(\rho_{12} + \rho_{xy})}{2} \tag{4.11}$$

$$\text{cov}_{\rho s} = \frac{.5 * ([(\rho_{1x} - \rho_{12}\rho_{2x})(\rho_{2y} - \rho_{2x}\rho_{xy})] + [(\rho_{1y} - \rho_{1x}\rho_{xy})(\rho_{2x} - \rho_{12}\rho_{1x})] + [(\rho_{1x} - \rho_{1y}\rho_{xy})(\rho_{2y} - \rho_{12}\rho_{1y})] + [(\rho_{1y} - \rho_{12}\rho_{2y})(\rho_{2x} - \rho_{2y}\rho_{xy})])}{(1 - \rho^2)^2} \tag{4.12}$$

$$q = |z_{\rho_{12}} - z_{\rho_{xy}}| \tag{4.13}$$

$$z_\delta = \frac{q\sqrt{n-3}}{\sqrt{2 - 2\text{cov}_{\rho s}}} \tag{4.14}$$

Example 4.4 Comparing Dependent Correlations, No Variables in Common

An example of this approach comes from the work of a former student and his advisor (Davis & Henry, 2008). They examined how strongly two variables correlated when measured in the research laboratory compared to measures of the same variables provided by the same participants online. Specifically, they addressed the correspondence of feelings toward African Americans and symbolic racism. The researchers predicted stronger correlations for data collected online compared to data collected in the laboratory. Using the authors' work as a template for designing a larger-scale investigation, the following example addresses the sample size necessary for power of .80.[1]

CALCULATIONS

This test requires all of the pairwise correlations, represented in a matrix of correlations in Table 4.7. Numbered labels designate the first set (correlations in the research laboratory) and letters designate the second set (Internet sample).

The calculations first find the average correlation between the two concepts of interest.

$$\bar{\rho} = \frac{(\rho_{12} + \rho_{xy})}{2} = \frac{.40 + .70}{2} = .55$$

This test requires application of Fisher's transformation to both correlations and then computation of the difference between the two to calculate the effect size q. This

Table 4.7 Correlations Between Variables for Comparing Two Dependent Correlations (No Shared Variables)

	1	2	x
1			
2	.40		
X	.30	.45	
Y	.10	.35	.70

example assumes a two-tailed test and so uses the absolute value of the difference. This corresponds to a test of the difference in magnitudes, disregarding sign. For a test that considers the direction of difference, use the signed difference rather than the absolute difference.

$$z_{\rho 12} = \frac{\ln(1+\rho) - \ln(1-\rho)}{2} = \frac{\ln(1+.40) - \ln(1-.40)}{2} = 0.424$$

$$z_{\rho xy} = \frac{\ln(1+\rho) - \ln(1-\rho)}{2} = \frac{\ln(1+.70) - \ln(1-.70)}{2} = 0.867$$

$$q = |z_{\rho_{12}} - z_{\rho_{xy}}| = |.424 - .867| = 0.443$$

The extensive calculation that follows is the covariance between the correlations.

$$cov_{\rho s} = \frac{\begin{array}{c} .5 * ([(\rho_{1x} - \rho_{12}\rho_{2x})(\rho_{2y} - \rho_{2x}\rho_{xy})] + [(\rho_{1y} - \rho_{1x}\rho_{xy})(\rho_{2x} - \rho_{12}\rho_{1x})] \\ + [(\rho_{1x} - \rho_{1y}\rho_{xy})(\rho_{2y} - \rho_{12}\rho_{1y})] + [(\rho_{1y} - \rho_{12}\rho_{2y})(\rho_{2x} - \rho_{2y}\rho_{xy})]) \end{array}}{(1 - \overline{\rho^2})^2}$$

$$= \frac{\begin{array}{c} .5 * ([(.3 - .4 * .45)(.35 - .45 * .7)] + [(.1 - .3 * .7)(.45 - .4 * .3)] \\ + [(.3 - .1 * .7)(.35 - .4 * .1)] + [(.1 - .4 * .35)(.45 - .35 * .70)]) \end{array}}{(1 - .55^2)^2}$$

$$= \frac{.5 * [(.12)(.035) + (-.11)(.33) + (.23)(.31) + (-.04)(.205)]}{(.6975)^2}$$

$$= \frac{.5 * (.0042 - .0363 + .0713 - .0082)}{.4865} = \frac{.0155}{.4865} = 0.0319$$

The final step involves computation of z_δ and then use of that value in conjunction with the $z_{critical}$ value (.05, two tailed in this example) to find power. In this case, power corresponds to the area above 0.65 on the standardized normal distribution. This area (power) is .26.

$$z_\delta = \frac{q\sqrt{n-3}}{\sqrt{2-2\,cov_{\rho s}}} \quad \frac{0.443\sqrt{20-3}}{\sqrt{2-(2*.0319)}} = \frac{1.827}{1.391} = 1.31$$

$$z_{power} = z_{critical} - z_\delta = 1.96 - 1.31 = 0.65$$

SPSS SYNTAX

Table 4.8 presents SPSS output for comparisons between dependent correlations with no variables in common. Like the other syntax files in this chapter, the syntax requires that the user provide correlations between all variables and decision criteria.

Table 4.8 Syntax for Comparing Correlations Between Variables for Comparing Two Dependent Correlations (No Shared Variables)

Syntax	Comments
INPUT PROGRAM.	
LOOP n=20 TO 120 by 10.	
END CASE.	
END LOOP.	
END FILE.	
END INPUT PROGRAM.	
EXECUTE.	
Compute r12 = .4.	Enter correlations here
Compute rxy = .7.	
Compute r1x = .3.	
Compute r1y = .1.	
Compute r2x = .45.	
Compute r2y = .35.	
Compute alpha = .05.	
Compute tails = 2.	
Compute z_r12 = 0.5 * (Ln((1 + r12) / (1 - r12))).	*** No changes here or below
Compute z_rxy = 0.5 * (Ln((1 + rxy) / (1 - rxy))).	Fisher's transformations
Compute q = abs(z_r12-z_rxy).	Formula 4.13 (effect size)
Compute r_ave = (r12+rxy)/2.	Formula 4.11 (average ρ)
Compute denom = (1-r_ave**2)**2 .	
Compute numer1 = (r1x -(r12*r2x))* (r2y-(r2x*rxy)).	
Compute numer2 = (r1y -(r1x*rxy))* (r2x-(r12*r1x)).	
Compute numer3 = (r1x -(r1y*rxy))* (r2y-(r12*r1y)).	

Table 4.8 Syntax for Comparing Correlations Between Variables for Comparing Two Dependent Correlations (No Shared Variables) (continued)

Syntax	Comments
Compute numer4 = (r1y -(r12*r2y))*(r2x-(r2y*rxy)).	
Compute numer = (numer1 + numer2 +numer3+numer4)/2.	
Compute cov = numer /denom.	Formula 4.12 (*SD* of ρs)
Compute z = (q*((n-3)**.5)) / ((2-(2*cov))**.5).	Formula 4.13 (z_8)
if tails = 1 prob = 1-alpha.	
if tails = 2 prob = 1-(alpha/2).	
Compute tabled = IDF. NORMAL(prob,0,1).	
Compute z_power = tabled – z.	
Compute power = 1-CDF. Normal(z_power,0,1).	Power based on normal distribution
Compute p = (1-CDF. Normal(z,0,1))*tails.	Probability for each sample result
execute.	

```
Matrix.
GET M /VARIABLES=n Power z p.
print M/title = "Power Analysis for
 Comparing Dependent Correlations
 (No shared variables)"
/clabels = "N" "Power" "z" "p"/
 format f10.4.
End Matrix.
```

The output in Table 4.9 shows that a sample of about 80 participants yields power of .80. Power reaches .90 with a sample of roughly 110. The output also includes *z* and *p*, so the syntax performs significance tests for existing data if desired.

NOTE ON EFFECT SIZES FOR COMPARING CORRELATIONS

The formulae presented in Formulae 4.4, 4.10, and 4.13 are applicable to tests that examine the magnitude of the differences between correlations and tests involving both magnitude and direction. For tests involving magnitude (e.g., is one variable a stronger predictor than another?), enter positive correlations for the values being compared in the test (i.e., the values inside the absolute value notation), regardless of direction. The reasoning for this is that two correlations may be similarly predictive

Table 4.9 Output for Comparing Correlations Between Variables for Comparing Two Dependent Correlations (No Shared Variables)

	Power Analysis for Comparing Dependent Correlations (No shared variables)		
N	Power	z	p
20.0	.2593	1.3146	.1887
30.0	.3808	1.6567	.0976
40.0	.4918	1.9394	.0525
50.0	.5893	2.1858	.0288
60.0	.6726	2.4071	.0161
70.0	.7421	2.6097	.0091
80.0	.7989	2.7977	.0051
90.0	.8447	2.9738	.0029
100.0	.8810	3.1401	.0017
110.0	.9096	3.2980	.0010
120.0	.9317	3.4487	.0006

but in opposite directions. For a test that examines both magnitude and direction, enter each correlation with its direction.

For example, consider a test that examines differences between dependent correlations with $\rho_{12} = .30$ and $\rho_{xy} = -.20$. For a test focused on magnitude only, the Fisher transformed correlations applied to the absolute value of each correlation yields, 0.31 and 0.20, respectively. This produces $q = 0.11$.

$$q = |z_{\rho_{12}} - z_{\rho_{xy}}| = |0.31 - 0.20| = 0.11$$

Now, consider a test focused on magnitude and direction, again with $\rho_{12} = .30$ and $\rho_{xy} = -.20$. For this test, the Fisher transformed correlations applied to the raw value of each correlation yields 0.31 and -0.20, respectively. This produces $q = 0.51$.

$$q = |z_{\rho_{12}} - z_{\rho_{xy}}| = |0.31 - (-0.20)| = 0.51$$

Clearly, the choice of approach influences the effect size and subsequent power. For the formulae presented in Formulae 4.4, 4.10, and 4.13, regardless of the type of test used, all correlations outside the absolute value notation should be entered with their appropriate direction (i.e., the raw correlation).

ADDITIONAL ISSUES

The procedures used for comparing correlations, particularly those for comparing dependent correlations, are but one of several approaches to these techniques. There remains considerable disagreement regarding the best procedures for comparing dependent correlations (see Silver, Hittner, & May, 2004, and Wilcox & Tian, 2008, for summaries and comparisons of other approaches). As a general consideration, most procedures for addressing these questions diverge from expected Type I error rates when data are nonnormal. As noted in the t-test chapter, transforming data to normality can be an important step in maintaining appropriate error rates. Some of the questions addressed in this chapter, in particular the comparison of two independent correlations, might also be tested as a regression interaction. Chapter 9 includes more information on this approach.

SUMMARY

This chapter examined power for zero-order correlations and for several tests comparing correlations. For zero-order correlations, the primary information required is the size of the correlation to detect (i.e., how large is a meaningful correlation). For tests comparing differences between correlations, power analyses require the size of a meaningful difference between the correlations and accurate estimates of correlations between all other variables (e.g., the correlation between the predictor variables compared).

NOTE

1. I take some liberties with the author's data to provide a simple example.

5

BETWEEN-SUBJECTS ANOVA (ONE FACTOR, TWO OR MORE FACTORS)

INTRODUCTION

Between-subjects analysis of variance (ANOVA) designs focus on approaches by which researchers either assign participants to or sample from independent groups. These tests often include planned or post hoc comparisons to detect differences between pairs of means or to clarify interactions. This chapter examines power for main effects, interactions, and contrasts/post hoc tests. Examples include one- and two-factor ANOVA, planned and post hoc contrasts, and simple effects tests. Additional issues include discussions of power for detecting all effects compared to power for an individual effect and artificial dichotomization.

NECESSARY INFORMATION

A good starting point is determining meaningful patterns of means (μs) and an estimate of standard deviation (σ) for each factor level. When approaching factorial ANOVA designs, it is necessary to determine cell means as well. Also important is a clear understanding of which effects are of interest (omnibus or contrast) as this impacts design.

FACTORS AFFECTING POWER

In addition to sample size and Type I error rate, larger differences between means and smaller standard deviations yield more power. Also relevant to power are decisions regarding follow-up tests, such as those involving planned comparisons between means and simple effects tests to examine interactions. Some approaches such as orthogonal contrasts make no adjustment for inflation of α, whereas others use some form of α adjustment (e.g., Bonferroni). Any adjustment to α, of course, reduces power.

OMNIBUS VERSUS CONTRAST POWER

This chapter examines power for both omnibus tests and tests involving planned contrasts and simple effects. Unless there is a firm theoretical reason for the omnibus F being the primary focus, power analyses should focus on contrasts corresponding to research hypotheses. For example, if you want to conclude that two groups both outperform a third, then design for adequate power for those contrasts rather than rather than for the omnibus test. Similarly, when hypotheses address specific interaction patterns, simple effects test power is often more central to the research hypotheses than power for the interaction effect.

KEY STATISTICS

There are two effect size statistics used for ANOVA power calculations. Partial eta-squared ($\eta^2_{partial}$) and f^2. Studies of statistical power often present f and f^2. The more commonly reported effect size statistic is $\eta^2_{partial}$. This value is termed partial η^2 because for designs with multiple factors the variance explained by all factors except the effect of interest is partialed out of the calculation. This distinction is not important for one-factor designs as there are no other effects to partial out of the equation. Formula 5.1 shows the relationship between $\eta^2_{partial}$ and f^2.

For the noncentrality parameter, some approaches use degrees of freedom for the error, whereas others use sample size. This produces small differences in power estimates, particularly when sample sizes or effect size are small. For this reason, some of the results produced in this text differ slightly from those produced by programs such as G*Power. Calculations in this text use df_{error} as it is more conservative (see Formula 5.2). Each of the calculations in Formulae 5.1–5.3 depends on sample size, so it is tricky to start with partial η^2 and design from there. I prefer a strategy that establishes meaningful differences between pairs of means and often a focus on power for contrasts rather than power for omnibus tests.

$$f^2 = \frac{\eta^2_{partial}}{1-\eta^2_{partial}}$$

(5.1)

For the omnibus ANOVA, tests calculate λ using Formula 5.2.

$$\lambda = f^2 df_{error} \tag{5.2}$$

$$\eta^2_{partial} = \frac{SS_{effect}}{SS_{effect} + SS_{error}} \tag{5.3}$$

Contrast tests require calculation of a noncentrality value δ that reflects the differences between the weighted (noted with c) means in a particular comparison. For the contrasts, examples present both λ and δ (Formulae 5.4 and 5.5). Both are correct ways to represent the noncentrality parameter, although λ is used in SPSS output.

$$\delta = \frac{\left| \sum c_i \mu_i \right|}{\sqrt{MS_{w/in} \left(\sum_{j=1}^{p} \frac{c_j^2}{n_j} \right)}} \tag{5.4}$$

$$\lambda = \delta^2 \tag{5.5}$$

One-Factor ANOVA Formulae

Formulae 5.6–5.9 are for equal sample sizes. With unequal sample sizes, replace n_j with the harmonic mean of the sample sizes (see Formula 3.13). The value j reflects the number of levels of the factor or, when used as a subscript, a notation to perform the operation for each group. The value μ_t reflects the grand mean (the mean of all scores irrespective of group).

$$MS_{w/in} = \sigma_p^2 \tag{5.6}$$

$$SS_{w/in} = MS_{w/in} * (n - j) \tag{5.7}$$

$$MS_{bg} = n_j \frac{\sum (\mu_j - \mu_t)^2}{j - 1} \tag{5.8}$$

$$SS_{bg} = n_j \sum (\mu_j - \mu_t)^2 \tag{5.9}$$

Factorial ANOVA Formulae

Calculations for factorial ANOVA follow a similar logic, with cell means and sample size replacing the j term. For main effects, A and B

note levels of the factor with the subscripts (A and B) used the same as j was. The $MS_{w/in}$ is the same as shown in Formula 5.6.

$$SS_{w/in} = MS_{w/in} * (n - cells) \qquad (5.10)$$

$$MS_{bg} = n_{cell} \frac{\sum (\mu_{cell} - \mu_t)^2}{cells - 1} \qquad (5.11)$$

$$SS_{bg} = n_{cell} \sum (\mu_{cell} - \mu_t)^2 \qquad (5.12)$$

$$SS_A = n_A \sum (\mu_A - \mu_t)^2 \qquad (5.13)$$

$$MS_A = n_A \frac{\sum (\mu_A - \mu_t)^2}{A - 1} \qquad (5.14)$$

$$SS_B = n_B \sum (\mu_B - \mu_t)^2 \qquad (5.15)$$

$$MS_B = n_B \frac{\sum (\mu_B - \mu_t)^2}{B - 1} \qquad (5.16)$$

$$SS_{AxB} = SS_{BG} - SS_A - SS_B \qquad (5.17)$$

$$MS_{AxB} = \frac{SS_{AxB}}{(A-1)(B-1)} \qquad (5.18)$$

Simple Effects Formulae

Test involving simple effects use the same logic as in the previous section but examine the impact of one factor isolated at the level of another.

$$SS_{AatB_i} = n_{AatB_i} \sum (\mu_{AatB_i} - \mu_{B_i})^2 \qquad (5.19)$$

$$MS_{AatB_i} = \frac{SS_{AatB_i}}{A - 1} \qquad (5.20)$$

Example 5.1: One-Factor ANOVA

This example presents a design to examine the effectiveness of dorm room interventions to improve intergroup attitudes. Based on previous work, college students score on average 80 (μ) with a standard deviation of 10 (σ) on an established scale of attitudes. There are three separate interventions with the opportunity to assign students randomly to one of the interventions or a control group. The first treatment is an inexpensive program that involves students rooming with a student of another ethnic group and some existing curricular enhancements by which the students take a one-unit course (1 hour per week) in their first semester on campus. The second treatment involves the same roommate pairing but develops a new curriculum for the one-unit class. This program would also be relatively inexpensive. The third treatment involves a roommate pairing with a more extensive (and expensive) program utilizing a three-unit course (3 hours per week) with structured intergroup experiences that involve both roommates.

In determining an effect size for our design, the primary question should address the sort of effect that would be meaningful. This question is complex, but for the present example, a cost–benefit approach is relevant. The first two treatments involve low-cost options, whereas the third program involves an expensive approach. To justify the high cost, it would be reasonable to expect better performance from the third program (i.e., a larger effect size). Previous studies examining predictors such as roommate contact in dorm rooms found moderate changes in ethnic attitudes predicted by roommate experiences such as living with students from other ethnic groups ($d \approx 0.30$; Van Laar, Levin, Sinclair, & Sidanius, 2005).

Based on these effects, combined with the cost of the interventions, we might decide to design to detect small effects for the inexpensive program ($d = 0.20$) but larger effects ($d = 0.60$) for the more expensive program. These effects would correspond to the following mean values: Control group with no intervention, $\mu = 80$; Treatment 1, $\mu = 82$; Treatment 2, $\mu = 82$; and Treatment 3, $\mu = 86$. Using these values with the standard deviation noted and $n = 60$ per group allows for several calculations.

$$MS_{w/in} = \sigma_p^2 = 10^2 = 100$$

$$MS_{bg} = n_{cell} \frac{\sum (\mu_{cell} - \mu_t)^2}{cells - 1} = 60 \frac{(80 - 82.5)^2 + (82 - 82.5)^2 + (82 - 82.5)^2 + (86 - 82.5)^2}{4 - 1}$$

$$= 60 * \frac{19}{3} = 380$$

$$SS_{w/in} = MS_{w/in} * (n - cells) = 100 * (240 - 4) = 23600$$

$$SS_{bg} = n_j \sum (\mu_j - \mu_t)^2 = 60 * [(80 - 82.5)^2 + (82 - 82.5)^2 + (82 - 82.5)^2 + (86 - 82.5)^2]$$

$$= 60 * 19 = 1140$$

$$\eta_{partial}^2 = \frac{SS_{effect}}{SS_{effect} + SS_{error}} = \frac{1140}{1140 + 23600} = .0461$$

$$f^2 = \frac{\eta_{partial}^2}{1 - \eta_{partial}^2} = \frac{.0461}{1 - .0461} = .0483$$

$$\lambda = f^2 df_{error} = 0.0483 * 236 = 11.4$$

For the η^2 and f^2 calculations, it is best to use several extra decimal places to ensure calculation accuracy. This likely will not make a great deal of difference in calculation of power, but rounding often produces results that differ slightly from SPSS and other sources. Many examples in the text use extra decimal places to ensure that calculations match SPSS output.

Calculation of power for ANOVA and other designs using the F distribution is complex and best left to a computer. However, an approximation technique exists. Formula 5.21 presents the unit normal approximation approach to calculating power. As in other chapters, I present approximate formulae and then computer approaches for obtaining exact power estimates. Formula 5.21 differs slightly from the version that appears in the work of Cohen (1988) to produce z-statistics consistent with the approaches discussed in Chapter 2.

$$z_{power} = \frac{\sqrt{(2df_{denom}-1)\dfrac{df_{num}F_{critical}}{df_{denom}}} - \sqrt{2(df_{num}+\lambda)-\dfrac{df_{num}+2\lambda}{df_{num}+\lambda}}}{\sqrt{\dfrac{df_{num}F_{critical}}{df_{denom}} + \dfrac{df_{num}+2\lambda}{df_{num}+\lambda}}} \qquad (5.21)$$

$$z_{power} = \frac{\sqrt{(2*236-1)\dfrac{3*2.643}{236}} - \sqrt{2(3+11.4)-\dfrac{3+2(11.4)}{3+11.4}}}{\sqrt{\dfrac{3*2.643}{236} + \dfrac{3+2(11.4)}{3+11.4}}} = -0.90$$

From z_{power}, we find an area of .817 (this is the area above $z = -0.90$ on the normal curve). An exact calculation is accomplished using λ in conjunction with the following line of SPSS syntax:

```
Compute Power = NCDF.F(F_Table,df_num, df_denom,Lambda).
```

Using the values yields

```
Compute Power = 1-NCDF.F(2.643, 3, 236, 11.4).
```

Using this approach, power = .812 (the .005 difference resulting from the approximation used Formula 5.21). This result suggests adequate power (> .80) for the omnibus test. However, detecting differences on the omnibus test may not be the primary effect of interest. For example, if our interest was whether the new programs outperform the older practices (no program and the current program), if the current program is better than no program, and whether one of the new programs is substantially better than the other, then planned comparisons rather than an omnibus test would be more relevant. The next section includes calculations for power for contrasts, then provides SPSS examples for both the omnibus and contrast tests.

Table 5.1 Contrast Weights (*c*) for One-Factor ANOVA Example

Contrast	Control	Current	New	New Extended
1	1	1	−1	−1
2	1	−1	0	0
3	0	0	1	−1

Example 5.2 One-Factor ANOVA With Orthogonal Contrasts

The present study allows for a set of three orthogonal contrasts. One contrast that makes sense involves comparing the control and current procedures (Groups 1 and 2) to the new and extended procedures (Groups 3 and 4). This contrast establishes whether the new programs differ from what the campus is currently doing. Contrast 2 is control versus current and Contrast 3 compares the two new programs (new vs. new extended). Calculating contrast values for each involves placing a weight on each mean as shown in Table 5.1 (for more on the contrast procedures, see Keppel, 1991, or Kirk, 1995). The weights in this table serve as the values of *c* in Formula 5.4.

I labeled each δ and λ with a subscript reflecting the contrast.

$$\delta_1 = \frac{\left|\sum c_i \mu_i\right|}{\sqrt{MS_{w/in}\left(\sum_{j=1}^{p} \frac{c_j^2}{n_j}\right)}} = \frac{\left|(1*80)+(1*82)+(-1*82)+(-1*86)\right|}{\sqrt{100\left(\frac{1^2}{60}+\frac{1^2}{60}+\frac{-1^2}{60}+\frac{-1^2}{60}\right)}} = \frac{6}{2.582} = 2.324$$

$$\lambda_1 = 2.324^2 = 5.40$$

$$\delta_2 = \frac{\left|(1*80)+(-1*82)+(0*82)+(0*86)\right|}{\sqrt{100\left(\frac{1^2}{60}+\frac{1^2}{60}+\frac{0^2}{60}+\frac{0^2}{60}\right)}} = \frac{2}{1.826} = 1.095$$

$$\lambda_2 = 1.095^2 = 1.20$$

$$\delta_3 = \frac{\left|(0*80)+(0*82)+(1*82)+(-1*86)\right|}{\sqrt{100\left(\frac{1^2}{60}+\frac{1^2}{60}+\frac{0^2}{60}+\frac{0^2}{60}\right)}} = \frac{4}{1.826} = 2.191$$

$$\lambda_3 = 2.191^2 = 4.80$$

Next, take the values for δ to SPSS, using the following syntax below:

```
Compute Power = NCDF.t(t_critical, df, delta).
```

Table 5.2 Power for $n = 60$ per Group for
Omnibus Test and Contrasts

	$\lambda(\delta)$	t_{power}	**Power**
Omnibus F	11.40	−0.90	.81
Contrast 1	5.40 (2.32)	−0.36	.64
Contrast 2	1.20 (1.10)	0.86	.19
Contrast 3	4.80 (2.19)	−0.23	.59

For this test, degrees of freedom correspond to *df* error from the ANOVA (236 in this case). The critical value for two-tailed t at $\alpha = .05$ is 1.97. Alternatively, the syntax presented for F and λ produces the same result. For the first contrast, the syntax is

```
Compute Power = 1-NCDF.t(1.97, 236, 2.32).
```

This yields power of .64. This suggests that if the first contrast involves a research question of interest, designing for adequate power (e.g., .80) requires a larger sample size.

Table 5.2 summarizes power for the remaining contrasts. Note that each contrast failed to produce power that approached the level of the omnibus test. This is not always the case, but outcomes like this are common enough that, unless there is a firm theoretical reason for omnibus F as the primary focus of the research, it is better to focus design efforts and power analyses on contrasts.

SPSS SYNTAX FOR THE ONE-FACTOR ANOVA

Table 5.3 presents SPSS syntax for completing the analyses detailed. Note that the syntax requires the descriptive statistics but no calculations.

Table 5.4 includes the entire SPSS output file generated by the syntax. Subsequent analyses omit much of this output. I present the complete output in Table 5.4 to give a sense of where to find the information of interest. Notations in bold indicate where to find each type of power (omnibus and contrasts).

At this point, it is important to consider which hypotheses are of the most interest and design for optimal power on those specific contrasts. For example, a reasonable decision is to focus on power for Contrasts 1 and 3. These tests address whether the new procedures outperform the old and whether the extended new procedure outperforms the new program without extension. As before, we can modify the sample sizes in the SPSS syntax in Table 5.3 and rerun the analysis until we find the

Table 5.3 SPSS Syntax for Omnibus *F* and Contrasts

Syntax	Comments
MATRIX DATA VARIABLES = Program ROWTYPE_ Attitude /FACTORS = Program.	Program is the IV, Attitude the DV. Factor defines the IV.
BEGIN DATA	
1 N 60	Each group (1, 2, 3, 4) has *N* and means
2 N 60	listed
3 N 60	
4 N 60	Standard deviations for each group are
1 MEAN 80	omitted as they are ignored in the
2 MEAN 82	calculation of MS Within
3 MEAN 82	
4 MEAN 86	
. Corr 1	
. STDDEV 10	This is the pooled *SD*
END DATA.	
MANOVA Attitude BY Program (1,4)	Specifies analysis; 1,4 indicates groups 1 through 4 are being analyzed
/MATRIX=IN(*)	Read data from the matrix above
/POWER EXACT t (.05) F (.05)	Produces power output; for Bonferroni
/CINTERVAL Joint (.95)	adjustment, change t (.05) to desired level
/OMEANS = Tables (Program)	Contrast (program) produces comparisons
/PRINT = Parameters (efsize)	The first set of weights (1 1 1 1) is
/CONTRAST (Program) = Special (1 1 1 1	required but does not produce analyses of interest
1 1 -1 -1,	First two groups versus last two
1 -1 0 0,	Group 1 versus Group 2
0 0 1 -1).	Group 3 versus Group 4

optimal level of power. The output in Table 5.5 shows that having 147 participants per cell produces power greater than .80 for Contrasts 1 and 3 (bold type in table).

OTHER CONTRAST OPTIONS FOR ONE-FACTOR ANOVA

SPSS provides a number of contrast options with accompanying power estimates. These include difference, Helmert, simple, repeated, and polynomial contrasts. Difference contrasts compare each level to the

Table 5.4 SPSS Output for One-Factor ANOVA (Omnibus Test and Contrast)

The default error term in MANOVA has been changed from WITHIN
 CELLS to WITHIN+RESIDUAL. Note that these are the same for all
 full factorial designs.
* * * * * * A n a l y s i s o f V a r i a n c e -- design 1 * * * * * *
Combined Observed Means for Program

	Variable .. Attitude	
Program		
1	WGT.	80.00000
	UNWGT.	80.00000
2	WGT.	82.00000
	UNWGT.	82.00000
3	WGT.	82.00000
	UNWGT.	82.00000
4	WGT.	86.00000
	UNWGT.	86.00000

* * * * * * A n a l y s i s o f V a r i a n c e -- design 1 * * * * * *

**Tests of Significance for Attitude using
UNIQUE sums of squares**

Source of Variation	SS	DF	MS	F	Sig of F
WITHIN CELLS	23600.00	236	100.00		
Program	1140.00	3	380.00	3.80	.011

Observed Power at the .0500 Level

Source of Variation	Noncentrality	Power	
Program	11.400	.812	**(Omnibus Power)**

Estimates for Attitude
--- Joint univariate .9500 SCHEFFE confidence intervals
--- two-tailed observed power taken at .0500 level

Program Parameter	Coeff.	Std. Err.	t-Value	Sig. t	Lower -95%	CL- Upper
2	-6.0000000	2.58199	-2.32379	.02099	-13.27028	1.27028
3	-2.0000000	1.82574	-1.09545	.27444	-7.14087	3.14087
4	-4.0000000	1.82574	-2.19089	.02944	-9.14087	1.14087

Parameter	ETA Sq.	Noncent.	Power	
2	.02237	5.40000	.638	**(Contrast 1: 1 and 2 vs. 3 and 4)**
3	.00506	1.20000	.194	**(Contrast 2: 1 vs. 2)**
4	.01993	4.80000	.588	**(Contrast 3: 3 vs. 4)**

Table 5.5 Power for One-Factor ANOVA with $n = 147$

Tests of Significance for Attitude
using UNIQUE sums of squares

Source of Variation	SS	DF	MS	F	Sig of F
WITHIN CELLS	39200.00	392	100.00		
Program	1881.00	3	627.00	6.27	.000

Observed Power at the .0500 Level

Source of Variation	Noncentrality	Power
Program	18.810	.965

Estimates for Attitude
--- two-tailed observed power taken at .0500 level

Program Parameter	Coeff.	Std. Err.	t-Value	Sig. t	Lower -95%	CL- Upper
2	-6.0000000	2.01008	-2.98496	.00301	-11.64363	-.35637
3	-2.0000000	1.42134	-1.40712	.16018	-5.99065	1.99065
4	-4.0000000	1.42134	-2.81425	.00514	-7.99065	-.00935

Parameter	ETA Sq.	Noncent.	Power
2	.02222	8.91000	.846
3	.00503	1.98000	.289
4	.01980	7.92000	.802

mean of the previous levels (e.g., Level 3 vs. mean of Level 1 and Level 2). Helmert contrasts compare each level to the mean of the next level(s) (e.g., Level 2 vs. mean of Level 3 and Level 4). Simple contrasts compare each level to a specific group (e.g., compare every group to the control group). Repeated contrasts compare each level to the next (e.g., Level 1 vs. Level 2; Level 2 vs. Level 3). Polynomial contrasts examine trends (e.g., linear, quadratic, cubic).

For each of the examples, replace the contrast statement found in the syntax of Table 5.3 with the line of syntax included in the contrast examples that follow. Each analysis reflects a sample of $n = 60$ to facilitate comparison with results in Table 5.4.

Example 5.3 Difference Contrasts

Difference contrasts focus on whether each level differs from the mean of the previous levels. For example, contrasts comparing Group 4 to the combined means of Groups 1, 2, and 3; Group 3 to the means of Groups 1 and 2; and Group 2 compared

Table 5.6 Difference Contrasts for One-Factor ANOVA with $n = 60$ with notes in bold

Parameter	Coeff.	Std. Err.	t-Value	Sig. t	Lower -95%	CL- Upper
2	2.00000000	1.82574	1.09545	.27444	-3.14087	7.14087
3	1.00000000	1.58114	.63246	.52770	-3.45212	5.45212
4	4.66666667	1.49071	3.13050	.00197	.46917	8.86417

Parameter	ETA Sq.	Noncent.	Power	
2	.00506	1.20000	.194	**(Group 2 vs. Group 1)**
3	.00169	.40000	.097	**(Group 3 vs. Mean Group 1 and 2)**
4	.03987	9.80000	.877	**(Group 4 vs. Means Group 1, 2, and 3)**

only to the mean of Group 1. Table 5.6 shows annotated and edited output to compare the current program and both new programs (Levels 2, 3, and 4) to the mean of the previous levels.

Syntax: Contrast (Program) = Difference.

The coefficient values reflect the differences between means. For example, the first contrast (Parameter 2), takes the difference between the group means of 82 and 80, producing a difference of 2.0. For Contrast 2, the means are 82 (Group 3) and 81 (the average of 80 for Group 1 and 82 for Group 2), producing a difference of 1.0. For Contrast 3, the means are 86 (Group 4) and 81.33 (the average of 80 for Group 1, 82 for Group 2, and 82 for Group 3), producing a difference of 4.67.

Example 5.4 Helmert Contrasts

Helmert contrasts ask whether each level differs from the mean of the levels that follow. This compares the control group, current program, and the new (short) program (Levels 1, 2, and 3, respectively) to the mean of each of the programs that follow. For example, the current program (Group 2) will be compared to the mean of the new short program and the new long program (Groups 3 and 4, respectively), whereas the control group (Group 1) is compared to the mean of all of the other programs (Groups 2, 3, and 4) (Table 5.7).

Syntax: Contrast (Program) = Helmert.

Example 5.5 Simple Contrasts

Simple contrasts focus on a comparison of each level with one specified level. This type of contrast is most useful for comparisons against a control group. The SPSS default is comparison to the last level. In the present study, the first group was the control

Table 5.7 Helmert Contrasts for One-Factor ANOVA with $n = 60$ with notes in bold

Parameter	Coeff.	Std. Err.	t-Value	Sig. t	Lower -95%	CL- Upper
2	-3.3333333	1.49071	-2.23607	.02628	-7.53083	.86417
3	-2.0000000	1.58114	-1.26491	.20715	-6.45212	2.45212
4	-4.0000000	1.82574	-2.19089	.02944	-9.14087	1.14087

Parameter	ETA Sq.	Noncent.	Power	
2	.02075	5.00000	.605	(Group 1 vs. Mean Group 2, 3, and 4)
3	.00673	1.60000	.243	(Group 2 vs. Mean Group 3 and 4)
4	.01993	4.80000	.588	(Group 3 vs. Group 4)

group, so we need to specify the group for comparison. To compare each level to the control group, note the level for comparison as shown in the Example 5.1. These are not orthogonal contrasts, so you may choose to adjust α for the contrasts (e.g., use .05/the number of comparisons = .05/3 = .0167). See Formulae 5.22 and 5.23 for techniques to adjust for inflation of α.

To adjust α, replace the power syntax line in Table 5.3 with this one: /Power exact t (.0167). Table 5.8 provides the unadjusted analysis and Table 5.9 an analysis that adjusts α for contrasts.

Syntax: Contrast (Program) = Simple (1).

Table 5.8 Simple Contrasts for One-Factor ANOVA with $n = 60$ and $\alpha = .05$ with notes in bold

Parameter	Coeff.	Std. Err.	t-Value	Sig. t	Lower -95%	CL- Upper
2	2.00000000	1.82574	1.09545	.27444	-3.14087	7.14087
3	2.00000000	1.82574	1.09545	.27444	-3.14087	7.14087
4	6.00000000	1.82574	3.28634	.00117	.85913	11.14087

Parameter	ETA Sq.	Noncent.	Power	
2	.00506	1.20000	.194	(Group 2 vs. Group 1)
3	.00506	1.20000	.194	(Group 3 vs. Group 1)
4	.04376	10.80000	.905	(Group 4 vs. Group 1)

Table 5.9 Simple Contrasts for One-Factor ANOVA with $n = 60$ and $\alpha = .0167$

Parameter	ETA Sq.	Noncent.	Power
2	.00506	1.20000	.096
3	.00506	1.20000	.096
4	.04376	10.80000	.809

Table 5.10 Repeated Contrasts for One-Factor ANOVA with $n = 60$ with notes in bold

Parameter	Coeff.	Std. Err.	t-Value	Sig. t	Lower -95%	CL- Upper
2	-2.0000000	1.82574	-1.09545	.27444	-7.14087	3.14087
3	.000000000	1.82574	.00000	1.00000	-5.14087	5.14087
4	-4.0000000	1.82574	-2.19089	.02944	-9.14087	1.14087

Parameter	ETA Sq.	Noncent.	Power	
2	.00506	1.20000	.194	(Group 1 vs. Group 2)
3	.00000	.00000	.050	(Group 2 vs. Group 3)
4	.01993	4.80000	.588	(Group 3 vs. Group 4)

Example 5.6 Repeated Contrasts

Repeated contrasts examine differences between each level and the next level. These would be useful when hypotheses focused on increasing benefits at each level of the factor (Table 5.10).

Syntax: Contrast (Program) = Repeated.

Example 5.7 Polynomial Contrasts

Polynomial contrasts produce trend analyses. There are four levels to our factor, allowing for tests of the linear, quadratic, and cubic trends. Chapter 7 includes a more detailed discussion of trend analyses (Table 5.11).

Contrast (Program) = Polynomial.

Example 5.8 Comparisons Among All Means

Although power analysis is an a priori venture, some research situations call for designs using conservative post hoc analyses. Conservative post hoc options (e.g., Tukey tests)

Table 5.11 Polynomial Contrasts (Trend Analysis) for One-Factor ANOVA with $n = 60$ with notes in bold

Parameter	Coeff.	Std. Err.	t-Value	Sig. t	Lower -95%	CL- Upper
2	4.02492236	1.29099	3.11769	.00205	.38978	7.66006
3	1.00000000	1.29099	.77460	.43935	-2.63514	4.63514
4	1.34164079	1.29099	1.03923	.29976	-2.29350	4.97678

Parameter	ETA Sq.	Noncent.	Power	
2	.03956	9.72000	.874	(Linear Trend)
3	.00254	.60000	.120	(Quadratic Trend)
4	.00456	1.08000	.179	(Cubic Trend)

involve comparisons between all pairs of means. Obtaining power for these analyses requires multiple test runs.

The syntax approach below takes each mean and assigns it as the comparison group for a simple contrast. This requires three separate MANOVA command files. There is considerable overlap between these analysis (i.e., some of the same comparisons appear several times).

The tests presented in Table 5.12 do not conduct tests such as the Tukey HSD (honestly significant difference). However, Bonferroni or Šidák adjustments provide a good approximation. Formulae 5.22 and 5.23 detail these adjustments. With four groups, there are six comparisons between means. To adjust for tests using $\alpha = .05$, we end up with $\alpha = .0083$ for Bonferroni and $\alpha = .0085$ for Šidák. Enter values from whichever test you plan to use in the following syntax (the example in Table 5.12 uses Bonferroni):

$$\alpha_{Bonferroni} = \frac{\alpha}{c} \tag{5.22}$$

$$\alpha_{Sidak} = 1 - (1-\alpha)^{1/c} \tag{5.23}$$

ANOVA WITH TWO FACTORS

Power for effects involving multiple factors in ANOVA have been described elsewhere, with a focus that begins with estimating the effect size associated with main effects and interactions. This approach is difficult as effect sizes for interactions are neither intuitive nor specific to the pattern of effects of interest. For example, designing for an interaction with a partial η^2 of .03 provides no information about whether this is a meaningful result or the pattern of effects underlying the interaction.

Because of these concerns, I prefer an approach that generates a set of meaningful pattern of cell means. That is, what is the specific pattern of result that is of interest, and what means correspond to the result? Determining meaningful means for cells requires considerable thought, far more than simply designing for a certain effect size. However, this approach likely provides better power and sample size estimates.

Example 5.9 Two-Factor ANOVA With Interactions

One of my long-standing areas of research involves examining attitudes toward affirmative action (AA). One project examined how policy features and the presence of policy justifications impact support for different forms of AA. There is considerable research on topics relevant to both justification and policy type. However, little is known about

Table 5.12 Comparisons among All Means for One-Factor ANOVA with $n = 60$ with notes in bold

```
MANOVA Attitude BY Program (1,4)
/MATRIX=IN(*)
/POWER EXACT t (.0083) F (.05)
/CONTRAST (Program) = Simple (1).

MANOVA Attitude BY Program (1,4)
/MATRIX=IN(*)
/POWER EXACT t (.0083) F (.05)
/CONTRAST (Program) = Simple (2).

MANOVA Attitude BY Program (1,4)
/MATRIX=IN(*)
/POWER EXACT t (.0083) F (.05)
/CONTRAST (Program) = Simple (3).
```

Parameter	Coeff.	Std. Err.	t-Value	Sig. t	Lower -95%	CL- Upper
2	-2.0000000	1.82574	-1.09545	.27444	-5.59683	1.59683
3	.000000000	1.82574	.00000	1.00000	-3.59683	3.59683
4	4.00000000	1.82574	2.19089	.02944	.40317	7.59683

Parameter	Noncent.	Power	
2	1.20000	.061	(Group 2 vs. Group 1)
3	1.20000	.061	(Group 3 vs. Group 1)
4	10.80000	.734	(Group 4 vs. Group 1)

Parameter	Coeff.	Std. Err.	t-Value	Sig. t	Lower -95%	CL- Upper
2	-2.0000000	1.82574	-1.09545	.27444	-5.59683	1.59683
3	.000000000	1.82574	.00000	1.00000	-3.59683	3.59683
4	4.00000000	1.82574	2.19089	.02944	.40317	7.59683

Parameter	Noncent.	Power	
2	1.20000	.061	(Group 1 vs. Group 2)
3	.00000	.008	(Group 3 vs. Group 2)
4	4.80000	.321	(Group 4 vs. Group 2)

Parameter	Coeff.	Std. Err.	t-Value	Sig. t	Lower -95%	CL- Upper
2	-2.0000000	1.82574	-1.09545	.27444	-5.59683	1.59683
3	.000000000	1.82574	.00000	1.00000	-3.59683	3.59683
4	4.00000000	1.82574	2.19089	.02944	.40317	7.59683

Parameter	Noncent.	Power	
2	1.20000	.061	(Group 1 vs. Group 3)
3	.00000	.008	(Group 2 vs. Group 3)
4	4.80000	.321	(Group 4 vs. Group 3)

Table 5.13 Means for Factorial ANOVA Example

	No Justification	Justified	M
Recruit	0.85	0.85	0.85
Tiebreak	0.0	0.60	0.30
M	0.425	0.725	0.575

justifications for specific applications of AA as most work on justification examined attitudes toward AA in general and did not manipulate policy type and justification in the same study.

The study in this example uses a 2 (Policy Type: Recruitment of Applications vs. Tiebreaker) by 2 (Justification: No Justification or Increased Diversity) design. The dependent measure was a four-item policy support scale used in a previous study, producing a standard deviation of 1.70. Table 5.13 details the expected cell means (an explanation of how I generated these values appears later). The primary hypothesis for the present study was that justifications influence evaluations of stronger policies like the tiebreaker policy by which minority applicants received preference when their qualifications were equal to those of a nonminority applicant. However, justifications were not expected to impact policies by which organizations made special outreach efforts to recruit minority applicants.

Several sources of information went into the determination of cell means. Results from a meta-analysis focusing on diversity justifications reported a correlation of .17 for differences between justified and not justified policies among studies examining attitudes toward AA in general (Harrison, Kravitz, Mayer, Leslie, & Lev-Arey, 2006). Analyses apply this effect size to the expected value for tiebreak (but not recruitment) conditions as previous work found individuals view tiebreakers as more typical of AA than is recruitment (Aberson, 2007). Converting r to d using Formula 4.1 yields $d = 0.35$. Given $\sigma = 1.7$, this corresponds to a difference of 0.60 between justified and not justified tiebreaker policies. Table 5.13 shows this difference in the row labeled "Tiebreak."

For policies presented without justifications, previous work in my lab found a difference in support for recruitment and tiebreaker policies that were presented without justification of roughly $d = 0.50$ favoring recruitment approaches. Given $\sigma = 1.7$ (the standard deviation from a previous use of the scale), this corresponds to a difference of 0.85 between recruitment and tiebreaker policies. The column of Table 5.13 labeled "No Justification" shows this difference.

The final cell mean is for the recruit-justified condition. Although there are no previous data on which to base this, part of the interaction hypothesis was that justification would not influence evaluations of the recruitment policy. Thus, analyses set the means to show no difference between the recruitment policies between not justified and justified conditions.

CALCULATIONS

Power for the factorial ANOVA may be calculated (mostly) by hand using the approaches that follow. Although the primary hypothesis involves the interaction, the calculation approach addresses all of the effects (but presents power only for the interaction). Calculations began with an estimate of $n = 100$ per cell. This may seem like a very large sample, but the study itself involved only a single page of measures that took participants roughly 2 minutes to complete, so large sample sizes were not unreasonable.

$$MS_{w/in} = \sigma_p^2 = 1.7^2 = 2.89$$

$$SS_{w/in} = MS_{w/in} * (n - cells) = 2.89 * (400 - 4) = 1144.4$$

$$MS_{bg} = n_{cell} \frac{\sum (\mu_{cell} - \mu_t)^2}{cells - 1} = 100 \frac{(0.85 - 0.575)^2 + (0.00 - 0.575)^2 + (0.85 - 0.575)^2 + (0.60 - 0.575)^2}{4 - 1}$$

$$= 100 \left(\frac{.4825}{3} \right) = 16.08$$

$$SS_{bg} = n_{cell} \sum (\mu_{cell} - \mu_t)^2 = 100[(0.85 - 0.575)^2 + (0.00 - 0.575)^2 + (0.85 - 0.575)^2 + (0.60 - 0.575)^2]$$

$$= 100(.4825) = 48.25$$

$$SS_A = n_A \sum (\mu_A - \mu_t)^2 = 200[(.425 - .575)^2 + (.725 - .575)^2] = 9.0$$

$$MS_A = n_A \frac{\sum (\mu_A - \mu_t)^2}{A - 1} = 200 \times \frac{(.425 - .575)^2 + (.725 - .575)^2}{2 - 1} = 9.0$$

$$SS_B = n_B \sum (\mu_B - \mu_t)^2 = 200[(.850 - .575)^2 + (.300 - .575)^2] = 30.25$$

$$MS_B = n_B \frac{\sum (\mu_B - \mu_t)^2}{B - 1} = 200 \times \frac{(.850 - .575)^2 + (.300 - .575)^2}{2 - 1} = 30.25$$

$$SS_{A \times B} = SS_{BG} - SS_A - SS_B = 48.25 - 9.0 - 30.25 = 9.0$$

$$MS_{A \times B} = \frac{SS_{A \times B}}{(A - 1)(B - 1)} = \frac{9.0}{(2 - 1)(2 - 1)} = 9.0$$

$$\eta_{partial}^2 = \frac{SS_{effect}}{SS_{effect} + SS_{error}} = \frac{9}{9 + 1144.4} = .0078$$

$$f^2 = \frac{\eta_{partial}^2}{1 - \eta_{partial}^2} = \frac{.0078}{1 - .0078} = .0079$$

$$\lambda = f^2 df_{error} = .0079 \times 396 = 3.11$$

Table 5.14 SPSS Syntax for Two-Factor ANOVA

Syntax	Comments
MATRIX DATA VARIABLES =	Matrix command facilitates analyses
Policy Justify ROWTYPE_	based on summary statistics
Support	Rowtype_ tells SPSS what will be in
	the row, factors precede this statement
/FACTORS = Policy Justify.	Specifies factors (Policy and Justify)
BEGIN DATA	Support is the dependent variable (DV)
1 1 N 100	1 1 indicate data for the cell (first level
1 2 N 100	of Policy, first level of Justify)
2 1 N 100	
2 2 N 100	Change N, mean, and SD
1 1 MEAN 0.85	.. In front of CORR and SD, need one
1 2 MEAN 0.85	period for each factor
2 1 MEAN 0.0	
2 2 MEAN 0.6	
. . CORR 1	CORR is correlation between DVs
. . SD 1.70	(with a single DV it is 1, CORR
END DATA.	statement is required)
MANOVA Support BY Policy,	First line specifies analysis; both
Justify (1,2)	factors have 2 levels so (1,2) is the
/MATRIX=IN(*)	specification
/POWER EXACT t (.05) F (.05)	If Policy had three levels and Justify four,
/CINTERVAL Joint (.95)	command would be Support By Policy
/OMEANS = Tables (Policy	(1,3), Justify (1,4)
Justify)	
/PRINT = Parameters (efsize)	*Note*: Order of factors/independent
/DESIGN.	variables (IVs) must be the same as
	in matrix

Taking $\lambda = 3.11$ to SPSS (using the single line of syntax demonstrated in Example 5.1) finds power of .42. A sample of $n = 100$ per cell is not adequate if we want power of .80.

SPSS SYNTAX FOR FACTORIAL ANOVA

The SPSS syntax in Table 5.14 completes all of the intermediate calculations and provides an estimate of power. Note that the syntax requires only means, standard deviations, and sample sizes. SPSS completes the remaining calculations. Table 5.15 presents output for the analysis using $n = 100$ per group. As in the preceding example, power $= .42$.

Table 5.15 Factorial ANOVA Output for $n = 100$ per Cell

Tests of Significance for Support using UNIQUE sums of squares

Source of Variation	SS	DF	MS	F	Sig of F
WITHIN CELLS	1144.44	396	2.89		
Policy	30.25	1	30.25	10.47	.001
Justify	9.00	1	9.00	3.11	.078
Policy BY Justify	9.00	1	9.00	3.11	.078

Observed Power at the .0500 Level

Source of Variation	Noncentrality	Power
Policy	10.467	.898
Justify	3.114	.421
Policy BY Justify	3.114	.421

Table 5.16 presents an analysis that increases the sample size to $n = 251$. This analysis finds power of roughly .80 for the interaction.

SIMPLE EFFECT TESTS

Of primary interest when examining interactions are simple effects tests. Much as contrasts offer a more precise explanation of effects than do omnibus F tests, simple effects tests address specific aspects of the interaction by focusing on the impact of one factor at the levels of the other. For the current example, the hypothesis stated that justification makes a difference for tiebreaker policies but not for recruitment policies. To test these predictions, we can examine differences in support for tiebreaker policies between the justified or not justified conditions and then differences in support for recruitment policies between the justification conditions. Addressing power for simple effects tests is important as these tests often relate directly to hypotheses.

$$SS_{AatB_i} = n_{AatB_i} \sum_i (\mu_{AatB_i} - \mu_{B_i})^2$$

$$SS_{Justify\_at\_Tiebreak} = 251(0.0 - 0.3)^2 + 251(0.6 - 0.3)^2 = 45.18$$

The following calculations yield $\lambda = 15.2$; for this value, power is .97, suggesting that the current design provides excellent power for detecting the simple effect of interest.

$$\eta^2_{partial} = \frac{SS_{effect}}{SS_{effect} + SS_{error}} = \frac{45.18}{3011.1} = .0150$$

$$f^2 = \frac{\eta^2_{partial}}{1 - \eta^2_{partial}} = \frac{.0150}{1 - .0150} = .0152$$

$$\lambda = f^2 df_{error} = .0152 \times 1000 = 15.2$$

Table 5.16 Syntax Modification and Output for $n = 251$

```
MATRIX DATA VARIABLES = Policy Justify ROWTYPE_ Support
    /FACTORS = Policy Justify.
BEGIN DATA
1 1 N 251
1 2 N 251
2 1 N 251
2 2 N 251
1 1 MEAN 0.85
1 2 MEAN 0.85
2 1 MEAN 0.0
2 2 MEAN 0.6
. . CORR 1
. . SD 1.7
END DATA.
```

Tests of Significance for Support
using UNIQUE sums of squares

Source of Variation	SS	DF	MS	F	Sig of F
WITHIN CELLS	2890.00	1000	2.89		
Policy	75.93	1	75.93	26.27	.000
Justify	22.59	1	22.59	7.82	.005
Policy BY Justify	22.59	1	22.59	7.82	.005

Observed Power at the .0500 Level

Source of Variation	Noncentrality	Power
Policy	26.272	.999
Justify	7.817	.798
Policy BY Justify	7.817	.798

SPSS SYNTAX FOR SIMPLE EFFECTS

This test involves a simple addition to the syntax file, noted in bold in Table 5.17. The prior matrix input is unchanged. To compare different simple effects such as how policies differed when justified and not justified, change the design statement to read Policy WITHIN Justify (1) and Policy WITHIN Justify (2).

Table 5.18 shows the output for simple effects. When running this analysis, the output includes both the information in Table 5.16 (the omnibus tests) and the simple effects tests.

Note that the power for the contrast of interest, listed as Justify Within Policy (2), is .97. The power for the other contrast, Justify Within Policy (1), is .05. Since the means for that contrast were equal, power is equal to α.

Table 5.17 Syntax for Simple Effects

```
MANOVA Support BY Policy, Justify (1,2)
/MATRIX=IN(*)
/POWER exact F (.05)
/CINTERVAL Joint (.95)
/Omeans = Tables (Policy Justify)
/Print = Parameters (efsize)
/DESIGN
/DESIGN = Justify WITHIN Policy (1)
/DESIGN = Justify WITHIN Policy (2).
```

Table 5.18 Output for Simple Effects

```
* * * * * A n a l y s i s o f V a r i a n c e -- design 2 * * * * *
             Tests of Significance for Support
                using UNIQUE sums of squares
```

Source of Variation	SS	DF	MS	F	Sig of F
WITHIN+RESIDUAL	3011.11	1002	3.01		
JUSTIFY WITHIN POLICY(1) Y(1)	.00	1	.00	.00	1.000

```
          Observed Power at the .0500 Level
```

Source of Variation	Noncentrality	Power
JUSTIFY WITHIN POLICY(1)	.000	.050

```
* * * * * A n a l y s i s o f V a r i a n c e -- design 3 * * * * *
Tests of Significance for Support using UNIQUE sums of squares
```

Source of Variation	SS	DF	MS	F	Sig of F
WITHIN+RESIDUAL	2965.93	1002	2.96		
JUSTIFY WITHIN POLICY(2)	45.18	1	45.18	15.26	.000

```
          Observed Power at the .0500 Level
```

Source of Variation	Noncentrality	Power
JUSTIFY WITHIN POLICY(2)	15.263	.974

ADDITIONAL ISSUES

Additional issues include power for detecting all effects versus power for an individual effect and artificial dichotomization of continuously scaled predictors.

Multiplicity[1]

Designs involving multiple factors address two forms of power. The first is power for a single effect (e.g., a main effect or an interaction). This is the sort of power examined in the current chapter. Another conceptualization of power involves the power for detecting all effects in a specific design. This is termed Power(All). For example, in a study with two factors designed to yield power for both main effects and the interaction as .50, power for single effects reflects three different estimates [Power(A), Power(B), and Power(AxB)]. Power for detecting all effects, on the other hand, reflects how likely it is to reject all three null hypotheses in the same study. You might be tempted to think this power would be .50 as well. This is not the case. As a thought exercise, consider flipping a coin three times. The probability of the coin coming up heads is .50 on each flip. This is analogous to Power(A), Power(B), and Power(AxB) with each set at .50. However, the probability that the coin comes up heads on all three flips is far less than .50. Using the binomial approximation approach, this probability would be .13. This is analogous to Power(All) or how likely any one study is to reject all three null hypotheses.

Table 5.19 reflects Power(All) corresponding to various levels of power for individual effects. This table is simplistic as it only examines when the same level of power exists for each effect. In addition, this assumes that the factors are independent (i.e., participants randomly assigned to levels of the factor). Power(Each Effect) refers to when both main effects and the interaction have equal power. The row labeled p(One or more reject H_0) is the probability that one or more of the effect are detected, and p(Two or more reject H_0) is the probability that two or more effects are detected. The row labeled p(Reject all H_0) is the probability that all three null hypotheses are rejected. Note that to obtain power = .80 for rejecting all three null hypotheses, we would need to design for each test to have power = .93. Table 5.20 shows the same calculations for a three-factor ANOVA. In this table, the probabilities for rejecting at least one H_0 and for rejecting all the H_0s become more extreme.

Table 5.19 Power for Rejecting All Effects (and at Least One) for Various Levels of Individual Effect Power for Two-Factor ANOVA

Power (Each effect)	.50	.60	.70	.80	.90	.93	.95
p(One or more reject H_0)	.88	.94	.97	.99	>.99	>.99	>.99
p(Two or more reject H_0)	.50	.65	.78	.90	.97	.99	>.99
p(Reject all H_0)	.13	.22	.34	.51	.73	.80	.86

Table 5.20 Power for Rejecting All Effects (and at Least One) for Various Levels of Individual Effect Power for Three-Factor ANOVA

Power (Each effect)	.50	.60	.70	.80	.85	.90	.95	.96
p(One or more reject H_0)	.98	>.99	>.99	>.99	>.99	>.99	>.99	>.99
p(Two or more reject H_0)	.89	.96	.99	>.99	>.99	>.99	>.99	>.99
p(Three or more reject H_0)	.66	.82	.93	.98	>.99	>.99	>.99	>.99
p(Four or more reject H_0)	.34	.54	.74	.90	.98	>.99	>.99	>.99
p(Five or more reject H_0)	.11	.23	.42	.66	.89	.97	.98	>.99
p(Reject all H_0)	.02	.05	.12	.26	.38	.53	.74	.80

Artificial Dichotomization

An approach sometimes used with ANOVA designs involves taking continuously scaled variables and dichotomizing those values to create a factor. For example, scores on a self-esteem scale might be collected for a sample, then participants classified as high or low in self-esteem based on a median split of scores to create two roughly equal groups.

The best advice regarding this approach is do not dichotomize. Use regression analysis instead. Artificially dichotomizing variables reduces power (see Cohen, 1984; Fitzsimons, 2008). Regression analysis is a more complicated statistical approach, but regression yields more power as the variable remains in its original continuously scaled format.

Other important reasons for avoiding dichotomization also deserve mention. It is possible that dichotomizing produces groups that do not reflect clearly differentiated categories. For example, analyses of self-esteem data indicated a tendency to dichotomize self-esteem scale scores into high and low self-esteem categories based on median scores (Aberson, Healy, & Romero, 2000). Much of this dichotomization resulted in questionable classification of individuals as having "low self-esteem." Many individuals who scored moderately high on the scale end up classified as having low self-esteem. For data on several major scales, participants with scores that reflected 70% of the total possible score (e.g., a score of 70 on a scale ranging from 1 to 100) were classified as having low self-esteem despite scores that would more accurately be termed "medium self-esteem."

Dichotomization impacts power through reduction of observed effect size. Formula 5.24 presents the attenuation factor statistic (Hunter & Schmidt, 1990), and Formula 5.25 presents the effect size attenuation statistic. In Formulae 5.24, a_d refers to attenuation due to dichotomization. The value $\phi(c)$ is the unit normal density function for the z-transformed cut point (i.e., the "height" of the normal distribution curve). The command used to compute this value with SPSS syntax is (PDF.NORMAL(0,0,1). The first 0 reflects the cut point. The 0 and 1 that follow are the mean and standard deviation, respectively (use 0 and 1 to make this a normal distribution calculation). The values p and q reflect the proportion of participants in each group. If using a median split approach, $p = .50$ and $q = .50$, producing $\phi(c) = .40$.

$$a_d = \frac{\phi(c)}{\sqrt{pq}} \tag{5.24}$$

Formula 5.25 demonstrates the impact of artificial dichotomization on the effect size. The attenuating factor a_d reduces the size of the observed effect.

$$d_{observed} = d_{actual} a_d \tag{5.25}$$

The following example reflects a typical study utilizing dichotomization based on a median split. If population effect size is 0.50 and $a_d = .80$, the observed effect size is 0.40.

$$a_d = \frac{.40}{\sqrt{.5 * .5}} = \frac{.40}{.50} = .80$$

$$d_{observed} = 0.50 * .80 = 0.40$$

Regarding the impact on power, a study designed to detect effects of $d = 0.50$ for a two-group design would require a sample size of $n = 128$ for power $= .80$. However, the true effect size does not reflect the observed effect. In this case, the observed effect size, $d_{observed} = 0.40$, with a sample of $n = 128$, yields power $= .61$. If you must dichotomize, then recognize the impact this has on effect sizes and adjust sample sizes accordingly.

SUMMARY

This chapter presented tests for one- and two-factor between-subjects designs. These designs require estimation of meaningful patterns of means and accurate standard deviations. One-factor designs require means across levels of each factor, whereas two-factor designs require cell means. A primary issue with both designs is whether hypotheses reflect omnibus tests or specific comparisons (e.g., planned contrast, simple effects). Well-developed hypotheses often predict outcomes best addressed through specific comparisons rather than omnibus tests. Power for specific comparisons often differs considerably from omnibus power.

NOTE

1. This section relies heavily on work by Maxwell (2004). I urge interested readers to consult this article as it details aspects of this issue that the present chapter does not address.

6

WITHIN-SUBJECTS DESIGNS

INTRODUCTION

Within subjects (also known as repeated measures) designs focus on approaches involving measurement of the same participants at multiple levels of a factor (also known as the independent variable). Often, these designs involve measurement over two or more time periods. This chapter examines power for one- and two-factor within-subject analysis of variance (ANOVA) designs and trend analyses. Examples focus on calculations and analyses using univariate and multivariate approaches and present SPSS syntax for primary analyses and for sphericity-adjusted tests.

NECESSARY INFORMATION

As with between-subjects ANOVA designs, a good starting point is determining meaningful patterns of means (μs) and estimates of standard deviation (σ) for each factor level or cell. Also necessary are the expected correlations (ρs) between dependent measures.

FACTORS AFFECTING POWER

Larger effect sizes and stronger positive correlations between dependent measures yield more power. Conceptually, correlations between measures explain variance that is otherwise attributed to error. The reduction of error when employing repeated measures makes within-subjects designs more powerful than between-subjects designs. As with other designs, increases in sample size, α, and decreases in standard deviation increase power.

Although within-subjects designs have great advantages regarding power, they also present an additional challenge. Designs that include three or more levels of the within-subjects factor come with an additional test assumption, namely, the sphericity assumption. Sphericity is a complex issue that is discussed nicely elsewhere (e.g., Field, 1998). A simple way to understand sphericity is that the assumption is satisfied if the correlations between each pair of measures are similar and variances across measures are homogeneous. Measures taken close together usually show higher correlations than those taken further apart, so the sphericity assumption is often violated. Sphericity assumption violations increase Type I error rates. As Type I error rates rise, so does power. This increase in power is fleeting; adjustments exist to account for this violation and drive the Type I error (and power) down.

This chapter presents two strategies for addressing violations of the sphericity assumption. The first approach involves downward adjustment of degrees of freedom in the univariate tests to account for inflated Type I error rates. This strategy, commonly termed *epsilon adjustment*, employs procedures such as the Greenhouse-Geisser (G-G) or Huynh-Feldt (H-F) statistics. The second strategy involves use of multivariate ANOVA (MANOVA; also called profile analysis). MANOVA does not assume sphericity, so adjustments are unnecessary. The univariate test is generally more powerful if its assumptions have been met and when effects are spread across the repeated measures. If the assumptions are violated or effects are concentrated (e.g., differences are found for one pair of measures but the others do not differ), the multivariate approach is usually more sensitive. MANOVA is, however, underpowered with smaller samples. Since a major advantage of within-subjects designs is that these designs allow for use of small samples, sometimes MANOVA is untenable. In general, when expecting a violation of the sphericity assumption, expecting measures to differ across the levels of the IV, and expecting a large sample (e.g., two or more cases per DV), then the multivariate approach is the preferred analysis (Tabachnick & Fidell, 2007b). The present chapter addresses both univariate tests with epsilon adjustments and MANOVA approaches to repeated measures.

KEY STATISTICS

Univariate ANOVA

This chapter does not include discussion of sums of squares and related statistics. These calculations are more involved than those for between-subjects ANOVA. For this reason, the techniques presented rely on computer-generated calculations for most values. Several sources provide excellent overviews of these calculations (e.g., Keppel, 1991).

Formulae 6.1 and 6.2 present two measures of effect size, partial η^2 and f^2. Partial η^2 is the more commonly presented effect size for ANOVA designs, reflecting the proportion of variance explained by a factor while partialing out the effects of other factors. In within-subjects ANOVA, there are several error terms, so take care to choose the right one for this calculation (more on this in the calculation example). The value f^2 is less commonly presented in conjunction with significance test statistics, but it is necessary for calculating the noncentrality parameter. The noncentrality parameter (Formula 6.3) is a function of the size of the effect size (partial η^2) and df_{error}.

$$\eta^2 = \frac{SS_{\text{Effect}}}{SS_{\text{Effect}} + SS_{\text{Error}}} \tag{6.1}$$

$$f^2 = \frac{\eta^2}{1 - \eta^2} \tag{6.2}$$

$$\lambda = f^2 df_{\text{error}} \tag{6.3}$$

The formulae presented in this text differ slightly from values used in other sources (e.g., G*Power3). With regard to effect size, some programs request partial η^2 but define this value using formulae that do not account for correlations among dependent measures (these approaches adjust for the correlations later). The value presented in this chapter is consistent with what SPSS calls partial η^2. Similarly, some sources calculate λ based on sample size and levels of the factor rather than degrees of freedom for error. I prefer to use sample size as it is more conservative (df_{error} is always less than the sample size). Different power estimates produced through different approaches likely reflect this choice.

Multivariate ANOVA

The noncentrality parameter for the multivariate effect uses Pillais V, as noted in Formulae 6.4 and 6.5. The calculation of Pillias V requires matrix algebra beyond the scope of the current text (interested readers should consult Tabachnick & Fidell, 2007b, for calculation details). SPSS calculates Pillias V. Formulae 6.4 and 6.5 include MV (multivariate) in the subscripts to avoid confusion with values in Formulae 6.2 and 6.3.

$$f^2_{\text{MV}} = \frac{V}{1 - V} \tag{6.4}$$

$$\lambda_{\text{MV}} = f^2_{\text{MV}} df_{\text{error(MV)}} \tag{6.5}$$

Sphericity Adjustments

Sphericity adjustment for univariate tests requires a value called epsilon (ε). Determining this value can be a bit tricky as adjustment values reflect patterns in the data. Two approaches to estimating the value exist. The first option is simply to choose a level for ε. For serious violations, a conservative estimate of ε is .50; for minor violations, a liberal estimate of ε is .80. As ε decreases, so does power.

The second option is to establish an empirical estimate for epsilon, requiring calculation of either the G-G or H-F statistic. SPSS calculates ε based on the pattern of variances and correlations. If you believe you can make a reasonable estimate of how standard deviations and correlations differ across measures, then the empirical approach is a good strategy. In the absence of that information, choosing a level of ε (liberal or conservative) is a better option. SPSS does not automatically provide power for sphericity-adjusted analyses, so a second analysis that adjusts power based on epsilon is necessary.

Example 6.1: Power for a One-Factor Within-Subjects Design

This example for power for a one-factor within-subjects design focuses on a project from my research laboratory designed to modify implicit attitudes through stereotype negation training. One study involved measures of implicit attitudes toward gay men taken at pretest, posttest (after training), 2 hours after posttest, and 6 hours after posttest. In between the pretest and posttest, participants engaged in a stereotype negation task that forced them to categorize nonstereotypical words with pictures of gay and heterosexual couples.

Determining the size of a meaningful effect required judgments regarding what size effect would be worth the time and effort required to develop and administer the test. Other researchers had success with similar approaches in improving attitudes toward other groups, so we were interested in detecting similar size outcomes. Others found raw score changes of +0.25 to +0.40 (meaning more positive attitudes) from pre to post and gradual increases thereafter. Based on this information, we judged +0.25 as the minimum value for a practically important pre–post change. That is, to term the technique effective, it was important to achieve at worst the same level of attitude change as the least-effective previous study.

We were also interested in whether attitudes continued to change over time and judged smaller increases as meaningful at 2 and 6 hours. Estimates of standard deviations relied on reported uses of similar dependent measures, yielding an estimate of $\sigma = 0.40$, with slight increases in variability for each subsequent measure. For the correlations between measures, large-scale studies of attitudes toward other groups reported test–retest correlation of .50. However, correlations tend to degrade over time, and the test–retest reliabilities for similar measures expressed a considerable range across studies, suggesting smaller correlations for measures further apart (e.g., correlations for pre-twohour = .30, correlations for pre-sixhour = .15).

Table 6.1 Descriptive Statistics for Within-Subjects ANOVA Example

	Pre	Post	2 hour	6 hour
Pre	$\mu = -0.25$ $\sigma = 0.40$			
Post	$\rho = .50$	$\mu = 0.00$ $\sigma = 0.50$		
2 hour	$\rho = .30$	$\rho = .50$	$\mu = 0.10$ $\sigma = 0.60$	
6 hour	$\rho = .15$	$\rho = .30$	$\rho = .50$	$\mu = 0.15$ $\sigma = 0.70$

Table 6.1 presents the estimates of population means, variances, and correlations needed for establishing power. Many of the values reflect conservative estimates. In general, smaller correlations between measures mean less power, larger standard deviations mean less power, and greater heterogeneity of variances means less power. Also, the divergent correlation values promote violation of the sphericity assumption.

The syntax in Table 6.2 creates the data file and the power analysis. The entry of the means and standard deviations corresponds to the order of the variable entry

Table 6.2 SPSS Syntax for Unadjusted Power Analysis

Syntax	Comments

```MATRIX DATA VARIABLES = ROWTYPE_```
 ``` pre post twohr sixhr.```
 ```BEGIN DATA```	

```Mean -0.25 0.00 0.10 0.15```	*M* and *SD* in order as above
```Stdev 0.40 0.50 0.60 0.70```	
```N 25 25 25 25```	Change *N* for different estimates
```Corr 1```	Correlations listed as …
```Corr .5 1```	Pre–post 1
```Corr .3 .5 1```	Pre–two post–two 1
```Corr .15 .3 .5 1```	Pre–four post–four two–four 1
```END DATA.```	The ones must be included
```MANOVA pre post twohr sixhr```	
```/WSFACTOR = time(4)```	Time is a name we provide for
```/MATRIX=IN(*)```	the within-subjects factor
```/POWER F (.05) t(.05) exact```	
```/PRINT signif (mult averf) signif```	
``` (AVERF HF GG EFSIZE)```	HF etc., produce adjusted tests
```/WSDESIGN = time.```	

(pre post twohr sixhr). The correlation matrix also follows the pre-post-twohr-sixhr order. In the MATRIX syntax portion, change the N line to obtain larger or smaller samples. Because the same people provide all four measures, sample size is the same across measures.

Table 6.3 presents highly edited output. However, there is still a considerable amount of information. For now, ignore the section for Multivariate tests (Pillais, etc.). Based on the univariate tests (also known as univariate unadjusted or sphericity assumed), a sample of 25 participants yields power of .809. Keep in mind that this is the power for a test that assumes sphericity. SPSS provides G-G and H-F adjustments to the F statistic but does not report power for those tests. Application of an adjustment (or as seen in the following section, use of the multivariate approach) provides an appropriate level of power for tests that account for sphericity assumption violations.

Regarding calculations, η^2 uses SS_{error} = SS Within + Residual = 14.53 and SS_{effect} = SS Time = 2.38 (underlined in Table 6.3). The noncentrality parameter (λ) uses the value labeled df Within + Residual = 72. Computations use Formulae 6.1, 6.2, and 6.3.

$$\eta^2 = \frac{SS_{Effect}}{SS_{Effect} + SS_{Error}} = \frac{2.38}{2.38 + 14.53} = .141$$

$$f^2 = \frac{\eta^2}{1 - \eta^2} = \frac{.141}{1 - .141} = .164$$

$$\lambda = f^2 df_{error} = .164 \times 72 = 11.8$$

Table 6.3 SPSS Output for Unadjusted Power Analysis

Tests involving 'TIME' Within-Subject Effect.

Mauchly sphericity test, W =	.70397
Chi-square approx. =	7.97609 with 5 D. F.
Significance =	.158
Greenhouse-Geisser Epsilon =	.81458
Huynh-Feldt Epsilon =	.91378
Lower-bound Epsilon =	.33333

EFFECT .. TIME

Multivariate Tests of Significance (S = 1, M = 1/2, N = 10)

Test Name	Value	Exact F Hypoth.	DF	Error DF	Sig. of F
Pillais	.32815	3.58188	3.00	22.00	.030
Hotellings	.48844	3.58188	3.00	22.00	.030
Wilks	.67185	3.58188	3.00	22.00	.030
Roys	.32815				

Table 6.3 SPSS Output for Unadjusted Power Analysis (continued)

Multivariate Effect Size and Observed Power
at .0500 Level

TEST NAME Effect	Size	Noncent.	Power
(All)	.328	10.746	.71

Tests involving 'TIME' Within-Subject Effect.

AVERAGED Tests of Significance for MEAS.1
using UNIQUE sums of squares

Source of Variation	SS	DF	MS	F	Sig of F
WITHIN+RESIDUAL	14.53	72	.20		
(Greenhouse-Geisser)	58.65				
(Huynh-Feldt)	65.79				
TIME	2.38	3	.79	3.92	.012
(Greenhouse-Geisser)	2.44			3.92	.018
(Huynh-Feldt)	2.74			3.92	.015

Effect Size Measures and Observed Power
at the .0500 Level

Source of Variation	Partial ETA Sqd	Noncentrality	Power
TIME	.141	11.767	.809

Example 6.2: Sphericity Adjustments

The first section of the output in Table 6.3 displays the ε adjustments (G-G, etc.). Often, data collected using within-subjects designs do have a sphericity problem, so I recommend a conservative approach that assumes a problem exists. Satisfying the conservative assumption yields adequate power when violating assumptions and even better power if there is no assumption violation. The output shows G-G ε = .815. Although there are some situations for which H-F is the preferred statistic for ε adjustment, I recommend G-G for use in power analysis because it is the more conservative approach. The sphericity adjustment is applied to the degrees of freedom. For example, the degrees of freedom involved in the significance test for time are 3 and 72. The G-G adjustment multiplies the G-G ε value of .815 by each degree of freedom, producing 2.44 (3 * .815) and 58.65 (72 * .815). These values become the degrees of freedom for that adjusted test. The degrees of freedom based on these adjustments are then used along with the F-statistic to calculate the probability [$F(2.44, 58.65) = 3.92$, $p = .018$].

For researchers who prefer the H-F adjustment, the approach detailed in Table 6.4 works in a same manner; simply substitute .914 for .815. Similarly, for a more conservative level of adjustment (e.g., ε = .50), substitute that value.

Table 6.4 Syntax for Sphericity Adjustments

Syntax	Comments
INPUT PROGRAM.	
LOOP n=25 TO 40 by 1.	Change this line to reflect the samples to test
END CASE.	Gives $n = 20$ to 40 by increments of 1
END LOOP.	
END FILE.	
END INPUT PROGRAM.	
EXECUTE .	
Compute Epsilon = 0.815.	Enter the G-G or H-F value here
Compute Measures = 4.	Number of levels of the WS factor
Compute Lambda = 11.767.	Listed as noncentrality in the output
Compute alpha = 0.05.	
Compute Initial_n = 25.	This is n from the analysis used to derive the sphericity estimate
Compute df_num = measures -1.	Leave everything here and below alone
Compute df_denom = (df_num * n) - df_num.	
Compute df_n_adj = df_num * Epsilon.	
Compute df_d_adj = df_denom * Epsilon.	
Compute n_adj = n * Epsilon.	
Compute lambda_adj = ((Lambda/ initial_n) * n_adj).	
Compute F_Table = IDF.F(1- alpha,df_n_adj, df_d_adj) .	
Compute Power = 1-NCDF.F(F_ table,df_n_adj, df_d_adj, lambda_adj) .	
EXECUTE .	
MATRIX.	
GET M /VARIABLES=n lambda_adj power.	
print M/title = "Sphericity Adjusted Power"/clabels = "n" "Lambda_Adj" "Power_Adj"/ format f9.3.	
End Matrix.	

Table 6.5 Sphericity Adjusted Power for $n = 25$ to 40

	Sphericity Adjusted Power	
n	Lambda_Adj	Power_Adj
25.0	9.590	.745
26.0	9.974	.764
27.0	10.357	.782
28.0	10.741	.798
29.0	11.125	.814
30.0	11.508	.829
31.0	11.892	.842
32.0	12.275	.855
33.0	12.659	.867
34.0	13.043	.878
35.0	13.426	.888
36.0	13.810	.897
37.0	14.193	.906
38.0	14.577	.914
39.0	14.961	.922
40.0	15.344	.929

The syntax in Table 6.4 is somewhat complex. The lines in bold are the only ones that require modification. This syntax creates the output shown in Table 6.5.

As shown in Table 6.5, to achieve power of .80 for a sphericity-adjusted test requires a sample of 28 or 29 rather than 25 as found for the unadjusted test. Three or four additional participants reflect a 12–16% increase in sample size.

MULTIVARIATE APPROACH TO REPEATED MEASURES

Multivariate analysis of variance (MANOVA) is an alternative approach to the univariate within-subjects ANOVA approach demonstrated. This section presents the MANOVA approach to a one-factor within-subjects design. Chapter 7 examines MANOVA for other designs.

An advantage of the MANOVA approach to repeated measures is that it does not require the sphericity assumption. This means there are no ε adjustments to reduce power. MANOVA is sometimes less powerful than univariate ANOVA, especially with small samples or when effects are concentrated across two levels (e.g., if the only difference between means in the example were between pretest and posttest). However, the trade-off between ε-adjusted power and MANOVA power often favors MANOVA, especially when violating the sphericity assumption.

The decision between approaches is not necessary for tests for which $df_{numerator} = 1$ (e.g., only two measurement periods). In those cases, the MV and univariate test are equivalent.

Example 6.3: Multivariate Approach

Returning to Table 6.3, we see the multivariate tests. SPSS gives Pillais, Hotellings, Wilks, and Roy's largest root. For a one-factor within-subjects design, the tests are equivalent; however, most researchers present Wilks λ.

Power calculations reflect the Pillais V statistic (or 1-Wilks λ) and the $df_{denominator}$ (reported by SPSS as df error). SPSS calculates the power for the MANOVA as .71. This is close to the ε-adjusted value of .745 found for $n = 25$ in Table 6.5. However, as will be shown, these values may diverge considerably.

$$f_{MV}^2 = \frac{V}{1-V} = \frac{.328}{1-.328} = .488$$

$$\lambda_{MV} = f_{MV}^2 df_{error(MV)} = .488 \times 22 = 10.7$$

These calculations highlight difference in the degrees of freedom between univariate and multivariate ANOVA. For the MANOVA, the degrees of freedom were 3 and 22, whereas for the univariate approach they were 3 and 72. This is one of the sources of differences in power calculations. The univariate $df_{denominator}$ is over three times the size of the multivariate. This may seem like a huge difference, but there are a couple of issues to keep in mind. First, ε adjustments to the degrees of freedom in univariate ANOVA drive the degrees of freedom downward (and thus closer to the MV value). Also, as sample size rises, the $df_{denominator}$ impacts power less. For this example, the critical value for F at $\alpha = .05$ is 3.05 for the MV test ($df_{denominator} = 22$), 2.73 for the univariate ($df_{denominator} = 72$), and 2.76 for the univariate tests G-G adjusted ($df_{denominator} = 58.65$). As sample sizes rise and problems with sphericity increase, power for the multivariate approach often surpasses the univariate test.

Example 6.4: A Serious Sphericity Problem

To demonstrate how power for the univariate and multivariate tests differ when violating the sphericity assumption, I modified the Example 6.3 to represent worse problems with sphericity. The matrix command shown in Table 6.6 demonstrates issues that contribute to violation of the sphericity assumption. When compared to the data used in Table 6.2, the standard deviations are more unequal and the correlations between measures more divergent. For this analysis, the G-G statistic is smaller than in the previous example (.662 vs. .815), reflecting greater deviation from the sphericity assumption. The power for the MANOVA far exceeds the univariate power (.50 vs. .12), even before applying an ε adjustment that reduces univariate power further.

Table 6.6 SPSS Syntax and Output for Serious Sphericity Problem Example

```
MATRIX DATA VARIABLES = ROWTYPE_ pre post twoweek sixweek.
BEGIN DATA
Mean -0.25 0.00 0.10 0.15
Stdev 0.40 0.50 2.5 2.0
N 25 25 25 25
Corr 1
Corr .5 1
Corr .3 .5 1
Corr .1 .3 .4 1
END DATA.

MANOVA pre post twoweek sixweek
   /WSFACTOR = time(4)
   /MATRIX=IN(*)
   /POWER F (.05) t(.05) exact
   /CONTRAST (time) = Polynomial
   /PRINT signif (mult averf) homogeneity (all) signif
    (AVERF HF GG EFSIZE)
   /WSDESIGN = time.
```

Greenhouse-Geisser Epsilon =   .66193

EFFECT .. TIME

Multivariate Tests of Significance (S = 1, M = 1/2, N = 10)

Test Name	Value	Exact F Hypoth.	DF	Error DF	Sig. of F
Wilks	.76036	2.31123	3.00	22.00	.104

Multivariate Effect Size and Observed Power at .0500 Level

TEST NAME Effect	Size	Noncent.	Power
(All)	.240	6.934	.50

AVERAGED Tests of Significance for MEAS.1 using UNIQUE sums of squares

Source of Variation	SS	DF	MS	F	Sig of F
WITHIN+ RESIDUAL	151.02	72	2.10		
(Greenhouse- Geisser)	47.66				

(continued)

Table 6.6 SPSS Syntax and Output for Serious Sphericity Problem Example (continued)

AVERAGED Tests of Significance for MEAS.1 using UNIQUE
sums of squares

Source of Variation	SS	DF	MS	F	Sig of F
TIME	2.38	3	.79	.38	.770
(Greenhouse-Geisser)	1.99		.38	.686	

Effect Size Measures and Observed Power
at the .0500 Level

Source of Variation	Partial ETA Sqd	Noncentrality	Power
TIME	.015	1.132	.121

TREND ANALYSIS

Often, research involving measures taken over time seek to examine trends. For example, a linear trend might exist by which scores rise (or fall) over time, or a quadratic (curvilinear) trend shows that scores improve initially but later return to pretest levels. This is a qualitatively different question than the one addressed in the example in which power analysis focused on tests examining whether the four means (one for each time) differed. Trend analyses ask whether means differ in a specific manner. Trend analyses do not require a sphericity adjustment. Trends involve a single degree of freedom in the numerator. Sphericity is not an issue when $df_{numerator} = 1$.

Example 6.5: Trend Analysis

Imagine that in the example from the previous section, hypotheses focused on steady and consistent changes in attitudes over each measurement period. For example, instead of predicting different levels of improvement across each measure (e.g., +0.25, then +0.10, then +0.05), we expected a +0.10 improvement in attitudes for each measurement period. This prediction reflects a hypothesis about a linear trend rather than an omnibus ANOVA test that simply specifies differences between means. This distinction is important as the two types of tests (omnibus vs. trend analysis) sometimes produce markedly different power analyses.

SPSS provides this test with some modification to the syntax used in Table 6.2. The primary modification is addition of a single line [Contrast (Time) = Polynomial] to produce the trend analysis. Also note that the mean values now represent a 0.10 improvement in attitudes for each measure. Table 6.7 presents both the syntax and the output

Table 6.7 SPSS Syntax and Output for Trend Analysis

```
MATRIX DATA VARIABLES = ROWTYPE_
 pre post twohr sixhr.
BEGIN DATA
Mean -0.25 -0.15 -0.05 0.05
Stdev 0.40 0.50 0.60 0.70
N 25 25 25 25
Corr 1
Corr .5 1
Corr .3 .5 1
Corr .15 .3 .5 1
END DATA.

   MANOVA pre post twohr sixhr
   /WSFACTOR = time(4)
   /MATRIX=IN(*)
   /POWER F (.05) t(.05) exact
   /CONTRAST (time) = Polynomial
   /PRINT signif (mult averf) homogeneity (all) signif
    (AVERF HF GG EFSIZE)
   /WSDESIGN = time.
EFFECT .. TIME
```

Multivariate Effect Size and Observed Power
at .0500 Level

TEST NAME	Effect Size	Noncent.	Power
(All)	.15308	6.68782	.52

Estimates for T2 (Comment: T2 is the Linear trend)

TIME		
Parameter	Noncent.	Power
1	6.445	.712

Estimates for T3 (Comment: T3 is the Quadratic trend)

TIME		
Parameter	Noncent.	Power
1	0.000	.050

Estimates for T4 (Comment: T4 is the Cubic trend)

Parameter	Noncent.	Power
1	0.000	.050

with additional annotations on the output (where it says Comment) as SPSS's labels for the trends are unclear. The bold part of the syntax is the only addition to the file used previously. The analysis uses $n = 25$.

Notice that the power for detecting the linear trend (.71) is considerably higher than the power for the multivariate test (.52) with $n = 40$. The pattern of means contains no quadratic or cubic component, so power for these trends is low.

Power for the specific contrasts or patterns of effect of interest often produce different power than omnibus tests. Clearly, in this case the linear trend power analysis suggests a smaller sample size requirement than the omnibus power analysis. The best question to ask is what the effect of interest is. Does the research hypothesis focus on the trend, the omnibus test, or both? In addition, what trend is important? Whatever your interest, design for detecting that effect.

Example 6.6: Two Within-Subjects Factors

The previous examples examined a single within-subjects factor. The example that follows adds a second within-subjects factor (length of negation task). Participants complete a short negation task (15 minutes; Condition A) then return a month later and complete a longer negation task (1 hour; Condition B). Both conditions involve pre, post, 2-hour, and 6-hour measures.

For simplicity, the syntax reflects all the correlations as .5. The means reflect the expectation that the longer test produces stronger attitude change. The difference between the means for the short and long tasks reflects the size of effect that justifies increasing the length of the intervention. For this design, there are two main effects and an interaction.

The WSFACTOR command shown in Table 6.8 requires careful attention. The variables are listed as all Condition A then all Condition B. This impacts the setup of the WSFACTOR statement. WSFACTOR requires listing the slowest-changing value first and the fastest-changing value second. The fastest-changing factor is Time. This is because as we move from the first to the second variable (pre_A to post_A), this changes the level of Time. Condition changes more slowly, not changing value until we move past the first four listed variables. Condition does not change until we move from sixhour_A to pre_b.

The analysis, presented in Table 6.9 with $n = 80$, demonstrates outstanding power for Time but lackluster power for Condition and the interaction. This table includes only the multivariate tests with the ε values and univariate tests deleted for brevity. If the research goal is to determine that one condition outperforms another, then a sample of 80 participants is too small to ensure adequate power. Note that Table 6.9 presents the univariate test for Condition. That is not a mistake. With $df_{numerator} = 1$, the univariate and multivariate tests are equivalent. SPSS MANOVA prints only the univariate test in these situations.

Table 6.10 finds the sample size for a design that yields power of 0.80 for both main effects. This analysis used a sample of $n = 335$.

Example 6.7: Simple Effects

As with between-subjects factorial ANOVA, when interactions exist, designs often probe interactions using simple effects tests. For example, we might be interested in showing

Table 6.8 SPSS Syntax for Doubly Within Design[a]

```
MATRIX DATA VARIABLES = ROWTYPE_ pre_A post_A twohour_A
 sixhour_A pre_b post_b twohour_b sixhour_b.
BEGIN DATA
Mean -0.25 0.00 0.10 0.15 -0.25 .10 .30 .35
Stdev 0.40 0.50 2.5 2.0 0.40 0.50 2.5 2.0
N 80 80 80 80 80 80 80 80
Corr 1
Corr .5 1
Corr .5 .5 1
Corr .5 .5 .5 1
Corr .5 .5 .5 .5 1
Corr .5 .5 .5 .5 .5 1
Corr .5 .5 .5 .5 .5 .5 1
Corr .5 .5 .5 .5 .5 .5 .5 1
END DATA.

MANOVA pre_A post_A twohour_A sixhour_A pre_b post_b
 twohour_b sixhour_b
  /WSFACTOR = condition(2) time(4)
  /MATRIX=IN(*)
  /POWER F (.05) t(.05) exact
  /CONTRAST (time) = Polynomial
  /PRINT signif (mult averf) homogeneity (all) signif
   (AVERF HF GG EFSIZE)
  /WSDESIGN = time condition time*condition.
```

[a] Please see comments in the syntax files and Chapter 11 regarding commonly encountered syntax run errors. The problems reported in Chapter 11 are particularly common for this analysis.

Table 6.9 Highly Edited SPSS Output for Doubly Within Design ($n = 80$)

Tests involving 'TIME' Within-Subject Effect.

```
EFFECT .. TIME
Multivariate Tests of Significance (S = 1, M = 1/2, N =
 37 1/2)
```

Test Name	Value	Exact F Hypoth.	DF	Error DF	Sig. of F
Wilks	.53690	22.13891	3.00	77.00	.000

(continued)

Table 6.9 Highly Edited SPSS Output for Doubly Within Design ($n = 80$) (continued)

Multivariate Effect Size and Observed Power at .0500 Level

TEST NAME	Effect Size	Noncent.	Power
(All)	.463	66.417	1.00

Tests involving 'CONDITION' Within-Subject Effect.

Tests of Significance for T5 using UNIQUE sums of squares

Source of Variation	SS	DF	MS	F	Sig of F
WITHIN+					
RESIDUAL	105.27	79	1.33		
CONDITION	2.50	1	2.50	1.88	.175

Effect Size Measures and Observed Power at the .0500 Level

Source of Variation	Partial ETA Sqd	Noncentrality	Power
CONDITION	.023	1.876	.272

Tests involving 'TIME * CONDITION' Within-Subject Effect.

EFFECT .. TIME * CONDITION

Multivariate Tests of Significance (S = 1, M = 1/2, N = 37 1/2)

Test Name	Value	Exact F Hypoth.	DF	Error DF	Sig. of F
Wilks	.96614	.89946	3.00	77.00	.445

Multivariate Effect Size and Observed Power at .0500 Level

TEST NAME	Effect Size	Noncent.	Power
(All)	.034	2.698	.24

significant improvements in attitudes for both groups individually. That is, that both techniques did in fact change attitudes for the better.

Table 6.11 shows the syntax and edited output for these analyses using the $n = 335$ sample size. The only change to the syntax is the addition of the bold lines. Based on this analysis, there exists considerable power to detect differences between means within each condition.[1]

Table 6.10 Output for Power ≥ .80 for Doubly Within Design

EFFECT .. TIME

TEST NAME	Effect Size	Noncent.	Power
(All)	.461	283.635	1.00

Effect Size Measures and Observed Power at the .0500 Level

Source of Variation	Partial ETA Sqd	Noncentrality	Power
CONDITION	.023	7.856	.798

EFFECT .. TIME * CONDITION

TEST NAME	Effect Size	Noncent.	Power
(All)	.034	11.524	.82

Table 6.11 Simple Effects Syntax and Output for Doubly Within Design

```
MANOVA pre_A post_A twohour_A sixhour_A pre_b post_b
twohour_b sixhour_b
  /WSFACTOR = condition(2) time(4)
  /MATRIX=IN(*)
  /POWER F (.05) t(.05) exact
  /PRINT signif (mult averf) homogeneity (all) signif
  (AVERF HF GG EFSIZE)
  /WSDESIGN = time condition time*condition
  /WSDESIGN = Time WITHIN Condition (1)
  /WSDESIGN = Time WITHIN Condition (2).
```

EFFECT .. TIME WITHIN CONDITION(1)

Test Name	Value	Exact F Hypoth.	DF	Error DF	Sig. of F
Pillais	.23795	34.55560	3.00	332.00	.000

Multivariate Effect Size and Observed Power at .0500 Level

TEST NAME	Effect Size	Noncent.	Power
(All)	.238	103.667	1.00

EFFECT .. TIME WITHIN CONDITION(2)

Test Name	Value	Exact F Hypoth.	DF	Error DF	Sig. of F
Pillais	.38301	68.69829	3.00	332.00	.000

Multivariate Effect Size and Observed Power at .0500 Level

TEST NAME	Effect Size	Noncent.	Power
(All)	.383	206.095	1.00

ADDITIONAL ISSUES

Issues related to detecting power for multiple effects, as discussed in Chapter 5, also pertain to within-subjects designs. Recall that the power to detect all the effects of interest is a function [termed Power(All)][2] of the product of the power of all the tests. In the example with $n = 335$, Power(All) reflects the product of the three power values (1 * .798 * .82 = .65). Designing to find significance for all three effects in the same study requires larger sample sizes.

With regard to appropriate sample size for use of MANOVA instead of univariate approaches, a reasonable suggestion is a minimum of two participants per cell, although other suggestions indicate only that more participants than measures is sufficient. In the example from Table 6.2, there are 25 participants and four measures, meeting the 2:1 criteria.

Chapter 7 covers special considerations when designing for optimal power for MANOVA. However, many of the issues discussed in that chapter (e.g., avoiding DVs with strong positive correlations) do not apply to tests of within-subjects effects and do not limit power in the MANOVA approach to repeated measures.

SUMMARY

This chapter examined one- and two-factor within-subjects designs. The primary information required for each design is meaningful patterns of means, standard deviations for each dependent measure, and correlations between measures. For standard deviations and correlations, accurate estimates improve power analysis. When expecting heterogeneous standard deviations or different correlations across measures (i.e., violation of the sphericity assumption), power analysis should address these issues through consideration of sphericity-adjusted approaches or use of MANOVA (provided there is a large enough sample). Power analysis results for hypotheses specifying trends or simple effects often diverge from results for omnibus tests, so power analysis should focus on the specific tests of interest.

NOTES

1. For the syntax represented in Table 6.11, I find that SPSS generally runs more smoothly if you run the two simple effects tests separately. The syntax file on the companion Web site contains an example of this approach.

2. Power(All) refers to the power of detecting all three effects as significant. The SPSS output includes a value labeled (All) (see Table 6.10, e.g.). The SPSS value is not Power(All). The (All) in this case refers to the multivariate tests, as in *all* the multivariate tests have the same value for power.

7

MIXED-MODEL ANOVA AND MULTIVARIATE ANOVA

INTRODUCTION

This chapter presents power analyses for mixed-model analysis of variance (ANOVA) and multivariate ANOVA (MANOVA). In this chapter, the term *mixed model* refers to ANOVA designs that include both within- and between-subjects factors. Some sources refer to these designs as mixed randomized-repeated or split-plot designs. MANOVA addresses designs with multiple dependent measures and at least one factor. This chapter examines power for mixed models with one between- and one within-subjects factor and for one-factor MANOVA, provides examples of SPSS syntax demonstrating designs that are more complicated, and discusses how different patterns of effect sizes and correlations in MANOVA influence power.

NECESSARY INFORMATION

As with the ANOVA designs in Chapters 5 and 6, power analysis requires means (μs) corresponding to meaningful differences (or patterns of differences) among factor levels, estimates of the standard deviation (σ) for each factor level, and the expected correlations (ρs) between dependent measures.

FACTORS AFFECTING POWER

For mixed-model ANOVA, larger effect sizes and stronger positive correlations between dependent measures yield more power. Sphericity impacts power for within-subjects factors as discussed in Chapter 6. As with other designs, larger sample sizes and α increase power.

For MANOVA, the pattern of correlations between variables and the pattern of differences between means (e.g., effect sizes for each dependent measure) influence power. This is a complex issue, so I devote a chapter section to it.

KEY STATISTICS

There are no new statistics introduced in this chapter. Calculation of effect sizes and noncentrality parameters use Formulae 6.1–6.5, presented in detail in Chapter 6. A full review of the statistics associated with these procedures and their calculation is outside the scope of this chapter. For a highly readable overview of the techniques, see the work of Tabachnick and Fidell (2007a, 2007b).

MIXED-MODEL DESIGNS

This section examines power for a mixed-model ANOVA. The term *mixed model* refers, in this chapter, to ANOVA designs with at least one within-subjects and one between-subjects factor. This does not connote a hierarchical linear model (HLM), which several sources also refer to as mixed-model designs. Information on resources for designs addressing HLM appears in Chapter 11.

Example 7.1: Mixed-Model ANOVA

The example in this section expands the one-factor within-subjects study from Chapter 6 through addition of a between-subjects factor. In the initial example, participants engaged in a stereotype negation procedure, and our interest was whether attitudes improved over time. Another reasonable question could be whether this level of change differed from the change in the control group. To address this issue, the study in this example includes a control group that completed a stereotype maintenance procedure (e.g., Kawakami, Dovidio, Moll, Herrasen, & Russin, 2000). Participants in this condition engaged in a task that forced them to respond in stereotype-consistent rather than stereotype-negating manners. Earlier work demonstrated that participants who completed a maintenance task showed consistent attitudes across all levels of measurement. Therefore, in this example, we did not expect participants in the maintenance condition to experience changes in their attitudes.

Table 7.1 details the means, standard deviations, and correlations for the measures. Note that the expected control group means (μ_c) remain constant, while the treatment group means (μ_t) change in the same manner as in the Chapter 6 example.

Table 7.2 presents the SPSS syntax for this analysis. The syntax addresses correlations for the overall sample rather than by group. The negation group is listed first

Table 7.1 Descriptive Statistics for Mixed-Model ANOVA Example

	Pre	Post	2 hour	6 hour
Pre	$\mu_t = -0.25,$ $\sigma_t = 0.40$ $\mu_c = -0.25,$ $\sigma_c = 0.40$			
Post	$\rho = .50$	$\mu_t = 0.0,$ $\sigma_t = 0.50$ $\mu_c = -0.25,$ $\sigma_c = 0.50$		
2 hour	$\rho = .30$	$\rho = .50$	$\mu_t = 0.10,$ $\sigma_t = 0.60$ $\mu_c = -0.25,$ $\sigma_c = 0.60$	
6 hour	$\rho = .15$	$\rho = .30$	$\rho = .50$	$\mu_t = 0.15,$ $\sigma_t = 0.70$ $\mu_c = -0.25,$ $\sigma_c = 0.70$

Note: Subscript t is the negation (treatment) group, and subscript c is the maintenance (control) group.

and noted with a "1" (e.g., 1 Mean -0.25 0.00 0.10 0.15), and the maintenance group appears second with a "2" (e.g., 2 Mean -0.25 -0.25 -0.25 -0.25).

Table 7.3 presents output for main effects and the interaction. The main hypothesis is that attitudes change in a different manner for each group. The statistical effect in this table that is most relevant to this hypothesis is the interaction (see the EFFECT . . . Condition BY TIME portion). For the interaction, 50 participants per condition yields a power of .80.

Example 7.2: Trend Analysis for Mixed Models

A slight variation on the Example 7.1 is a situation in which hypotheses specify a steady improvement for the treatment group at each measurement period (e.g., attitudes improve by 0.10 for each measurement) and, as before, no change across measures for the control group. As discussed in Chapter 6, this pattern of effects reflects a prediction of a linear trend for the treatment group. For the control group, there is no trend predicted. In this study, the hypothesis specifies a condition-by-time linear trend interaction. Specifically, the hypothesis predicted the negation group to show a steady improvement in attitudes (a linear trend) and the maintenance group to show no change in attitudes (no linear trend). The presence of a condition-by-time linear trend indicates that different linear trends exist for each

Table 7.2 Syntax for Mixed-Model ANOVA Example

Syntax	Comments
MATRIX DATA VARIABLES = Condition Rowtype_ pre post twohour sixhour /Factor = Condition.	
BEGIN DATA	*M* and *SD* in order as above
1 Mean -0.25 0.00 0.10 0.15	
1 N 50 50 50 50	Change *N* for different estimates
2 Mean -0.25 -0.25 -0.25 -0.25	
2 N 50 50 50 50	Correlations listed as ...
. Corr 1	
. Corr .5 1	Pre-post 1
. Corr .3 .5 1	Pre-two post-two 1
. Corr .15 .3 .5 1	Pre-four post-four two-four 1
. Stdev 0.40 0.50 0.60 0.70	The ones must be included
END DATA.	
MANOVA pre post twohour sixhour by condition (1,2)	List DVs in order
/WSFACTOR = time(4)	"By" precedes the between subject factor
/MATRIX=IN(*)	Time is a name we provide for the within-subjects factor
/POWER F (.05) t(.05) exact	
/PRINT signif (mult averf) homogeneity (all) signif (AVERF HF GG EFSIZE)	HF (Hyunh-Feldt), etc., produce adjusted tests
/WSDESIGN = time.	

condition, so power for this effect is particularly relevant to the hypothesis. SPSS does not provide this test as a default, but modifications to the syntax produce the analysis.

The syntax in Table 7.4 presents syntax and output for a power analysis using means that represent a 0.10 improvement in attitudes each time the treatment group is measured. In the syntax, the bold contrast line specifies the trend analysis. The test of the linear trend for the interaction produced power of .516, suggesting a larger sample is needed to attain adequate power for this test. This test could also be conceptualized as a regular interaction (i.e., one that does not focus specifically on a trend). The power for detecting such an interaction is .37. We have considerably more power to detect the interaction on the linear trend than the standard interaction. An important point highlighted by this analysis is that researchers should focus on tests that address the most specific aspects of their hypotheses.

Table 7.3 Output for Mixed-Model ANOVA Example

```
Tests of Between-Subjects Effects.
```

```
Tests of Significance for T1 using UNIQUE sums of squares
```

Source of Variation	SS	DF	MS	F	Sig of F
WITHIN+RESIDUAL	64.14	98	.65		
Condition	6.25	1	6.25	9.55	.003

Effect Size Measures and Observed Power at the .0500 Level

Source of Variation	Partial ETA Sqd	Noncentrality	Power
Condition	.089	9.549	.864

EFFECT .. Condition BY TIME
Multivariate Tests of Significance (S = 1, M = 1/2, N = 47)

Test Name	Value	Exact F Hypoth.	DF	Error DF	Sig. of F
Pillais	.10684	3.82776	3.00	96.00	.012

Multivariate Effect Size and Observed Power at .0500 Level

TEST NAME Effect	Size	Noncent.	Power
(All)	.107	11.483	.80

EFFECT .. TIME
Multivariate Tests of Significance (S = 1, M = 1/2, N = 47)

Test Name	Value	Exact F Hypoth.	DF	Error DF	Sig. of F
Pillais	.10684	3.82776	3.00	96.00	.012

Multivariate Effect Size and Observed Power at .0500 Level

TEST NAME Effect	Size	Noncent.	Power
(All)	.107	11.483	.80

Designs With Three or More Factors

Table 7.5 shows syntax for a few variations on the mixed-model ANOVA design. These tests involve simple modifications to the syntax presented in this chapter and in Chapters 5 and 6. For example, addition of a

Table 7.4 Syntax and Output for Trends

```
MATRIX DATA VARIABLES = Condition Rowtype_ pre post
 twohour sixhour
    /Factor = Condition.
```

```
BEGIN DATA
1 Mean -0.25 -0.15 -0.05 0.05
1 N 50 50 50 50
2 Mean -0.25 -0.25 -0.25 -0.25
2 N 50 50 50 50
. Corr 1
. Corr .5 1
. Corr .3 .5 1
. Corr .15 .3 .5 1
. Stdev 0.40 0.50 0.60 0.70
END DATA.
```

```
    MANOVA pre post twohour sixhour by condition (1,2)
    /WSFACTOR = time(4)
    /MATRIX=IN(*)
    /POWER F (.05) t(.05) exact
    /PRINT signif (mult averf) homogeneity (all) signif
    (AVERF HF GG EFSIZE)
    /CONTRAST (time) = polynomial
    /WSDESIGN = time.
```

EFFECT .. Condition BY TIME

TEST NAME	Effect Size	Noncent.	Power
(All)	.04302	4.31591	.37

Estimates for T2 (Note: This is the linear trend)
Condition BY TIME

Noncent.	Power
4.03096	.516

Estimates for T3 (Note: This is the quadratic trend)
Condition BY TIME

Noncent.	Power
.00000	.050

Estimates for T4 (Note: This is the cubic trend)
Condition BY TIME

Noncent.	Power
.00000	.050

Table 7.5 Syntax for Mixed-Model Designs With Three Factors

Two Within, One Between	Two Between, One Within
| ```
MATRIX DATA VARIABLES = A
 ROWTYPE_ X1Y1 X2Y1 X3Y1
X4Y1 X1Y2 X2Y2 X3Y2 X4Y2
  /Factors = A.

BEGIN DATA
1 Mean -0.25 0.00 0.10 0.15
 -0.25 0.10 0.30 0.35
1 N 335 335 335 335 335 335
335 335
2 Mean 0.0 0.00 0.05 0.05
 -0.35 0.00 .10 .25
2 N 335 335 335 335 335 335
335 335
. Corr 1
. Corr .5 1
. Corr .5 .5 1
. Corr .5 .5 .5 1
. Corr .5 .5 .5 .5 1
. Corr .5 .5 .5 .5 .5 1
. Corr .5 .5 .5 .5 .5 .5 1
. Corr .5 .5 .5 .5 .5 .5
.5 1
. Stdev 0.40 0.50 2.5 2.0
0.40 0.50 2.5 2.0
END DATA.



MANOVA X1Y1 X2Y1 X3Y1 X4Y1
X1Y2 X2Y2 X3Y2 X4Y2 by
A (1,2)
   /WSFACTOR = y(2) x(4)
   /MATRIX=IN(*)
   /POWER F (.05) t(.05)
   exact
   /WSDESIGN = x y x*y.
``` | ```
MATRIX DATA VARIABLES = A B
 ROWTYPE_ dv1 dv2 dv3 dv4


  /Factor = A, B.



BEGIN DATA

1 1 Mean -0.25 0.00 0.10
 0.15
1 1 N 50 50 50 50

1 2 Mean 0.25 0.25 0.25 0.25

1 2 N 50 50 50 50
2 1 Mean 0.50 0.25 0.10 0.15
2 1 N 50 50 50 50
2 2 Mean 0.75 0.50 0.25 0.25
2 2 N 50 50 50 50
. . Corr 1
. . Corr .5 1
. . Corr .5 .5 1

. . Corr .5 .5 .5 1

. . Stdev 0.40 0.50 0.60
 0.70
END DATA.

MANOVA dv1 dv2 dv3 dv4 by
 a, b (1,2)

   /WSFACTOR = time(4)
   /MATRIX=IN(*)
   /POWER F (.05) t(.05)
   exact
   /WSDESIGN = time.
``` |

second within-subjects variable with two levels (noted here as Y1 and Y2) requires only that the mean, sample size, and standard deviation lines include information for all of the dependent variables, that the correlation matrix expands to 8 × 8 to account for all correlations among DVs, and that the WSFACTOR command adds a second factor (Y). Addition of a second between-subjects factor as shown in the right-hand side of Table 7.5 adds numbers to note levels of each factor and now includes two periods in front of the correlations. The two numbers on the left (e.g., 1 1; 1 2) correspond to the levels of Factors A and B, respectively (e.g., 1 2 is first level of A, second level of B). The correlation statement now includes two periods in front of the Corr term as the syntax requires a period preceding that aspect of the matrix for every between-subjects factor.

MULTIVARIATE ANOVA

The MANOVA procedures address comparisons across groups on two or more dependent variables. For power analysis, MANOVA brings additional complexity. With MANOVA, patterns of effect sizes across the dependent measures and patterns of correlations between dependent measures influence power considerably. For that reason, discussion of how these patterns affect power appears before coverage of MANOVA power because understanding these relationships is important in designing for adequate power. As suggested throughout the text, when in doubt (and when it is feasible) it is good practice to design conservatively. An understanding of how the patterns of correlations and effects impact power helps to determine what is and what is not a conservative design decision.

Patterns of Effects and Correlations

Aside from the basic issues influencing power for all ANOVA designs, two new issues affect MANOVA power. The first involves the type of effect sizes observed for each dependent measure. In general, if all the effect sizes are consistent, one pattern of power results exist, whereas for inconsistent effects there is a different pattern. In this context, *consistent* means roughly the same effect size across all dependent measures. When effects are inconsistent (e.g., some dependent measures differ strongly across the between-subjects factor and others show small differences), a different pattern of power results exists.

Power also depends on correlations between dependent measures. For consistent effects (e.g., Small–Small), power increases as we move from strongly positive to strongly negative correlations. For inconsistent effects (e.g., Small–Strong), power increases when moving toward more extreme relationships (either stronger positive or stronger negative correlations). Regardless of the relationship, negative correlations between predictors usually produce more power than positive correlations of the same magnitude (but see the discussion that follows regarding recoding variables).

Table 7.6 Power as a Function of Effect Size and Correlation Patterns

Correlation Between Measures	Small–Small $d = 0.2$, 0.2	Moderate–Moderate $d = 0.5$, 0.5	Strong–Strong $d = 0.8$, 0.8	Small–Moderate $d = 0.2$, 0.5	Small–Strong $d = 0.2$, 0.8	Moderate–Strong $d = 0.5$, 0.8
.9	.14	.26	.59	.52	.98	.72
.8	.14	.27	.61	.34	.84	.60
.7	.15	.29	.64	.29	.72	.57
.6	.15	.30	.67	.26	.64	.56
.5	.16	.32	.70	.25	.60	.57
.4	.17	.34	.73	.25	.58	.59
.3	.18	.36	.76	.25	.57	.61
.2	.19	.39	.80	.26	.57	.64
.1	.20	.42	.83	.27	.57	.68
.0	.22	.46	.87	.28	.59	.72
−.1	.24	.50	.90	.30	.62	.76
−.2	.26	.55	.93	.33	.65	.81
−.3	.30	.61	.96	.36	.70	.86
−.4	.34	.69	.98	.41	.75	.91
−.5	.40	.77	.99	.47	.82	.95
−.6	.49	.86	1.0	.56	.89	.98
−.7	.61	.94	1.0	.69	.96	1.0
−.8	.80	.99	1.0	.86	.99	1.0
−.9	.98	1.0	1.0	.99	1.0	1.0

Table 7.6 summarizes these relationships for a MANOVA with two dependent measures (see also Cole, Maxwell, Arvey, & Salas, 1994, for a technical description). All situations in the table use $n = 20$ except for the small–small effect column, in which tests used $n = 50$ to more clearly demonstrate the pattern of results. In the table, *small* refers to a $d = 0.20$ between two conditions on a single DV. *Moderate* refers to $d = 0.50$, and *strong* indicates $d = 0.80$. The column labeled "Small–Small" reflects when two dependent variables both show $d = 0.20$; in the "Small–Strong" column, one measure has $d = 0.20$ and the other $d = 0.80$, and so on. All effects in the table represent results in the same direction (e.g., both positive).

One interpretation drawn from Table 7.6 is that negative correlations increase power. This leads to an obvious question. In fact, every time I teach or present on this topic someone asks, "If negative correlations between dependent measures increase my power, does this mean I can reverse code one of my DVs to yield more power?" The answer is no.

Table 7.6 presents power for situations for which predictors relate to the dependent measure in the same manner (e.g., Group 1 scores higher than Group 2 on both measures). That is, the IV-DV relationships are all in the same direction. If one variable were reversed coded (e.g., high scores converted to low scores), a reversal of the direction of the effect size would follow for that variable. To obtain values for situations for which one IV has a positive and one has a negative relationship with the DV, the values in the correlation table reverse. For example, with $d = 0.5$ for one IV and $d = -0.5$ for the other and the DVs correlated at $-.40$, the power would be .34 (the value listed for $r = .40$) rather than .69, which is the value for $r = -.40$ (see the "Additional Issues" section for a more detailed explanation).

Table 7.6 illustrates several other important considerations for MANOVA. First, power tends to be higher when negative correlations exist between dependent measures. Practically, if IV–DV relationships are in the same direction, strong negative correlations between dependent measures are not common. When negative correlations are present, they are usually small. However, small negative correlations give more power than small positive correlations. Second, in several cases strong positive correlations between dependent measures reduce power. If strong positive correlations exist between dependent measures, consider a design that collapses across these values and conduct power analyses using the collapsed variables to address whether that approach improves power. Finally, the table highlights the importance of accurate estimates of correlations between dependent measures when designing for optimal power. In the absence of accurate estimates for correlations between dependent measures, I recommend a conservative approach by which the choice of correlations reflects values that limit power. For example, if we had no information about the size of the expected correlations in the present example and were designing to detect a combination of small and strong effects, setting correlations between .1 and .3 provides the most conservative power analysis.

Example 7.3 Multivariate ANOVA

Taking the example used in the mixed-model section, imagine we chose to address whether differences existed across conditions on several dependent measures (i.e., a cross-sectional design) instead of examining change over time. Specifically, we are interested in whether differences exist between groups across different measures of attitudes rather than whether there are differential changes between groups in attitudes over time. This design includes the implicit attitude measure as before but adds paper-and-pencil measures addressing other aspects of bias (e.g., stereotype endorsement, anxiety, and dislike). MANOVA addresses whether the combination of the dependent measures differs between the two conditions.

Although it may be difficult to estimate correlations between measures, especially for research addressing measures that have not been used together previously, reference to other sources helps establish reasonable estimates. For example, several studies of attitudes toward African Americans used similar dependent measures, so in the absence of information specific to our study targets, relationships found in this work provide some useful estimates of correlations. In examining other studies, correlations between the anxiety, stereotyping, and dislike measures ranged from .35 to .45 (e.g., Tropp & Pettigrew, 2005), and comparatively small correlations (.10) existed between implicit attitudes and the other measures (Aberson & Gaffney, 2009). Table 7.7 shows the pattern of correlations used for the present analysis.

Previous examples discussed the mean differences shown in Table 7.7 for implicit attitudes but did not address the mean differences for the other measures. We established a meaningfully sized effect for implicitly held attitudes (see Chapter 6). With regard to the effects for the other variables, we can consider both the size of the implicit effect and content of the experimental manipulation. First, since the experimental manipulation focuses on negating stereotypes, it is reasonable to expect a strong effect for stereotype endorsement. For this reason, I set the differences for the stereotyping measures at the same level as the implicit attitude measure. Note that this reflects a moderately strong effect size ($d \approx 0.60$). The liking and anxiety measures are less closely related to the manipulation, so an expectation of smaller effects is reasonable ($d = 0.25$).

As seen in Table 7.7, there are small effects for some variables across condition (anxiety and liking) and moderate-to-strong effects for others (implicit and stereotyping). The correlations between the dependent measures were set between .10 and .45. The column in Table 7.6 labeled "Small–Moderate" indicates that even if correlations were substantially larger, power would remain relatively constant.

Table 7.7 Descriptive Statistics for MANOVA Example

	Implicit	Stereotype	Anxiety	Dislike
Implicit	$\mu_t = 0.0,$ $\sigma_t = .40$ $\mu_c = -.25,$ $\sigma_c = .40$	$\rho = .10$	$\rho = .10$	$\rho = .10$
Stereotype	$\rho = .10$	$\mu_t = 1.0,$ $\sigma_t = 5.0$ $\mu_c = -2.0,$ $\sigma_c = 5.0$	$\rho = .35$	$\rho = .45$
Anxiety	$\rho = .10$	$\rho = .35$	$\mu_t = 2.4,$ $\sigma_t = 1.6$ $\mu_c = 2.0,$ $\sigma_c = 1.6$	$\rho = .40$
Dislike	$\rho = .10$	$\rho = .45$	$\rho = .40$	$\mu_t = -0.7,$ $\sigma_t = 1.2$ $\mu_c = -1.0,$ $\sigma_c = 1.2$

The syntax in Table 7.8 produces the output found in Table 7.9. The results show that 40 participants per group provide adequate power for the MANOVA (.82). The output provides power for univariate tests of each dependent measure as well. The DVs with smaller effect sizes, of course, produce less power. If research hypotheses specified rejection of both the multivariate hypothesis and hypotheses for each univariate test, then a larger sample size would be desirable. However, keep in mind that power for detecting multiple effects in the same study is generally lower than power for detecting a single effect (see the discussion of power for multiple tests found in Chapters 5 and 6).

Direction of Correlations in MANOVA

To demonstrate further the impact of patterns of correlations in MANOVA, Table 7.10 shows the analysis from Tables 7.8 and 7.9 for a situation in which some of the dependent variables expressed negative correlations with each other (stereotyping, anxiety, and liking in this case). When small positive correlations are replaced with small negative correlations while retaining the same pattern of effect sizes, power for the MANOVA jumps from .82 (Table 7.9) to .95 (Table 7.10). Power

Table 7.8 SPSS Syntax for Multivariate ANOVA

Syntax	Comments
MATRIX DATA VARIABLES Condition ROWTYPE_ implicit stereotype anxiety liking /Factor = Condition.	
BEGIN DATA	Means listed by group for each DV
1 Mean 0.0 1.0 2.4 -0.7	
1 N 40 40 40 40	
2 Mean -0.25 -2.0 2.0 -1.0	
2 N 40 40 40 40	Correlations listed as …
. Corr 1	Implicit-Implicit
. Corr .1 1	Stereo-Imp St-St
. Corr .1 .35 1	Anxiety-Imp Anx-St Anx-Anx
. Corr .1 .45 .40 1	Liking-Imp Lik-St Lik-Anx Lik-Lik
. Stdev 0.40 5.0 1.6 1.2	
END DATA.	
MANOVA implicit stereotype anxiety liking by Condition (1,2)	
/MATRIX=IN(*)	Compare to Table 7.2; there is no
/POWER F (.05) t (.05)	WSFACTOR command here but
/PRINT signif (mult averf)	everything else is the same
param (estim efsize).	

Table 7.9 SPSS Output for Multivariate ANOVA

EFFECT .. Condition

Multivariate Tests of Significance (S = 1, M = 1 , N = 36 1/2)

Test Name	Value	Exact FHypoth.	DF	Error DF	Sig.of F
Pillais	.14962	3.29901	4.00	75.00	.015
Hotellings	.17595	3.29901	4.00	75.00	.015
Wilks	.85038	3.29901	4.00	75.00	.015
Roys	.14962				

Observed Power at .0500 Level

TEST NAME	Noncent.	Power
(All)	13.196	.82

EFFECT .. Condition (Cont.)

Univariate F-tests with (1,78) D. F.

Variable	Hypoth. SS	Error SS	Hypoth. MS	Error MS	F	Sig. of F
implicit	1.25000	12.48000	1.25000	.16000	7.81250	.007
stereoty	180.00000	1950.00000	180.00000	25.00000	7.20000	.009
anxiety	3.20000	199.68000	3.20000	2.56000	1.25000	.267
liking	1.80000	112.32000	1.80000	1.44000	1.25000	.267

Variable	Noncent.	Power
implicit	7.81250	.78611
stereoty	7.20000	.75246
anxiety	1.25000	.19537
liking	1.25000	.19537

Table 7.10 SPSS Syntax and Output for Multivariate ANOVA Examining Different Correlations

```
MATRIX DATA VARIABLES = Condition ROWTYPE_ implicit stereotype anxiety liking
  /Factor = Condition.
BEGIN DATA
1 Mean 0.0 1.0 2.4 -0.7
1 N 40 40 40 40
2 Mean -0.25 -2.0 2.0 -1.0
2 N 40 40 40 40
. Corr 1
. Corr .1 1
. Corr .1 -.3 1
. Corr .1 -.2 -.2 1
. Stdev 0.40 5.0 1.6 1.2
END DATA.
MANOVA implicit stereotype anxiety liking
by Condition (1,2)
  /MATRIX=IN(*)
  /POWER F (.05) t (.05)
  /PRINT signif (mult averf) param(estim efsize).
```

EFFECT .. Condition

Test Name	Value	Exact F Hypoth.	DF	Error DF	Sig. of F
Pillais	.20747	4.90847	4.00	75.00	.001

TEST NAME	Noncent.	Power
(All)	19.634	.95

Univariate F-tests with (1,78) D. F.

Variable	Hypoth. SS	Error SS	Hypoth. MS	Error MS	F	Sig. of F
implicit	1.25000	12.48000	1.25000	.16000	7.81250	.007
stereoty	180.00000	1950.00000	180.00000	25.00000	7.20000	.009
anxiety	3.20000	199.68000	3.20000	2.56000	1.25000	.267
liking	1.80000	112.32000	1.80000	1.44000	1.25000	.267

Variable	Noncent.	Power
implicit	7.81250	.78611
stereoty	7.20000	.75246
anxiety	1.25000	.19537
liking	1.25000	.19537

for the univariate tests remains the same for the two analyses. Note, however, that in this example the direction of mean differences remains consistent across analyses.

ADDITIONAL ISSUES

As mentioned, a common question asked by students and researchers regarding MANOVA is whether reverse coding variables in MANOVA to produce negative correlations improves power. Typically, the question goes something like this: "If I have two positively correlated dependent variables, can I reverse the scale on one of them to yield negatively correlated dependent variables that produce more power?" The short answer is no, this will not affect power.

To demonstrate this, Table 7.11 shows a MANOVA with two variables with a positive correlation (.40). Table 7.12 shows the same variables with

Table 7.11 SPSS Syntax and Output for Multivariate ANOVA Without Reverse-Coded Variables

```
MATRIX DATA VARIABLES = Condition ROWTYPE_ implicit
 stereotype
    /Factor = Condition.
BEGIN DATA
1 Mean 0.0 1.0
1 N 20 20
2 Mean -0.25 -2.0
2 N 20 20
. Corr 1
. Corr .4 1
. Stdev 0.40 5.0
END DATA.
MANOVA implicit stereotype by Condition (1,2)
    /MATRIX=IN(*)
    /POWER F (.05) t (.05)
    /PRINT signif (mult averf) param(estim efsize).
```

EFFECT .. Condition

Test Name	Value	Exact F Hypoth.	DF	Error DF	Sig. of F
Pillais	.12371	2.61171	2.00	37.00	.087

Observed Power at .0500 Level

TEST NAME	Noncent.	Power
(All)	5.223	.49

Table 7.12 SPSS Syntax and Output for Multivariate ANOVA With Reverse-Coded Variables

```
MATRIX DATA VARIABLES = Condition ROWTYPE_ implicit
 stereotype
/Factor = Condition.
BEGIN DATA
1 Mean 0.0 -1.0
1 N 20 20
2 Mean -0.25 2.0
2 N 20 20
. Corr 1
. Corr -.4 1
. Stdev 0.40 5.0
END DATA.
```

(syntax for MANOVA deleted)

<table>
<tr><td colspan="6" align="center">EFFECT .. Condition</td></tr>
<tr><td></td><td></td><td colspan="3" align="center">Exact F</td><td>Sig.</td></tr>
<tr><td>Test Name</td><td>Value</td><td>Hypoth.</td><td>DF</td><td>Error DF</td><td>of F</td></tr>
<tr><td>Pillais</td><td>.12371</td><td>2.61171</td><td>2.00</td><td>37.00</td><td>.087</td></tr>
<tr><td colspan="6" align="center">Observed Power at .0500 Level</td></tr>
<tr><td>TEST NAME</td><td>Noncent.</td><td>Power</td><td></td><td></td><td></td></tr>
<tr><td>(All)</td><td>5.223</td><td>.49</td><td></td><td></td><td></td></tr>
</table>

the scale for the second variable reversed so that the correlation between the two variables is −.40 and the signs on the means are reversed for the second variable in both groups.

Output in Tables 7.11 and 7.12 finds the same power estimate (.49). This is because, for the second example, although there is a negative correlation between the predictors, the effects now run in opposite directions. When effects run in opposite directions, the power estimates found in Table 7.6 reverse, as shown in Table 7.13.

SUMMARY

Power for mixed-model ANOVA designs and MANOVA require estimates of patterns of means, standard deviations for each dependent measure, and the correlation between dependent measures. For both designs, accurate estimates of standard deviation and correlations are particularly important. In addition, careful consideration of the

Table 7.13 Power as a Function of Effect Size and Correlation Patterns for Effects in Opposite Directions

Correlation Between Measures	Small–Small $d = +0.2, -0.2$	Moderate–Moderate $d = 0.5, -0.5$	Strong–Strong $d = 0.8, -0.8$
.9	.98	1.00	1.00
.8	.80	.99	1.00
.7	.61	.94	1.00
.6	.49	.86	1.00
.5	.40	.77	.99
.4	.34	.69	.98
.3	.30	.61	.96
.2	.26	.55	.93
.1	.24	.50	.90
.0	.22	.46	.87
−.1	.20	.42	.83
−.2	.19	.39	.80
−.3	.18	.36	.76
−.4	.17	.34	.73
−.5	.16	.32	.70
−.6	.15	.30	.67
−.7	.15	.29	.64
−.8	.14	.27	.61
−.9	.14	.26	.59

specific test reflecting hypotheses (e.g., omnibus tests vs. tests of trends) is necessary as different types of tests often produce different power estimates. Power for MANOVA is particularly sensitive to estimates of correlations. In the absence of correlation information, the chapter provides guidance for choosing conservative correlation estimates.

8

MULTIPLE REGRESSION

INTRODUCTION

Multiple regression focuses on the prediction of a criterion variable (also known as dependent variable, outcome variable, response variable) from two or more predictors (also known as independent variables, regressors). The criterion must be continuously scaled. Predictors may be continuously scaled or dichotomous. Predictors with three or more categories are converted to a set of dichotomous predictors via dummy coding (see Cohen, Cohen, West, & Aiken, 2003). This chapter presents power analyses for the R^2 *model, R^2 change*, and regression coefficients in designs using multiple predictors. In addition, the chapter includes tests that examine differences between independent and dependent predictors as well as tests comparing R^2 across independent samples. The "Additional Issues" section includes discussions of the impact of reliability on power and detecting multiple effects.

NECESSARY INFORMATION

Power analyses for regression focus on the size of meaningful correlations between predictors and the criterion measure. Unlike experimental designs in which predictors (i.e., factors) are unrelated, predictors in regression analysis often correlate to some degree. This correlation between predictors, discussed in this chapter as *multicollinearity*, requires accurate estimation of correlations between predictors to establish realistic estimates of power.

FACTORS AFFECTING POWER

Several forms of power are of interest for multiple regression. The most common issues are power for the set of all predictors (R^2 model), power for tests of one set of predictors over another set (R^2 change), and power for a single predictor within a model (regression coefficients). Researchers may seek to address power on some or all forms, depending on their research goals. Additional questions addressed in this chapter involve power for detecting whether predictors are different in size and whether predictors from one sample are stronger than predictors in another sample are. Power considerations differ for each approach, but for all tests, larger sample sizes and more liberal α increase power.

Many research questions involving regression analysis focus on the R^2 model, R^2 change, and tests of coefficients. Power for a set of predictors is tested through estimation of the variance explained by all predictors, termed here the R^2 model. The power for the R^2 model is impacted by the amount of variance explained (larger effect size = more power) and the number of predictors. More predictors can lower power because predictors add degrees of freedom to the numerator of the F statistic used to test null hypotheses. However, more predictors may increase the R^2 model and thus increase power. A small number of predictors that explain a considerable amount of variance is more powerful than a large number of predictors that explain the same amount of variance.

Power for R^2 change involves explanation afforded by the addition of a set of predictors over predictors already entered into the prediction model (also known as control variables). This value is of interest for hierarchical multiple regression (MR), in which the goal is often to address whether addition of variables explains variance over and above existing predictors. Power for change statistics is stronger for predictors that correlate more strongly with the criterion.

Another form of power is for a single predictor within a model. The statistic reflecting this effect is the regression coefficient, either the unstandardized (b) or standardized (β). This is often called the *slope*. The regression coefficient reflects the strength of the unique relationship between predictor and criterion, that is, what the variable predicts that others cannot. The presentation in this chapter focuses on power for the coefficient. However, the test for the coefficient is equivalent to a test of partial and semipartial correlations for the predictor as well. As with the other approaches, the strength of correlations with the criterion variable affects power. For sets with a single predictor, the power for R^2 change is equivalent to power for the coefficient if the R^2 change reflects the final step of the regression model.

Regardless of the test of interest, multicollinearity is a concern. *Multicollinearity* refers to how strongly the predictors of interest correlate with each other. The unique explanation afforded by predictors determines the value of R^2 *change* and the coefficient. The more strongly correlated the predictors, the less unique variance explanation exists, so multicollinearity reduces power. A predictor may be highly correlated with the criterion; however, if that predictor correlates strongly with other predictors in the model, the variance it explains over and above the other predictors may be limited. For this reason, deriving accurate estimates of the correlations between predictor variables is essential for establishing accurate power estimates.

Other issues covered in this chapter focus on differences between predictors. The primary factors affecting power in these cases are the magnitudes of the differences between the predictors (or sets of predictors).

KEY STATISTICS

Calculations for R^2 and coefficients are useful for understanding power. Several formulae included here present values for demonstration purposes. Several of the formulae are not necessary for most power calculations but do facilitate an understanding of how multicollinearity influences power. I present formulae for models with two predictors. Adding predictors to a model expands most formulae to increasing levels of complexity such that most texts present only the two-predictor formulae. SPSS syntax for calculation of R^2 and coefficients for designs with more than two predictors (Example 8.2) handles complex calculations nicely.

Formulae for R^2 and Coefficient Tests

Formula 8.1 presents the calculation of R^2 for a model with two predictors. The unstandardized coefficient seen in Formula 8.2 technically reflects a population coefficient. Often, the symbol beta (β) denotes the unstandardized coefficient for the population. However, β is also used to note the standardized regression coefficient, so I use b to reference the unstandardized population regression coefficient in Formula 8.2 and elsewhere. Formula 8.3 presents the calculation for the standardized coefficient (β). I use population values for correlations to reflect that in power analysis we make estimates of population values for correlations rather than using values derived from samples.

$$R^2_{y.12} = \frac{\rho^2_{y1} + \rho^2_{y2} - 2\rho_{y1}\rho_{y2}\rho_{12}}{1 - \rho^2_{12}} \tag{8.1}$$

$$b_{y1.2} = \frac{\rho_{y1} - \rho_{y2}\rho_{12}}{1 - \rho_{12}^2} \times \frac{\sigma_y}{\sigma_1} \tag{8.2}$$

$$\beta_{y1.2} = \frac{\rho_{y1} - \rho_{y2}\rho_{12}}{1 - \rho_{12}^2} \tag{8.3}$$

For Formulae 8.1–8.3, y refers to the criterion; 1 refers to the first predictor and 2 to the second. For example, $y.12$ means y predicted from both 1 and 2; $y1.2$ means y predicted from 1 while controlling for predictor 2; ρ_{y2} refers to the correlation between the criterion variable and the second predictor; ρ_{12} reflects the correlation between predictors; and $b_{y1.2}$ is the unstandardized coefficient for the predictor of the criterion by the first predictor while controlling for the second predictor.

The numerators for each term are a product of the strength of the relationship of interest minus a value that multiplies the correlation between the other predictor and dependent measure by the correlation between predictors. The numerator gets smaller when the predictors overlap more strongly (e.g., predictors positively correlated and predictor–DV relationships in same direction), making for smaller effect sizes. As shown in Formulae 8.1–8.3, under these conditions, the correlation between the predictors (called *collinearity* with two predictors and *multicollinearity* with three or more) reduces the size of the R^2 and coefficients. In this way, overlapping predictors limit power.

For designs with a single predictor, Formula 8.4 presents the calculation of the unstandardized coefficient (b). For these designs, the standardized coefficient (β) is equal to the correlation.

$$b_{y1} = \rho_{y1} \times \frac{\sigma_y}{\sigma_1} \tag{8.4}$$

The noncentrality parameter for tests of R^2 is the same as for analysis of variance (ANOVA) since significance tests use the F distribution. Both f^2 and λ may be derived for either the model or the change value; however, the approach differs slightly for both tests with regard to the calculation of the effect size (f^2). This effect size estimate is sometimes called partial f^2 as it removes the influence of the other predictors from the denominator.

$$f_{\text{Model}}^2 = \frac{R_{\text{Model}}^2}{1 - R_{\text{Model}}^2} \tag{8.5}$$

$$\lambda_{\text{Model}} = f^2_{\text{Model}} df_{\text{error}} \tag{8.6}$$

$$f^2_{\text{Change}} = \frac{R^2_{\text{Change}}}{1 - R^2_{\text{Model}}} \tag{8.7}$$

$$\lambda_{\text{Change}} = f^2_{\text{Change}} df_{\text{error}} \tag{8.8}$$

For tests of coefficients, Formulae 8.9–8.12 present calculations of standard errors and the noncentrality parameter for unstandardized and standardized values. These formulae use Variable 1 as an example but maybe adapted to Variable 2 by changing references to Variable 1 to Variable 2 (i.e., change subscripts from 1 to 2). These tests use δ for tests as the noncentrality parameter. For these tests, $\delta^2 = \lambda$.

$$se_{b_1} = \sqrt{\frac{1 - R^2_{y.12}}{\left(1 - R^2_{12}\right) * (n - k - 1)}} \times \frac{\sigma_y}{\sigma_1} \tag{8.9}$$

$$\delta_{b1} = \frac{b_1}{se_{b_1}} \tag{8.10}$$

$$se_{\beta_1} = \sqrt{\frac{1 - R^2_{y.12}}{\left(1 - R^2_{12}\right) * (n - k - 1)}} \tag{8.11}$$

$$\delta_{\beta_1} = \frac{\beta_1}{se_{\beta_1}} \tag{8.12}$$

Formulae for Detecting Differences Between Two Independent Coefficients

Tests that address power for detecting differences between two independent coefficients compare coefficients from samples comprised of different people. Analyses comparing a single predictor across two independent samples use Formulae 8.13–8.18. Several formulae use the value i to refer to the predictor. We complete this calculation for both coefficients separately with yi referring to the relationship between the dependent measures and the predictor of interest. Calculations address either unstandardized (b) or standardized coefficients (β); however, when using the SPSS options presented in the chapter, the unstandardized approach simplifies analyses.

Calculations first address standard error for each predictor (Formulae 8.13 or 8.16). After calculating the standard error for each of the two bs or βs (depending on which is used for the analyses), calculate the standard error of the differences (Formulae 8.14 or 8.17). Next, calculate the noncentrality parameter using Formulae 8.15 or 8.18 (depending on whether using standardized or unstandardized coefficients).

For tests using unstandardized coefficients, refer to Formulae 8.13–8.15.

$$se_{b_i} = \frac{\sigma_y}{\sigma_i}\sqrt{\frac{1}{1-R_i^2}}\sqrt{\frac{1-R_y^2}{n-k-1}} \tag{8.13}$$

$$se_{b_1-b_2} = \sqrt{se_{b_1}^2 + se_{b_2}^2} \tag{8.14}$$

$$\delta = \frac{|b_1|-|b_2|}{se_{b_1-b_2}} \tag{8.15}$$

Tests using standardized coefficients refer to Formulae 8.16–8.18.

$$se_{\beta_i} = \sqrt{\frac{1}{1-R_i^2}}\sqrt{\frac{1-R_y^2}{n-k-1}} \tag{8.16}$$

$$se_{\beta_1-\beta_2} = \sqrt{se_{\beta_1}^2 + se_{\beta_2}^2} \tag{8.17}$$

$$\delta = \frac{|\beta_1|-|\beta_2|}{se_{\beta_1-\beta_2}} \tag{8.18}$$

The calculations represented in Formulae 8.15 and 8.18 test differences in magnitude, that is, whether one predictor is stronger than another is. If you are interested in tests that involve magnitude and direction, simply remove the absolute value symbols.

Formulae for Detecting Differences Between Two Dependent Coefficients

Dependent coefficients are those that come from the same analysis. The primary question addressed when comparing dependent coefficients is whether two predictors in the same model differ significantly.

Formula 8.19 defines the noncentrality parameter for this test. The formula requires values from the calculation of the inverse of the correlation matrix (ρ^{ii}, ρ^{jj}, and ρ^{ij}). SPSS syntax presented in the chapter completes these matrix calculations. Cohen et al. (2003) includes calculation details for interested readers.

$$\delta = \frac{|b_1| - |b_2|}{\sqrt{se_{b_1}^2 + se_{b_2}^2 - 2se_{b_1} se_{b_2} \left(\dfrac{\rho^{ij}}{\rho^{ii}\rho^{jj}} \right)}} \tag{8.19}$$

Formulae for Comparing Two Independent R^2 Values

A question similar to that addressed by comparing coefficients from independent samples compares R^2 values from different samples. In this case, hypotheses address whether a set of variables predicts more strongly in one analysis than another. Formula 8.20 is appropriate for model or change values.

$$\delta = \frac{|R_1^2 - R_2^2|}{\sqrt{\left(\dfrac{4R_1^2\left(1-R_1^2\right)^2(n_1 - k - 1)^2}{\left(n_1^2 - 1\right)(n_1 + 3)} \right) + \left(\dfrac{4R_2^2\left(1-R_2^2\right)^2(n_2 - k - 1)^2}{\left(n_2^2 - 1\right)(n_2 + 3)} \right)}} \tag{8.20}$$

Example 8.1: Power for a Two-Predictor Model (R^2 *Model* and Coefficients)

This example focuses on predicting behavioral intentions relevant to affirmative action policies (Intent; y) from two predictors: internal motivation to control prejudice (1) and external motivation to control prejudice (2). Table 8.1 presents correlations between two predictors (internal and external) and a criterion variable (intention). Correlations between the predictors of interest and the criterion should reflect meaningful observed relationships, that is, what sort of effect would be important to detect. The correlations between predictors should be estimated as accurately as possible, as should predictor–criterion relationships when the researcher is not interested in power for that particular predictor.

Of the three forms of power available to us, my interest here is detecting significant coefficients for internal and external, as well as a significant R^2 *model*. The variable modern racism shown in the table is not used for the two-predictor example. Another example in the chapter with three predictors makes use of that variable.

Based on commonly observed effect sizes in the affirmative action literature, I determined that a meaningful correlation between each predictor and criterion would have a minimum value of $\rho = .40$. Many predictors of affirmative action beliefs exist, so additional variables would have to show moderately large effects to make an impact on

Table 8.1 Correlations and *SD*s for Two- and Three-Predictor Examples

	Intent	Internal	External	Modern Racism
Intent (*y*)	$\mu = 1.0$ $\sigma = 7.0$			
Internal (1)	$\rho = .40$	$\mu = 1.0$ $\sigma = 1.0$		
External (2)	$\rho = .40$	$\rho = -.15$	$\mu = 1.0$ $\sigma = 1.0$	
Modern racism (3)	$\rho = -.40$	$\rho = -.60$	$\rho = .25$	$\mu = 1.0$ $\sigma = 2.0$

the literature. In short, for the present study, I was not interested in trying to find weak predictors, so I set the correlations relatively high. Here, a meaningful relationship is a relatively large one.

Correlations between predictors are not values when it is important to establish the size of a meaningful relationship. For these values, it is more important to have an accurate estimate of the strength of the relationship. That is, how strongly can we expect the predictors to be associated? This is because accurately estimating power for predictor–criterion relationships is dependent on the size of the predictor–predictor correlations. A good source for information when using existing measures is empirical studies that present these correlations. A scale development study presenting correlations between internal and external motivations (Plant & Devine, 1998) suggested a correlation of −.15 between the two variables.

The distinction between predictor–criterion and predictor–predictor relationships is an important one. When dealing with the criterion variable, focus on the size of a meaningful relationship. When dealing with correlations between predictors, use the literature (or pretesting) to establish a reasonable estimate. One exception is a design in which predictors serve as control variables, for example, when entering a set of variables in the first step of a hierarchical regression analysis and then assessing the impact of one or more variables over and above that set. In that case, the control variables should reflect the accurate instead of meaningful approach (see the three-predictor section for an example of this approach).

Calculations based on Formula 8.1 yield the R^2 *model* = .376. One item of interest is that the sum of the squared correlations ($.40^2 + .40^2 = .32$) is smaller than the R^2 *model*. This may seem counterintuitive, but this is a product of the direction of the correlations between the predictors. As shown in the following calculation, negative correlations (ρ_{12}) between predictors increase effect sizes, provided that the predictor–DV correlations (ρ_{y1} and ρ_{y2}) are in the same direction (i.e., both negative or both positive). Following the R^2 calculation is calculation of the effect size (Formula 8.5) and noncentrality parameter (Formula 8.6).

$$R^2_{y.12} = \frac{\rho_{y1}^2 + \rho_{y2}^2 - 2\rho_{y1}\rho_{y2}\rho_{12}}{1 - \rho_{12}^2} = \frac{.40^2 + .40^2 - 2(.40*.40*-.15)}{1 - (-.15)^2} = .376$$

$$f^2_{Model} = \frac{R^2_{Model}}{1 - R^2_{Model}} = \frac{.376}{1-.376} = .603$$

$$\lambda_{Model} = f^2_{Model} df_{error} = .603(27) = 16.3$$

As demonstrated in Chapter 5, computer approaches allow for calculation of power given λ, df, and an $F_{critical}$ value. For example, with a sample of 30 participants, for a test with $\alpha = .05$, with $df_{numerator} = 2$ (the number of predictors) and $df_{denominator} = 27$ (n – Number of predictors – 1), $F_{critical} = 3.35$, and $\lambda - 16.3$, power is .94.
The following line of syntax calculates power:

```
Compute Power = 1-NCDF.F(3.35, 2, 27, 16.3).
```

Table 8.2 presents SPSS syntax for conducting power analyses for the R^2 *model* and the coefficient. As in other chapters, the SPSS syntax requires only the descriptive statistics. The primary information for entry are the correlations. Estimates of the *M* (mean) and *SD* (standard deviation) can be set at arbitrary values for most analyses. The standard deviation affects the coefficient but not the power analysis for the coefficient. This is because the ratio of the coefficient to its standard error is a function of the correlations.

If you want to conduct power analyses involving the intercept (known as the constant in SPSS), the analysis requires accurate *M* and *SD* estimates. However, this is generally a less-common question of interest than analyses focusing on coefficient and R^2 estimates.

Table 8.2 SPSS Syntax for Two Predictors

Syntax	Comments
`MATRIX DATA VARIABLES = ROWTYPE_` `Intention Internal External.`	

`BEGIN DATA`
`Mean 1 1 1`
`Stdev 7 1 1`
`N 30 30 30`
`Corr 1`
`Corr .40 1`
`Corr .40 -.15 1`
`END DATA.`
 	
`MANOVA Intention with Internal`
`  External`
`/MATRIX=IN(*)`
`/POWER exact t (.05) F (.05)`
`/CINTERVAL Joint (.95)`
`/DESIGN.`
	M and *SD* necessary for syntax but do not impact power
	Change for other power estimates
	
	Matrix here is in order listed above
	The MANOVA command carries out ANOVA, regression, ANCOVA, and MANOVA; the "with" statement addresses continuously scaled predictors

Table 8.3 Power Analysis ($n = 30$) for the R^2 Model

Tests of Significance for Intention using UNIQUE sums of squares Source of Variation

	SS	DF	MS	F	Sig of F
WITHIN CELLS	886.04	27	32.82		
REGRESSION	534.96	2	267.48	8.15	.002
CONSTANT	430.91	1	430.91	13.13	.001

Observed Power at the .0500 Level

Source of Variation	Noncentrality	Power
Regression	16.302	.937

Table 8.3 includes the output relevant to power for the R^2 *model*. The bold line reflects that estimate. With a sample of 30 participants, given the correlations presented in Table 8.1, power is 94%. Keep in mind that power for the R^2 *model* does not necessarily suggest the same level of power to detect effects for both coefficients in the model.

Tests of coefficients involve calculation of the coefficient, its standard error, and the noncentrality parameter. As an example, I present calculation of one of the unstandardized coefficients, standard error, and the noncentrality parameter using Formulae 8.2, 8.9, and 8.10.

$$b_{y1.2} = \frac{\rho_{y1} - \rho_{y2}\rho_{12}}{1 - \rho_{12}^2} \times \frac{\sigma_y}{\sigma_1} = \frac{.40 - .40(-.15)}{1 - (-.15)^2} \times \frac{7}{1} = 3.294$$

$$se_{b_1} = \sqrt{\frac{1 - R_{y.12}^2}{\left(1 - R_{12}^2\right) * (n - k - 1)}} \times \frac{\sigma_y}{\sigma_{x_1}} = \sqrt{\frac{1 - .376}{(1 - .15^2) * (30 - 2 - 1)}} \times \frac{7}{1} = 1.076$$

$$\delta_{b1} = \frac{b_1}{se_{b_1}} = \frac{3.294}{1.076} = 3.061$$

A sample of 30 participants, for a test with $\alpha = .05$, $df = 27$ (n – Number of predictors – 1) yields $t_{critical} = 2.05$. With $\delta = 3.061$ (alternatively, we can square this value to produce $\lambda = 9.37$), the following line of syntax calculates power as .84:

```
Compute Power = 1-NCDF.t(2.05, 27, 3.061).
```

Table 8.4 shows power analysis for the coefficients for each predictor. This comes from the same analysis produced by the syntax in Table 8.2. With a sample of 30, power

Table 8.4 Power Analysis ($n = 30$) for Coefficients

COVARIATE	B	Beta	Std. Err.	t-Value	Sig. of t
Internal	3.29412	.	1.076	3.062	.005
External	3.29412	.	1.076	3.062	.005

COVARIATE	Lower -95%	CL- Upper	Noncent.	Power
Internal	.507	6.081	9.374	.839
External	.507	6.081	9.374	.839

is around 84% for both predictors. These values are equal as both predictor–DV correlations were .40. Although power is good for both predictors, power for the coefficients are less than the power for R^2 *model*.

Example 8.2 Power for Three-Predictor Models

The three-predictor model expands on Example 8.1 through addition of a third predictor (modern racism). In this example, the interest is power for R^2 *change* for a set including internal and external after considering the impact of modern. Set analyses of this sort would be the preferred approach for dummy-coded predictors (e.g., a predictor with three categories coded into two dichotomous variables then entered as a set). Also addressed is power for coefficients within a three-predictor model.

This analysis controls for the impact of modern racism, so this is not a test in which we are interested in a meaningful relationship between this predictor and the criterion per se. This analysis investigates the impact of internal and external over modern because modern racism is an established predictor of affirmative action-relevant beliefs that may be correlated with internal and external motivations to control prejudice. Estimates for the modern racism variable correlations came from two sources. Information from meta-analyses (Harrison et al., 2006) and a scale development article (Plant & Devine, 1998), suggested correlations for modern racism and the other variables found in Table 8.1.

Analyses for R^2 *change* involve more steps than tests for coefficients or R^2 *model*. I present a two-stage process. The first step involves obtaining R^2 *change* for the set of interest (based on our correlations). This step also provides R^2 *model*. The second step uses another syntax file to calculate power for a range of sample sizes using the R^2 values from the first analysis.

The technique presented in Tables 8.5 through 8.7 is flexible. For those who prefer thinking in terms of R^2, simply use this approach instead of the coefficient approach in the previous example by entering the variable of interest in the final step. The syntax in Table 8.5 is a shortcut procedure. You can also calculate these values by hand or provide your own estimates of R^2 *model* and R^2 *change* directly using the syntax in Table 8.7.

Table 8.6 yields R^2 *model* = .467 and R^2 *change* = .307. Enter these values along with the number of predictors for the full model and for the set associated with the change, α, and the desired sample sizes in the syntax file in Table 8.7. The bold values are the only pieces to change for this analysis.

Table 8.5 Syntax for Creating Matrix and Calculating R^2 Model and Change

Syntax	Comments
MATRIX DATA VARIABLES = ROWTYPE_ Intention Internal External Modern.	
BEGIN DATA Mean 1 2 3 4 Stdev 7 1 1 2 N 30 30 30 30 Corr 1 Corr .40 1 Corr .40 -.15 1 Corr -.40 -.60 .25 1 END DATA.	Matrix created as before, with addition of Modern N can be set at any value, R^2 will not change
REGRESSION /MATRIX=IN(*) /MISSING LISTWISE /STATISTICS change /CRITERIA=PIN(.05) POUT(.10) /NOORIGIN /DEPENDENT Intention /METHOD=ENTER Modern /METHOD=ENTER Internal External.	This analysis calculates the R^2 values The separate enter statements create two "blocks" of variables

Table 8.8 shows that we need 24 participants for power of .80 or more for R^2 *change*. In this example, small increases in sample size influence power considerably. This result focuses on R^2 *change* for a set of variables. Researchers often desire an outcome in which not only was R^2 *change* significant but also the individual contribution of each variable within that set was significant. Addressing this issue requires power analysis for the coefficients for our predictors (the internal and external motivation variables).

Table 8.6 Output for Step 1 (Calculation Step)

					Change Statistics
Model Summary					
Model	R	R^2	Adjusted R^2	Standard Error of the Estimate	R^2 Change
1	.400[a]	.160	.130	6.5291653	.160
2	.683[b]	.467	.405	5.3989553	.307

[a] Predictors: (Constant), Modern
[b] Predictors: (Constant), Modern, External, Internal

Table 8.7 Syntax for R^2 Change Power

Syntax	Comments
INPUT PROGRAM.	
LOOP n=20 TO 40 by 1.	Modify this line to get different sample
END CASE.	size values; 20 to 40 by 1 yields
END LOOP.	estimates for 20, 21, 22, etc.
END FILE.	
END INPUT PROGRAM.	
EXECUTE.	
Compute R2model = .467.	Modify these values; be sure you have
Compute R2change = .307.	all the decimals in place
Compute modelpred = 3.	
Compute changepred = 2.	
Compute alpha = .05.	
Compute df_change = changepred.	Do not change values not bolded[a]
Compute df_denom = (n - modelpred) -1.	
Compute k2 = 1 - R2model.	
Compute multiplier = df_denom.	
Compute f2 = R2change/k2.	
Compute lambda = f2*multiplier .	
Compute F_Table = IDF.F(1-alpha,df_change,df_denom).	
Compute power = 1 - NCDF.F(F_Table,df_change,df_denom,Lambda).	
EXECUTE.	
matrix.	
GET M /VARIABLES-n lambda Power .	
print M/title = "Power for R2 Change"/clabels = "N" "Lambda" "Power"/format f10.4.	
End Matrix.	

[a] I use a calculation approach for λ based on df_{error}. Other sources (e.g., G*Power) use sample size. If you prefer calculations based on n, replace "compute multiplier = df_denom" with "compute multiplier = n."

Keep in mind that the sample size yielding adequate power for the model and the set (change) will not necessarily yield high power for each coefficient.

Table 8.9 shows that with $n = 24$, the power for the coefficients (.90 for external and .47 for internal) is divergent. The output also shows power for R^2 *model* (.90). Power for the coefficients diverges because of differences in the predictor's correlation with modern racism (the control variable). Internal motivation had a stronger

Table 8.8 Power Analysis for R^2 Change Power ($n = 20$ to 40)

Power for R2 Change		
N	Lambda	Power
20.0	9.2158	.6943
21.0	9.7917	.7274
22.0	10.3677	.7577
23.0	10.9437	.7853
24.0	11.5197	.8103
25.0	12.0957	.8329
26.0	12.6717	.8532
27.0	13.2477	.8713
28.0	13.8236	.8875
29.0	14.3996	.9018
30.0	14.9756	.9145
31.0	15.5516	.9257
32.0	16.1276	.9356
33.0	16.7036	.9443
34.0	17.2795	.9519
35.0	17.8555	.9585
36.0	18.4315	.9643
37.0	19.0075	.9693
38.0	19.5835	.9737
39.0	20.1595	.9774
40.0	20.7355	.9807

relationship with modern racism; as a result, internal motivation is a weaker unique predictor of intentions.

To achieve power of .80 (or more) for both internal and external coefficients requires a larger sample. Table 8.10 presents an analysis producing the desired level of power for the coefficients. To run this analysis, simply change the MATRIX (Table 8.9) line for N and run the MATRIX and MANOVA commands until you find the desired power. For this analysis, I changed the syntax to read N 110 110 110 110.

The differences between sample size requirements for tests of the model, change, and coefficients highlight important considerations in multiple regression designs. First, different research questions correspond to different power estimates. Researchers should first decide on the question that is most relevant then design for appropriate power for that question. Second, multicollinearity impacts power. When predictors are highly correlated, power for coefficients drop considerably. Tests of coefficients examine variability explained uniquely by a predictor. The more strongly predictors correlate, the less unique variance there is to go around. This can be seen by examining power in the three-predictor design. External motivation had small correlations with the other predictors, but internal had a strong correlation with modern. External has greater power because it explains more variance that the other variables cannot account for.

Table 8.9 Syntax and Output for Coefficient Power ($n = 24$)

```
MATRIX DATA VARIABLES = ROWTYPE_
Intention Internal External Modern.
BEGIN DATA
Mean 1 2 3 4
STDEV 7 1 1 2
N 24 24 24 24
Corr 1
Corr .40 1
Corr .40 -.15 1
Corr -.40 -.60 .25 1
END DATA.
MANOVA Intention with Internal External Modern
   /MATRIX=IN(*)
   /POWER exact t (.05) F (.05)
   /CINTERVAL Joint (.95)
   /DESIGN.
```

Tests of Significance for Intention using UNIQUE sums of squares

Source of Variation	SS	DF	MS	F	Sig of F
WITHIN CELLS	601.07	20	30.05		
REGRESSION	525.93	3	175.31	5.83	.005
CONSTANT	57.82	1	57.82	1.92	.181

Observed Power at the .0500 Level

Source of Variation	Noncentrality	Power
Regression	17.500	.904

Dependent variable .. Intention

COVARIATE	B	Beta	Std. Err.	t-Value	Sig. of t
Internal	1.75000	.	1.429	1.225	.235
External	3.73333	.	1.181	3.162	.005
Modern	-1.34167	.	.730	-1.839	.081

COVARIATE	Lower -95%	CL-Upper	Noncent.	Power
Internal	-2.606	6.106	1.500	.215
External	.134	7.333	10.000	.853
Modern	-3.566	.882	3.382	.417

Table 8.10 SPSS Output for Coefficient Power ≥ .80 ($n = 110$)

Tests of Significance for Intention using UNIQUE sums of squares					
Source of Variation	SS	DF	MS	F	Sig of F
WITHIN CELLS	2848.53	106	26.87		
REGRESSION	2492.47	3	830.82	30.92	.000
CONSTANT	273.68	1	273.68	10.18	.002

Observed Power at the .0500 Level		
Source of Variation	Noncentrality	Power
Regression	92.750	1.000

COVARIATE	B	Beta	Std. Err.	t-Value	Sig. of t
Internal	1.75000	.	.621	2.820	.006
External	3.73333	.	.513	7.280	.000
Modern	-2.68333	.	.634	-4.234	.000

COVARIATE	Lower -95%	CL- Upper	Noncent.	Power
Internal	-.013	3.513	7.950	.798
External	2.276	5.190	53.000	1.000
Modern	-4.484	-.883	17.926	.987

POWER FOR DETECTING DIFFERENCES BETWEEN TWO DEPENDENT COEFFICIENTS

This section deals with determining if one predictor in a model is significantly stronger than another predictor in the same model. For example, an analysis designed to test whether internal motivation was a stronger predictor than external motivation within Example 8.2 involves dependent coefficients as the coefficients come from the same participants. It is tempting to think that if one predictor is statistically significant and the other is not that this would mean that one predictor is stronger than the other is. However, imagine an analysis in which one coefficient in the model was barely significant (e.g., $p = .049$) and the other missed the mark (e.g., $p = .051$). In this case, one predictor is not likely stronger than the other.

Example 8.5 Comparing Dependent Coefficients

For this example, imagine that we wanted to design to conclude that internal motivations were stronger predictors of intentions than external motivations. Using the data from Table 8.1, output from Table 8.10, and some additional calculations allows for determination of the noncentrality parameter using Formula 8.19.

One aspect of this calculation that deserves special mention are the values noted ρ^{ii}, ρ^{ij}, and ρ^{jj}. These values come from the inverse of the correlation matrix. For those with matrix algebra backgrounds, the calculation is simple. For those without, computer protocols easily accomplish these calculations.

Table 8.10 provides values for the coefficients, yielding $b_1 = 3.73$ and $b_2 = 1.75$ with the corresponding standard errors of $SE_{b1} = 0.513$ and $SE_{b2} = 0.621$. Based on the inverted matrix of predictor correlations (calculated by the computer), $\rho^{ii} = 1.56$, $\rho^{ij} = 0.00$, and $\rho^{jj} = 1.07$. Using Formula 8.19, this produces $\delta = 2.46$.

$$\delta = \frac{|b_1| - |b_2|}{\sqrt{se_{b_1}^2 + se_{b_2}^2 - 2se_{b_1}se_{b_2}\left(\frac{\rho^{ij}}{\rho^{ii}\rho^{jj}}\right)}}$$

$$= \frac{3.73 - 1.75}{\sqrt{0.513^2 + 0.621^2 - 2*0.513*0.621\left(\frac{0}{1.56*1.07}\right)}} = 2.46$$

For a sample of $n = 110$, plug $\delta = 2.46$ with $df = 106$ (n minus the total number of predictors minus 1; $110 - 3 - 1$) and a $t_{critical}$ value of 1.98 (.05, two tailed) into the following syntax lines. Another approach is to square δ to get λ. Either approach yields Power = .68.

```
Compute Power = 1-NCDF.t(1.98, 106, 2.46)

Compute Power = 1-NCDF.F(3.93, 1, 106, 6.05)
```

The SPSS syntax in Table 8.11 conducts these tests but does not require the calculations. I omit several lines as the file is very long and involves multiple procedures necessary for inverting the matrix. The syntax file presented in Table 8.11 compares two predictors that are in a three-predictor model.

Some aspects of the syntax require explanation over and above the comments in Table 8.11. These analyses require a full correlation matrix (i.e., top and bottom) for the predictor variables only. Entry of correlations between predictors and the dependent variable occur later. This approach is necessary to perform the matrix inversion calculations for this analysis. Another requirement for this analysis is that the two predictors to compare are listed as the first and second variables. The file requires running analyses with several sample sizes to converge on adequate power.

Table 8.11 Syntax for Comparing Dependent Coefficients

```DATA LIST LIST /a b c.ᵃ```
```BEGIN DATA```
```1 -.15 -.60```
```-.15 1 .25```
```-.60 .25 1```
```END DATA.```
 	
```(syntax deleted)```
	For this matrix, include on the bottom diagonal the correlations with those values mirrored on the upper diagonal; the matrix would look like this:
	
	a b c
	
	a
	
	b
	
	c

```****Add the four values```
``` below```
```Compute ry1 = .4.```
	These are ONLY the correlations between predictors; the DV is not involved at this point of the analysis

```Compute ry2 = .4.```
```Compute ry3 = -.4.```
```Compute R2 = .467.```
 	
```(syntax deleted)```
	On the diagonal (where the 1s are now), place the *SD* for each variable
	
	ry1, ry2, ry3 = Correlations between predictors and DV R2 is for the full model

```Compute N = 110.```
```Compute alpha = .05.```
```Compute tails = 2.```
 	
```(syntax deleted)```
	N for each analysis; you will have to run this several times using a new sample size each time

ᵃ This syntax uses a print matrix function that takes values from output and imports them to the data file. Much of this work would not be possible without an uncredited file from http://spsstools.net called "invert a matrix."

Table 8.12 shows that power for $n = 110$ is about .68. A sample of 143 would achieve 80% power for the test of differences. Output for the analysis includes confidence limits on the difference. This syntax can be used to obtain confidence limits on the differences between predictors in a model for existing data.

Table 8.12 Output for Comparing Dependent Coefficients ($n = 110$ and $n = 147$)

Comparing two dependent predictors			
n	LL	UL	power
110.000	.055	.511	.685
Comparing two dependent predictors			
n	LL	UL	power
143.000	.085	.482	.800

POWER FOR DETECTING DIFFERENCES BETWEEN TWO INDEPENDENT COEFFICIENTS

Another possible question is whether a predictor is stronger for one group than another. For example, in the internal and external motivation example, a reasonable argument might be that a sample of college students might respond more strongly to external motivations than an older, noncollege sample.

Example 8.4: Comparing Two Independent Coefficients

This example uses the data from the previous example to represent a college student sample and adds a second set of values to represent a noncollege (adult) sample. Table 8.13 shows these values.

The basic approach is to take the difference between the unstandardized regression coefficients divided by the standard error of the differences between coefficients using Formulae 8.15 or 8.18. As with other aspects of analyses in this chapter, the shortcut syntax is useful for deriving several values (i.e., skipping hand calculations). As before, both samples need a correlation matrix for calculations.

The analysis approach is twofold. First, derive the coefficients (unstandardized) and R^2 values using the SPSS shortcut file (or calculate them by hand). Next, plug the coefficients, R^2 values, standard deviations, and desired sample sizes into another SPSS file. This example uses the same standard deviations for measures across samples; however, the syntax allows for use of different standard deviations if desired. The calculations that follow demonstrate that the calculation approaches and SPSS approaches produce equivalent results.

The first step is to run the "shortcut" syntax to find coefficients, R^2_y, and R^2_i for calculations or input into the power analysis syntax. For each of the two samples, we derive R^2 for prediction of the dependent variable. Tables 8.14–8.16 present output from these analyses.

The output in Table 8.14 shows $R^2_y = .467$, reflecting how well the criterion variable is predicted by predictors in the student sample. Also from this output, we take $b_1 = 3.733$, the unstandardized coefficient for external. Table 8.15 presents syntax and output for R^2_i. From the table, $R^2_i = .063$, reflecting how well the predictor of interest (external) is predicted by the other predictor variables (again for the student sample). Since the predictors show the same correlations across both samples, I present this analysis only once (it produces $R^2_i = .063$ for both samples). Using these values and

Table 8.13 Correlations for Both Populations With Student Sample on Lower Diagonal and Adult Sample on Upper Diagonal

	Intent	Internal	External	Modern Racism
Intent (y)	$\sigma = 7.0$	$\rho = .40$	$\rho = .10$	$\rho = -.40$
Internal (1)	$\rho = .40$	$\sigma = 1.0$	$\rho = -.15$	$\rho = -.60$
External (2)	$\rho = .40$	$\rho = -.15$	$\sigma = 1.0$	$\rho = .25$
Modern racism (3)	$\rho = -.40$	$\rho = -.60$	$\rho = .25$	$\sigma = 2.0$

Table 8.14 Student Sample ($n = 50$) Shortcut Syntax and Output for Predicting the DV

```
MATRIX DATA VARIABLES = ROWTYPE_ Intention Internal
 External Modern.
BEGIN DATA
Mean 1 2 3 4
Stdev 7 1 1 2
N 50 50 50 50
Corr 1
Corr .40 1
Corr .40 -.15 1
Corr -.40 -.60 .25 1
END DATA.

REGRESSION
   /MATRIX=IN(*)
   /MISSING LISTWISE
   /STATISTICS COEFF OUTS R ANOVA COLLIN TOL zpp change
   /CRITERIA=PIN(.05) POUT(.10)
   /NOORIGIN
   /DEPENDENT Intention
   /METHOD=ENTER Modern Internal External.
```

Model Summary

Model	R	R^2	Adjusted R^2	Standard Error of the Estimate
1	.683[a]	.467	.432	5.2761426

Coefficients[b]

Model	b	Standard Error	β	t	Significance
1 (Constant)	-8.333	3.963		-2.103	.041
Modern	-1.342	.481	-.383	-2.789	.008
Internal	1.750	.942	.250	1.857	.070
External	3.733	.778	.533	4.796	.000

[a] Predictors: (constant), external, internal, modern
[b] Dependent variable: intention

Formula 8.13, we can calculate the standard error of each coefficient (shown only for the college sample).

$$se_{b_1} = \frac{\sigma_y}{\sigma_1} \sqrt{\frac{1}{1-R_i^2}} \sqrt{\frac{1-R_y^2}{n-k-1}} = \frac{7}{1} \sqrt{\frac{1}{1-.063}} \sqrt{\frac{1-.467}{50-3-1}} = 0.778$$

Table 8.15 Student Sample ($n = 50$) Shortcut Syntax and Output for R^2_i

```
MATRIX DATA VARIABLES = ROWTYPE_ Internal External Modern.

BEGIN DATA
Mean 2 3 4
Stdev 1 1 2
N 50 50 50
Corr 1
Corr -.15
Corr -.60 .25 1
END DATA.

REGRESSION
   /MATRIX=IN(*)
   /MISSING LISTWISE
   /STATISTICS change
   /CRITERIA=PIN(.05) POUT(.10)
   /NOORIGIN
   /DEPENDENT External
   /METHOD=ENTER Internal Modern.
```

Model Summary

Model	R	R^2	Adjusted R^2	Standard Error of the Estimate
1	.250[a]	.063	.023	.9886322

[a] Predictors: (constant), modern, internal

Note that in Table 8.14, the standard error for external is 0.778, just as found in the calculation. Table 8.16 provides the necessary values for the adult sample, with $b_2 = 1.493$ and $se_{b2} = 0.928$. These values and those from the student sample allow for calculation of the standard error of the differences (Formula 8.14) and then the noncentrality parameter (Formula 8.15).

$$se_{b_1-b_2} = \sqrt{se_{b_1}^2 + se_{b_2}^2} = \sqrt{0.778^2 + .928^2} = 1.211$$

$$\delta = \frac{|b_1| - |b_2|}{se_{b_1-b_2}} = \frac{3.733 - 1.493}{1.211} = \frac{2.24}{1.211} = 1.85$$

Power for $\delta = 1.85$, using $t_{critical}$ for a two-tailed test with $\alpha = .05$ and $df = 92$ (Total sample size – Number of predictors in first model – Number of predictors in second model – 2) comes to .45.

Table 8.16 Adult Sample ($n = 50$) Shortcut Output

(Syntax omitted; same as Table 8.14 with different correlations)

Model Summary

Model	R	R^2	Adjusted R^2	Standard Error of the Estimate
1	.493[a]	.243	.193	6.2872496

Coefficients[b]

Model	Unstandardized Coefficients b	Standard Error	Standardized Coefficients β	t	Significance
1 (Constant)	1.513	6.445		.235	.815
Modern	-2.123	1.146	-.303	-1.852	.070
Internal	1.750	1.123	.250	1.559	.126
External	1.493	.928	.213	1.610	.114

[a] Predictors: (constant), external, internal, modern
[b] Dependent variable: intention

SPSS syntax in Table 8.17 completes this calculation for a range of sample sizes. This syntax requires a number of pieces of information but does not require the standard error values.

As shown in the calculation that yielded $\delta = 1.85$, the output in Table 8.18 indicates that $n = 50$ per group produces Power = .45. For $n = 115$ per sample, power is .82. As with the test of dependent predictors, I also provide the confidence limits on the difference between the coefficients, noted as LL and UL.

POWER FOR COMPARING TWO INDEPENDENT R^2 VALUES

Another option with regression is to compare overall prediction across samples. For example, if our interest was to test if our ability to predict intentions was significantly better in the student sample compared to the adult sample, this sort of question involves comparison of the R^2 *model* values for each analysis.

Example 8.5: Comparing Two Independent R^2 Values

This example examines the R^2 for both samples. Although the example presents comparisons of the R^2 *model*, this approach works for R^2 *change* comparisons as well. Again, the shortcut syntax used in the previous example does this calculation easily, producing

Table 8.17 SPSS Syntax for Comparing Independent Coefficients

Syntax	Comments
INPUT PROGRAM.	
LOOP n=100 TO 300 by 10.	Modify to change sample size; currently it will
END CASE.	yield analyses for overall n of 100, 110, 120, etc.
END LOOP.	
END FILE.	
END INPUT PROGRAM.	
EXECUTE.	
	Prop_N1 is proportion of total sample in the
Compute Prop_N1 = 0.5.	first group; use .5 for equal sample sizes
Compute b1 = 3.733.	b1, b2 are the unstandardized coefficients
Compute r2y1 = .467.	r2y1, r2y2 are R^2 for the full models
Compute r2_1 = .063.	
Compute b2 = 1.493.	
Compute r2y2 = .243.	r2_1, r2_2 are R^2 for predicting the IV of interest
Compute r2_2 = .063.	from the other predictors
Compute sdy 1= 7.	
Compute sdy 2= 7.	sdy1 and sdy2 refer to the DVs in each sample
Compute sd1 = 1.	
Compute sd2 = 1.	sd1, sd2 are standard deviations for the IVs
Compute alpha = .05.	
Compute tails = 2.	k = number of predictors in the full model
Compute k = 3.	(No modifications beyond this point)

```
Compute N1 = N * Prop_N1.
Compute N2 = N * (1-Prop_N1).
Compute seb1 = (sdy/sd1)* (1/(1-r2_1)**.5)*(((1-r2y1)/
 (n1-k-1))**.5).
Compute seb2 = (sdy/sd2)*(1/(1-r2_2)**.5)*(((1-r2y2)/
 (n2-k-1))**.5).
Compute df = n1+n2-k-k-2.
Compute alpha_tails = alpha/tails.
Compute fail = 1-alpha_tails.
Compute slope_diff = abs(b1-b2).
Compute sediff = Sqrt((seb1**2) + (seb2**2)).
Compute delta = slope_diff / sediff.
Compute t_tabled = IDF.t(fail,df).
Compute Power = 1-NCDF.t(t_tabled,df,delta).
Compute LL_diff = slope_diff - (t_tabled*sediff).
Compute UL_diff = slope_diff + (t_tabled*sediff).
execute.
MATRIX.
GET M /VARIABLES=n1 n2 ll_diff ul_diff power.
print M/title = "Comparing two independent predictors"/
 clabels = "n1" "n2" "LL" "UL" "power"/format f9.3.
End Matrix.
```

Table 8.18 SPSS Output for Comparing Independent Coefficients

Comparing two independent predictors				
n1	n2	LL	UL	Power
50.0	50.0	-.165	4.645	.448
55.0	55.0	-.041	4.521	.488
60.0	60.0	.065	4.415	.525
65.0	65.0	.158	4.322	.561
70.0	70.0	.240	4.240	.595
75.0	75.0	.313	4.167	.626
80.0	80.0	.379	4.101	.656
85.0	85.0	.438	4.042	.684
90.0	90.0	.492	3.988	.711
95.0	95.0	.541	3.939	.735
100.0	100.0	.587	3.893	.758
105.0	105.0	.629	3.851	.779
110.0	110.0	.667	3.813	.798
115.0	115.0	.704	3.776	.816
120.0	120.0	.738	3.742	.833
125.0	125.0	.769	3.711	.848
130.0	130.0	.799	3.681	.862
135.0	135.0	.827	3.653	.875
140.0	140.0	.853	3.627	.887
145.0	145.0	.878	3.602	.897
150.0	150.0	.902	3.578	.907

LL = lower limit; UL = upper limit

R^2 for the student sample of .467 and .243 for the adult sample. Table 8.19 presents R^2 for each sample. Apply these values to Formula 8.20 to calculate the noncentrality parameter. The example begins with $n = 115$ for each group (230 overall), reflecting the sample size found for differences between coefficients as a starting point.

$$\delta = \frac{|R_1^2 - R_2^2|}{\sqrt{\left(\frac{4R_1^2\left(1-R_1^2\right)^2(n_1-k-1)^2}{\left(n_1^2-1\right)(n_1+3)}\right) + \left(\frac{4R_2^2\left(1-R_2^2\right)^2(n_2-k-1)^2}{\left(n_2^2-1\right)(n_2+3)}\right)}}$$

$$= \frac{|.467-.243|}{\sqrt{\left(\frac{(4\times.467)(1-.467)^2(115-3-1)^2}{(115^2-1)(115+3)}\right) + \left(\frac{(4\times.243)(1-.243)^2(115-3-1)^2}{(115^2-1)(115+3)}\right)}}$$

$$= 2.43$$

Table 8.19 SPSS Shortcut Output for Comparing Two Independent R^2s

Model Summary				
Model	R	R^2	Adjusted R^2	Standard Error of the Estimate
1	.683[a]	.467	.432	5.2761426

Model Summary				
Model	R	R^2	Adjusted R^2	Standard Error of the Estimate
1	.493[b]	.243	.193	6.2872496

[a] Predictors: (constant), external, internal, modern
[b] Predictors: (constant), external, internal, modern

Evaluating power for $\delta = 2.43$ requires a t-critical value for a two-tailed test with $\alpha = .05$ and $df = 222$ (that is, Total sample size − Number of predictors in first model − Number of predictors in second model − 2). Using the procedures detailed, $\delta = 2.43$ corresponds to Power = .68.

The SPSS syntax in Table 8.20 completes power calculations for a range of sample sizes. As with several of the other files in this chapter, I include confidence limits. The primary information required for the syntax are R^2 values (either model or change) and the number of predictors.

Table 8.21 shows that for this analysis power of .80 requires a sample of 320 overall, given that there are equal numbers of participants in each group.

ADDITIONAL ISSUES

Reliability

Reliability plays a major role in regression analysis with continuously scaled variables. Less-reliable measures reduce the size of correlations observed in samples (e.g., Hunter & Schmidt, 1994). Since poor reliability attenuates observed relationships, less-reliable measures produce smaller effect sizes and reduce power. For example, two variables might have a .60 correlation in the population (ρ_{true}); however, unreliable measures may reduce the observed correlation (ρ_{obs}). Formula 8.21 shows how reliability impacts the observed correlation (α_1 is the reliability for the predictor, α_y is for the criterion).

$$\rho_{obs} = \rho_{true} \sqrt{\alpha_1 \alpha_y} \qquad (8.21)$$

In the following example, both the variables demonstrate mediocre reliability ($\alpha_1 = \alpha_y = .50$). In this case, the observed correlation is half the size of the population correlation. Of course, if the effect size observed

Table 8.20 Syntax for Comparing Two Independent R^2s

Syntax	Comments
```INPUT PROGRAM.```	Modify to change sample size; currently
```LOOP n=230 to 400 by 10.```	it will yield analyses for overall *n* of 230,
```END CASE.```	240, etc.
```END LOOP.```	
```END FILE.```	
```END INPUT PROGRAM.```	
```EXECUTE.```	Prop_N1 is proportion of total sample in
	the first group; use .5 for equal sample
```Compute Prop_N1 = 0.5.```	sizes
```Compute R2_1 = .467.```	
```Compute R2_2 = .242.```	R2_1 and R2_2 are the R^2 values to compare
```Compute k =3.```	
```Compute alpha = .05.```	k = number of predictors in the full model
	(No modifications beyond this point)

```
Compute tails = 2.
Compute N1 = N * Prop_N1.
Compute N2 = N * (1-Prop_N1).
Compute SER2_1 = ((4*R2_1)*(1-R2_1)**2)*((n1-k-1)**2)/
 ((n1**2 - 1)* (n1+3)).
Compute SER2_2 = ((4*R2_2)*(1-R2_2)**2)*((n2-k-1)**2)/
 ((n2**2 - 1)* (n2+3)).
Compute SER2 = (SER2_1 + SER2_2)**.5.
Compute diff = abs(r2_1-r2_2).
Compute alpha_tails = alpha/tails.
Compute fail = 1-alpha_tails.
Compute df = n1+n2-k-k-2.
Compute delta = diff/SER2.
Compute t_tabled = IDF.t(fail,df).
Compute Power = 1-NCDF.t(t_tabled,df,delta).
Compute LL_diff = diff - (t_tabled*SER2).
Compute UL_diff = diff + (t_tabled*SER2).
execute.

MATRIX.
GET M /VARIABLES=n1 n2 ll_diff ul_diff power.
print M/title = "Comparing two independent R-Square
 Values"/clabels = "n1" "n2" "LL" "UL" "power"/format
 f9.3.
End Matrix.
```

Table 8.21 Output for Comparing Two Independent R^2s

Comparing two independent R-Square Values				
n1	n2	LL	UL	Power
115.0	115.0	.042	.408	.677
120.0	120.0	.046	.404	.694
125.0	125.0	.049	.401	.710
130.0	130.0	.052	.398	.725
135.0	135.0	.055	.395	.740
140.0	140.0	.058	.392	.754
145.0	145.0	.061	.389	.768
150.0	150.0	.064	.386	.780
155.0	155.0	.066	.384	.793
160.0	160.0	.068	.382	.804
165.0	165.0	.071	.379	.815
170.0	170.0	.073	.377	.826
175.0	175.0	.075	.375	.836
180.0	180.0	.077	.373	.846
185.0	185.0	.079	.371	.855
190.0	190.0	.081	.369	.863
195.0	195.0	.082	.368	.871
200.0	200.0	.084	.366	.879

LL = lower limit; UL = upper limit

is considerably smaller than the expected effect in the population (i.e., the value used in power analysis), power falls.

$$.30 = .6\sqrt{.5 * .5}$$

The next calculation shows a situation in which both variables have strong reliabilities ($\alpha_1 = \alpha_y = .90$). In this case, the observed correlation is closer to the population value.

$$.54 = .6\sqrt{.9 * .9}$$

Reliability is also important for experimental designs but often to a lesser extent. For experimental designs, factors based on random assignment are considered perfectly reliable (i.e., $\alpha_1 = 1.0$), so the impact of reliability on observed relationships comes only from the dependent variable rather than the DV and the factor.

Multiplicity and Direction of Predictor Correlations

As discussed in Chapter 5, designs involving two or more predictors open the door for different conceptualizations of power. Power might be discussed in terms of power for a single effect (as this chapter covers) or as power for detecting all the effects of interest [Power(All)]. Thinking about the example in Table 8.4, the power for internal was .84 [Power(A)] and the power for external [Power(B)] was also .84. For either effect, we have an 84% chance of detection. Power(All) reflects the power for detecting a significant effect for both internal and external *at the same time*. If predictors are uncorrelated, as in the case of ANOVA with random assignment, Power(All) = Power (A) × Power (B). Predictors in multiple regression, however, often correlate.

The size and direction of correlations between predictors impact power to detect effects. Provided that the predictors relate to the criterion in a consistent manner (i.e., all positively correlated or all negatively correlated), predictors that positively correlate with each other reduce Power(All). However, when predictors negatively correlate, Power(All) increases (see Maxwell, 2004, for a detailed discussion of these issues).[1] Negative correlations of this form, outside of cases with small negative correlations, are less common than positive correlations between predictors. This potentially leads to cases for which, despite adequate power for each predictor, poor power for detecting all the effects in a single study exists. Clearly, this is not ideal; most researchers want all their effects to turn out significant, not just some of them.

Given these issues, I offer several recommendations for designs for which the goal is to detect multiple effects. First, whenever possible use uncorrelated or slightly negatively correlated predictors. If predictors demonstrate strong positive correlations, recognize that this increases sample size requirements. Second, consider factor or components analyses to help identify uncorrelated predictors. Third, if your goal is to have Power(All) = .80, design for greater power on individual predictors. With uncorrelated predictors, power for two predictors at .89 for both will yield Power(All) ≈ .80 ($.89^2 = .80$); for three, power would need to be .93 ($.93^3 = .80$); for four, you would need .95 ($.95^4 = .80$). Finally, consider set analyses for highly correlated predictors. In general, tests of R^2 *change* for the set are more powerful than tests of the unique contribution of each predictor when the predictors are highly correlated.

SUMMARY

This chapter presented power for R^2 *model*, R^2 *change*, and coefficients for multiple regression. For these tests, the primary information required is the correlations between variables or estimates of R^2. Estimates of correlations between predictors and the dependent measure (as well as R^2) should reflect meaningful levels of association, whereas estimates for correlations between predictors focus on accuracy. This chapter also presented tests for comparisons between independent coefficients, dependent coefficients, and independent R^2 values. Each test requires estimates of the value of interest and correlations between all predictors and/or R^2 values.

NOTE

1. I discuss these issues in terms of the directions of the correlations between variables. Maxwell (2004) focuses on correlations between *coefficients*. A positive correlation between predictors would reflect a negative relationship among coefficients (i.e., as one coefficient rises the other tends to fall).

9

COVARIATE ANALYSES AND
REGRESSION INTERACTIONS

INTRODUCTION

This chapter examines analysis of covariance (ANCOVA), multivariate analysis of covariance (MANCOVA), and regression interaction designs. Analyses in this chapter expand on work in Chapters 6–8 and in some cases continue examples from those chapters. Additional issues include reliability impacts on detection of regression interactions. I present few new formulae because calculations of some effect sizes and other values for the analyses are outside the scope of this text. For details on these calculations, see the work of Tabachnick and Fidell (2007a, 2007b), Cohen et al. (2003), and Aguinis (2004).

ANALYSIS OF COVARIANCE

Necessary Statistics

Covariate analyses require means and standard deviations for each group or cell (as with analysis-of-variance [ANOVA] designs) and estimates of correlations between the covariate and dependent measure (as with regression).

Factors Affecting Power

Inclusion of covariates often increases power. Ideally, a covariate explains variability in the dependent variable that the factors do not explain. This reduces the error variance. Reducing error variance causes F and the noncentrality parameter (λ) for factors to become larger because the denominator of the test gets smaller. As F and λ increase, power increases. Well-chosen covariates do wonders for power. As with other designs, larger sample size, more liberal α error criteria, larger differences between means, and smaller standard deviations yield more power.

The value of a covariate is limited to the extent that it is unrelated to the factors. This issue is similar to multicollinearity considerations discussed in Chapter 8. If factors relate to the covariate, then the covariate explains some of the variability in the dependent variable that the factors would otherwise explain. This causes a reduction in the F statistic for the factors of interest. Poorly selected covariates reduce power by removing variance explained by factors and reducing error degrees of freedom.

An important assumption of ANCOVA is that the covariate and DV demonstrate the same relationship across every level of the IV. This is equivalent to assuming that there is no interaction between the covariate and the factors. This assumption is stated formally as the homogeneity of covariance or homogeneity of regression assumption. If you expect a covariate-by-factor interaction, then do not use ANCOVA. Regression approaches described in this chapter handle violations of this assumption nicely.

Example 9.1: Analysis of Covariance

In Chapter 5, an example focused on a two-factor between-subjects ANOVA design involving prediction of attitudes toward specific affirmative action (AA) policies based on policy type (recruitment vs. tiebreaker) and justification (none vs. increased diversity) for the policy. That design required a sample of over 1,000 participants to produce power of roughly 80% for the test of the interaction. Example 9.2 examines how adding a covariate (general AA attitudes) reduces the sample size requirements.

Previous work found correlations between general AA attitudes and attitudes toward specific policies of around .40 for several applications of AA (e.g., Aberson, 2007). That is, how people feel about AA in general (e.g., "I support affirmative action") relates to their evaluations of specific AA policies regardless of policy content. Based on this information, the example uses an estimated correlation between general attitudes and attitudes toward each policy of .40. Like the process involved in addressing correlations between control variables in regression analysis, this estimate should focus on accuracy rather than meaningfulness (i.e., what we expect the value to be in the population rather than how large the effect would be to have practical importance).

The syntax in Table 9.1 adds a covariate to the analyses found in Chapter 5. Note that the syntax differs only slightly from that used for factorial ANOVA. Specifically, the syntax file now includes general AA attitudes (the variable called General) as the covariate. In the matrix command, enter the covariate as any other continuous variable would be.

Table 9.1 SPSS Syntax for Two-Factor ANCOVA

Syntax	Comments
MATRIX DATA VARIABLES = Policy Justify ROWTYPE_ Support General /FACTORS = Policy Justify.	Support is the DV; general is the covariate Specifies factors (Policy and Justify)
BEGIN DATA	
1 1 N 251 251	1 1 identifies the cell (first level of
1 2 N 251 251	Policy, first level Justify)
2 1 N 251 251	
2 2 N 251 251	
1 1 MEAN 0.85 2.5	Need *M, SD, N* for DV and covariate
1 2 MEAN 0.85 2.5	.. In front of CORR and *SD*, need
2 1 MEAN 0.0 2.5	one period for each factor; 4 is
2 2 MEAN 0.6 2.5	DV and covariate correlation
. . CORR 1	
. . CORR .4 1	
. . STDEV 1.70 1.0	
END DATA.	
MANOVA Support BY Policy, Justify (1,2) with General	
/MATRIX=IN(*)	The statement "with" adds the
/POWER exact t (.05) F (.05)	covariate to the analysis; multiple
/CINTERVAL Joint (.95)	covariates can be used
/OMEANS = Tables (Policy Justify)	
/PRINT = Parameters (efsize)	
/DESIGN.	

Then, in the multivariate analysis of variance (MANOVA) portion, the statement "with" adds the covariate.

SPSS output, shown in Table 9.2, lists the covariate as "regression." When using multiple covariates, SPSS lists all of them together on this single line. Comparing power from the covariate analysis to power for the original analysis found in Table 9.3 (this reproduces information from Table 5.16 in Chapter 5) shows there is more power for detecting effects for the factors and the interaction following addition of the covariate.

Note that the sum of squares for Policy, Justify, and Policy by Justify are the same across the two analyses. That is, the effects explain the same amount of variance in attitudes. The difference between the two analyses is that the error variance (noted as "within cells") is smaller for the covariate analysis (2,427.60) than for the ANOVA without the covariate (2,890.00). The addition of the covariate accounts for 462.40 sums of squares toward the explanation of the dependent measure (note that 462.40 is the difference between 2,427.60 and 2,890.00).

Calculations using Formulae 5.1–5.3 illustrate how the covariate increases power in this analysis. The first calculations are based on the ANCOVA, using information from

Table 9.2 SPSS Output for Two-Factor ANCOVA

```
       Tests of Significance for Support using UNIQUE
                      sums of squares
```

Source of Variation	SS	DF	MS	F	Sig of F
WITHIN CELLS	2427.60	999	2.43		
REGRESSION	462.40	1	462.40	190.29	.000
Policy	75.93	1	75.93	31.25	.000
Justify	22.59	1	22.59	9.30	.002
Policy BY Justify	22.59	1	22.59	9.30	.002

```
          Observed Power at the .0500 Level
```

Source of Variation	Noncentrality	Power
Regression	190.286	1.000
Policy	31.245	1.000
Justify	9.296	.861
Policy BY Justify	9.296	.861

Table 9.2. The interaction, with the covariate included in the analysis, yields $\eta^2 = .009$. The noncentrality parameter λ gets larger as the effect size increases.

$$\eta^2_{partial} = \frac{SS_{effect}}{SS_{effect} + SS_{error}} = \frac{22.59}{22.59 + 2427.6} = .00922$$

Table 9.3 SPSS Output for Two-Factor ANOVA for Comparison to Table 9.2 Results

```
       Tests of Significance for Support using UNIQUE
                      sums of squares
```

Source of Variation	SS	DF	MS	F	Sig of F
WITHIN CELLS	2890.00	1000	2.89		
Policy	75.93	1	75.93	26.27	.000
Justify	22.59	1	22.59	7.82	.005
Policy BY Justify	22.59	1	22.59	7.82	.005

```
          Observed Power at the .0500 Level
```

Source of Variation	Noncentrality	Power
Policy	26.272	.999
Justify	7.817	.798
Policy BY Justify	7.817	.798

$$f^2 = \frac{\eta^2_{partial}}{1-\eta^2_{partial}} = \frac{.00922}{1-.00922} = .00931$$

$$\lambda = f^2 df_{error} = 0.00931 * 999 = 9.30$$

Next are calculations for the analysis using the values in Table 9.3. This analysis reflects the two-factor ANOVA that did not include a covariate.

$$\eta^2_{partial} = \frac{SS_{effect}}{SS_{effect}+SS_{error}} = \frac{22.59}{22.59+2890} = .00776$$

$$f^2 = \frac{\eta^2_{partial}}{1-\eta^2_{partial}} = \frac{.00776}{1-.00776} = .00782$$

$$\lambda = f^2 df_{error} = .00782 \times 1000 = 7.82$$

Comparing the calculations for ANCOVA and ANOVA shows that the inclusion of the covariate reduced the error variance, which in turn increased the effect size and the noncentrality parameter. The covariate also consumed a degree of freedom (999 vs. 1,000). In the present example, the degree-of-freedom loss does little to influence the analysis. However, with small samples, that degree of freedom has more of an impact on power. Well-chosen covariates make up for the lost degrees of freedom.

The next step in this analysis examines how large a sample (with the covariate included) is necessary for adequate power. Table 9.4 shows that a sample of $n = 213$ per group yields power of approximately 80% for the interaction. Although still a large sample (852 participants), there is a net savings of 152 participants over the factorial ANOVA without the covariate. At this point, a good question is whether the sample size savings justifies inclusion of the covariate measures. In this study, the covariate measure is a five-item general AA attitudes scale, requiring only about a minute of the participant's time to complete. Adding this short measure reduces the sample size requirement by 15%.

MODERATED REGRESSION ANALYSIS (REGRESSION WITH INTERACTIONS)

Moderated regression analysis focuses on regression models with inter-actions. Interactions can be between categorical variables, continuous variables, or both. However, ANOVA procedures handle categorical-by-categorical interactions more simply. This section includes three approaches to moderated regression analysis. Two expand on the covariate and multiple regression tests found in this chapter and in Chapter 8. These techniques work for interactions between categorical and continuous predictors as well as interactions between continuously scaled

Table 9.4 SPSS Output for Two-Factor ANCOVA ($n = 213$ per Group)

Tests of Significance for Support using UNIQUE sums of squares					
Source of Variation	SS	DF	MS	F	Sig of F
WITHIN CELLS	2058.60	847	2.43		
REGRESSION	392.12	1	392.12	161.33	.000
Policy	64.43	1	64.43	26.51	.000
Justify	19.17	1	19.17	7.89	.005
Policy BY Justify	19.17	1	19.17	7.89	.005

Observed Power at the .0500 Level		
Source of Variation	Noncentrality	Power
Regression	161.333	1.000
Policy	26.510	.999
Justify	7.887	.801
Policy BY Justify	7.887	.801

predictors. The third approach focuses on interactions between a dichotomous variable and a continuous variable. Necessary statistical values for each approach differ and are presented in the sections that address each procedure.

Factors Affecting Power

A number of issues affect power for moderated effects in regression. The first are measurement issues associated with use of continuously scaled variables. These issues include range restriction, artificial dichotomization (see Chapter 5), and poor reliability (see Aguinis, 2004). In short, if one first-order predictor (i.e., main effect) possesses poor psychometric properties, these shortcomings also appear in the interaction term. If both first-order predictors possess poor psychometric properties, the problems are amplified for the interaction. The additional issues section of this chapter addresses this problem with regard to reliability. Another issue is the strength of the relationship between the first-order predictors and the criterion variable. Broadly, interaction effects are constrained by the size of these relationships. The less variance the first-order predictors explain, the smaller the possible interaction effect size (for a technical description, see Rogers, 2002). The size of the interaction effect is discussed in the section that follows. As with other designs, larger sample sizes and more liberal α increase power.

Size of Interaction Effects

The techniques discussed in this section focus on either estimating patterns of correlations or the amount of variance explained by the interaction. The effect size reflects the relationship between the interaction term and the dependent variable. Many forms of interactions typically produce small effects. For example, Aiken and West (1991) note in discussing interactions between continuous variables, that "[o]bserved effect sizes for interactions are very small, accounting for about 1% of the variance in outcomes. . . . The social scientist is forewarned" (p. 170). Similarly, a review of 30 years of publications in applied psychology and management found the median effect size for regression interactions between categorical and continuous predictors was $f^2 = .002$ or 0.2% variance explained by the interaction on the dependent variable (Aguinis, Beaty, Boik, & Pierce, 2005).

In considering these findings, it is important to note that Aguinis et al. (2005) concentrated on areas of investigation that tend to employ designs addressing interactions between demographic variables such as gender and a measured variable. In many of these studies, tests were exploratory (e.g., does gender moderate the predictor–DV relationship?) rather than theoretically derived. Although complimentary meta-analyses examining designs that include a manipulated variable that interacts with a measured variable are not available, a cursory examination of work in fields such as social psychology suggest that when manipulated variables are included in the interaction, larger effect sizes are common. Similarly, it is reasonable to expect that when interaction hypotheses follow from theory, larger effects are likely.

Previous chapters discussed the importance of designing for "meaningful" effects. When discussing interactions, it is difficult to determine what size of effect would be meaningful, but there are several useful approaches to obtaining estimates. First, focus on the sort of effects detected typically in your area of inquiry. Examination of a handful of studies presenting regression interactions can give a sense of the typical effect size for the topical area. Second, it appears that regression interactions are strongest when one variable is manipulated and predictions are theoretically supported. Interactions are weakest when neither variable is manipulated and tests are exploratory. This should serve as a reality check for power analyses. For example, effects approaching even 1% explained variance represent a relatively large interaction for a correlational design focused on exploratory analyses of interactions between two measured variables.

Regression Analogy Approaches

What I term the *regression analogy approach* is conceptually the same as the multiple-regression approach for coefficients found in Chapter 8. This approach treats the interaction in the same manner as the other predictors. This strategy requires estimates of correlations between all variables in the model, including the interaction. In practice, the inter-action–DV correlation is often difficult to estimate, so the discussion regarding commonly observed effect sizes is particularly relevant.

A second approach is to estimate the R^2 *change* provided by the addition of the interaction to a model that includes the other predictors. This analysis proceeds according to the R^2 *change* analyses in Chapter 8. This approach requires particular attention to effect size estimation for the inter-action and an estimate of the variance explained by all the predictors.

Comparison of Correlations/Simple Slopes Analogy Approach

An alternative approach uses calculations presented by Aguinis (2004). The primary difference between this approach and the regression anal-ogy approach is that it is limited to situations with a single dichotomous predictor and a single continuous predictor. This approach focuses on the size of the correlation (or the unstandardized regression coefficient) for the relationship between the continuous predictor and the depen-dent measure in each of the two groups.

The analyses presented in this section use Formula 9.1 to calculate the effect size. The primary advantage of this formula is that it provides an adjustment for heterogeneity of variance that is represented in the formula through the consideration of standard deviations across the levels of the categorical moderator. Homogeneity of variance violations are common in studies examining categorical-by-continuous predictor interactions (Aguinis, Petersen, & Pierce, 1999).

$$f^2_{\text{modified}} = \frac{\sum (n_j -1)\rho^2_j \sigma^2_{y_j} - \dfrac{\left(\sum (n_j -1)\rho_j \sigma_{y_j} \sigma_{x_j}\right)^2}{\sum (n_j -1)\sigma^2_{x_j}}}{\sum (n_j -2)(1-\rho^2_j)\sigma^2_{y_j}} \qquad (9.1)$$

The correlation/simple slope approach may be more intuitive than the first two approaches discussed in this chapter. For this approach, we address relationships between the continuously scaled predictor and dependent variable for each category (i.e., estimates of correlations between the predictor and dependent variables in Group 1 and Group 2). Hypotheses that specify relationships between the predictor and dependent measure for one condition but not another can be modeled nicely with this approach.

Moderated Regression Examples

The following examples show each of the approaches discussed. Many of the estimates required for moderated regression analysis are not obvious, so I devote considerable space to approaches used to derive estimates from a published article.

Ayduk, Gyurak, and Luerssen (2008) examined the moderating effects of rejection sensitivity on the relationship between social rejection and aggression. The researchers exposed participants to a manipulation in which a potential partner either rejected or did not reject them. Participants then aggressed by allocating hot sauce to the partner after being informed that he or she disliked spicy food. This example follows the design of a study to replicate these findings. The initial step takes information from the study as a guide to expected effect sizes. Ideally, authors provide a correlation matrix and standard deviations for the dependent variable and predictors with these values also presented for each level of the categorical predictor. Of course, a single study does not necessarily provide an accurate estimate of the population effect size.

Regarding effect sizes, Ayduk et al. (2008) reported the effect for condition as $d = 0.34$ and the interaction as $d = 0.53$ based on $n = 122$. Using Formula 9.2 for converting d to ρ, these values become .17 and .26, respectively. The authors did not report the sensitivity–aggression or condition–sensitivity relationships; however, the article suggested that these were very small relationships, so it is reasonable to estimate them with zero or near-zero effect sizes. Similarly, the authors did not present correlations between the interaction term and the first-order variables. Theoretically, the covariate was not expected to relate to the condition, so estimating a correlation of zero is a reasonable approach, as is using a small correlation (e.g., $\rho = .05$). Since the authors did not report these values, you may have to plug and play a bit to find values that reproduce the analyses found in the research report (alternatively, you can contact the authors). Table 9.5 presents estimates of the correlations and standard deviations.

$$\rho = \sqrt{\frac{d^2}{d^2 + \dfrac{1}{P_1 P_2}}} \tag{9.2}$$

Table 9.5 Descriptive Statistics for Moderated Regression Example

	Aggression	**Condition**	**Sensitivity**	**C × S**
Aggression	σ = 2.72			
Condition	ρ = .17	σ = 0.50		
Sensitivity	ρ = .00	ρ = .00	σ = 3.25	
C × S interaction	ρ = .26	ρ = .05	ρ = .05	σ = 1.00

Example 9.2 Regression Analogy (Coefficients)

Table 9.6 presents SPSS syntax for producing the power analysis for the coefficient approach. The first set of analyses found in Table 9.7 is the regression shortcut syntax from Chapter 8. This analysis verifies that the relationships specified corresponded to the relationships Ayduk et al. (2008) reported. Of particular interest are the interaction results for which the authors reported $F(1, 118) = 8.3$. As seen

Table 9.6 SPSS Syntax-Moderated Regression (Test of Coefficient Approach)

Syntax	Comments
`MATRIX DATA VARIABLES = ROWTYPE_` `  aggress condition sensitive sxc`	Interaction variable entered last

`BEGIN DATA`
`Mean 4 1 1 1`
`N 122 122 122 122`
`Stdev 2.72 0.50 3.25 1.00`
`Corr 1`
`Corr .17 1`
`Corr .00 .00 1`
`Corr .26 .05 .05 1`
`END DATA.`
	M and *SD* for interaction do not impact power of interaction, so I usually enter 1 and 1

`REGRESSION`
`   /MATRIX=IN(*)`
`   /MISSING LISTWISE`
`   /STATISTICS R change`
`   /DEPENDENT aggress`
`   /METHOD=ENTER condition sensitive`
`   /METHOD=ENTER sxc.`
	This syntax for checking results (shortcut syntax) Interaction entered in final step of the regression analysis to check result (see Table 9.7); not necessary for all analyses

`MANOVA aggress with condition`
`  sensitive sxc`
`   /MATRIX=IN(*)`
`   /POWER F (.05)`
`   /PRINT signif (mult averf)`
`   /NOPRINT param(estim)`
`   /DESIGN.`
	Interaction entered as with other regression analysis; must be in same order as above (see Table 9.8)

Table 9.7 SPSS Output R^2 Values

				Model Summary					—
				Standard Error of the Estimate	Change Statistics				
Model	R	R^2	Adjusted R^2		R^2 Change	F Change	df1	df2	Significance of F Change
1	.170[a]	.029	.013	2.7028384	.029	1.771	2	119	.175
2	.304[b]	.092	.069	2.6239228	.064	8.266	1	118	.005

[a] Predictors: (constant), condition, sensitive
[b] Predictors: (constant), condition, sensitive, sxc

in Table 9.7 under F change for the second model, our data yielded $F(1, 118) = 8.27$, matching the authors' results. This step is not required if you are not trying to reproduce results.

Table 9.8 presents the power analysis for coefficients. A sample of $n = 122$ produces power of .81 for the interaction (noted as sxc in the output).

Table 9.8 SPSS Output Regression Coefficient Analysis for Interaction

Tests of Significance for aggress using UNIQUE sums of squares

Source of Variation	SS	DF	MS	F	Sig of F
WITHIN CELLS	812.43	118	6.88		
REGRESSION	82.78	3	27.59	4.01	.009
CONSTANT	125.39	1	125.39	18.21	.000

Observed Power at the .0500 Level

Source of Variation	Noncentrality	Power
Regression	12.02326	.827

Regression analysis for WITHIN CELLS error term
Dependent variable .. aggress

COVARIATE	B	Beta	Std. Err.	t-Value	Sig. of t
conditio	.85605	.	.478	1.792	.076
sensitiv	-.01058	.	.073	-.144	.886
sxc	.68752	.	.239	2.874	.005

COVARIATE	Lower -95%	CL- Upper	Noncent.	Power
conditio	-.099	1.802	3.211	.428
sensitiv	-.156	.135	.021	.052
sxc	.214	1.161	8.266	.814

Another important question is whether we are comfortable using the previously reported effect size as the target effect size for power. Recall that throughout the text, I encourage designing for meaningful effects, so we need to add some additional context to the discussion. The f^2 value (.07), calculated using Formula 8.7, for the interaction is large when compared to the meta-analytic results discussed, likely because the researchers experimentally manipulated one of the variables (rejection).

$$f^2_{Change} = \frac{R^2_{Change}}{1 - R^2_{Model}} = \frac{.064}{1 - .092} = .07$$

At this point, a conservative approach suggests designing for a smaller effect size. Keep in mind that the reported effect size may or may not be a good representation of the population effect. The population effect may be larger or smaller than observed in any single study. A conservative approach when replicating studies is to reduce the effect size (f^2) to design for a study that was sensitive to the detection of smaller effects.

Example 9.3 Regression Analogy (R^2 *Change*)

The R^2 *change* syntax easily handles changes in effect size specifications. The example that follows reduces the effect size (f^2 *change*) by cutting it in half to .035. Rearranging the f^2 *change* formula yields R^2 *change* of 0.032. Note that this calculation used the R^2 *model* estimate of .092 from Table 9.7. Although this value would likely be smaller if the R^2 *change* were smaller, using the larger estimate is more conservative.

$$R^2_{Change} = f^2_{Change}\left(1 - R^2_{Model}\right) = .035 * (1 - .092) = .032$$

Next, take the R^2 *change* value of .032 to the syntax in Table 9.9. The R^2 for the model includes .032 from the two predictors prior to the entry of the covariate plus the R^2 *change* (coincidentally, also .032), to give .064.

Table 9.10 presents output for this analysis. With this smaller R^2 *change* value, to attain power of .80 we require $n = 240$, almost double that in the original analysis.

Example 9.4 Comparison on Correlations/Simple Slopes

The third approach to power analysis for moderated regression involves comparing relationships across the experimental conditions. The present example requires estimates of the sensitivity–aggression correlation (or regression coefficients) for the control group and the rejection group as well as standard deviations for sensitivity and aggression for each of the conditions. This approach is intuitive as it provides a direct comparison of descriptive values (rather than the effect size for the interaction).

Table 9.9 SPSS Syntax for R^2 Change Analysis for Interaction

```
INPUT PROGRAM.
LOOP n=100 TO 400 by 20.
END CASE.
END LOOP.
END FILE.
END INPUT PROGRAM.
EXECUTE.

Compute r2model = .064.
Compute r2change = .032.
Compute modelpred = 3.
Compute changepred = 1.
Compute alpha = .05.

Compute df_change = changepred.
Compute df_denom = (n - modelpred) -1.
Compute k2 = 1 - r2model.
Compute multiplier = df_denom.
Compute f2 = r2change/k2.
Compute lambda = f2*multiplier .
Compute F_Table = IDF.F(1-
 alpha,df_change,df_denom).
Compute power = 1 - NCDF.F
 (F_Table,df_change,df_denom,Lambda).
execute.

matrix.
GET M /VARIABLES=n lambda Power .

print M/title = "Power for R2 Change
 Interaction"/clabels = "N" "Lambda"
 "Power"/format f10.4.
End Matrix.
```

To get model power set
model and change as
same values

This approach is more accurate than the others are when the distribution of variances on the dependent variable across levels of the categorical moderator is unequal (i.e., heterogeneity of variance).

The article (Ayduk et al., 2008) reported the standard deviations for aggression as 3.22 and 2.10 for the rejection and control conditions, respectively. However, the authors reported the standard deviation for the sensitivity score for only the entire sample (3.25). This may seem problematic, but unless there is an expectation of heterogeneity of variances, we can use the same standard deviation for both groups. The authors reported unstandardized regression coefficients (b) for the sensitivity–aggression relationship in the control condition as $b = -0.17$ and as $b = 0.25$ for the rejected condition. Using Formula 9.3 to convert these values finds correlations

Table 9.10 SPSS Output for R^2 Change Analysis for Interaction

Power for R2 Change Interaction		
N	Lambda	Power
100.0	3.2821	.4340
120.0	3.9658	.5060
140.0	4.6496	.5719
160.0	5.3333	.6313
180.0	6.0171	.6843
200.0	6.7009	.7310
220.0	7.3846	.7720
240.0	8.0684	.8076
260.0	8.7521	.8383
280.0	9.4359	.8646
300.0	10.1197	.8870
320.0	10.8034	.9061
340.0	11.4872	.9221
360.0	12.1709	.9357
380.0	12.8547	.9470
400.0	13.5385	.9564

of $-.26$ and $.25$, respectively. Table 9.11 summarizes the descriptive statistics used in the analysis.

$$\rho = b\frac{\sigma_x}{\sigma_y} \tag{9.3}$$

$$\rho_{control} = -0.17\frac{3.25}{2.10} = -.26$$

$$\rho_{rejected} = 0.25\frac{3.25}{3.22} = .25$$

The key to this analysis is the calculation of the f^2 statistic from the group-based statistics. An example of this calculation, using a sample of $n = 61$ per group follows. Given $\lambda = 7.92$ with $df = 1, 118$ and $\alpha = .05$, power is $.797$. This result is consistent with

Table 9.11 Descriptive Statistics by Group for Moderated Regression

	Control	Rejected
σ_x	3.25	3.25
σ_y	2.10	3.22
ρ	-.26	.25

the prior analysis using coefficients. Table 9.12 presents syntax for completing these calculations, and Table 9.13 presents results.

$$f^2_{modified} = \frac{\sum_j (n_j - 1)\rho_j^2 \sigma_{y_j}^2 - \dfrac{\left(\sum_j (n_j - 1)\rho_j \sigma_{y_j} \sigma_{x_j}\right)^2}{\sum_j (n_j - 1)\sigma_{x_j}^2}}{\sum_j (n_j - 2)\left(1 - \rho_j^2\right)\sigma_{y_j}^2} =$$

$$\frac{[(60*-.26^2*2.10^2) + (60*.25^2*3.22^2)] - \dfrac{[(60*-.26*2.10*3.25) + (60*.25*3.22*3.25)]^2}{(60*3.25^2) + (60*3.25^2)}}{(59*(1-.26^2)*2.10^2) + (59*(1-.25^2)*3.22^2)} = .0671$$

$$\lambda = f^2 df_{error} = .0671 * 118 = 7.92$$

Table 9.12 SPSS Syntax for Group-Based Interaction Tests

```
INPUT PROGRAM.
LOOP n=100 TO 130 by 2.
END CASE.
END LOOP.
END FILE.
END INPUT PROGRAM.
EXECUTE.

Compute Estimates = 1.
Compute Group1 = -.26.
Compute Group2 = .25.
Compute Sx1 = 3.25.
Compute Sx2= 3.25.
Compute Sy1= 2.10.
Compute Sy2= 3.22.
Compute alpha = .05.
Compute Prop_N1 = 0.5.
Compute N1 = N * Prop_N1.
Compute N2 = N * (1-Prop_N1).
If Estimates = 1 r1 = Group1.
If Estimates = 1 r2 = Group2.
If Estimates = 2 r1 = Group1*(Sx1/Sy1).
If Estimates = 2 r2 = Group2*(Sx2/Sy2).
Compute sx1_sq = Sx1**2.
Compute sx2_sq = Sx2**2.
Compute sy1_sq = Sy1**2.
Compute sy2_sq = Sy2**2.
```

For estimates: Enter 1 for correlations, enter 2 for unstandardized slopes
Group 1 is estimate for first group
Sx1 is the standard deviation of predictor for first group
Sy1 is the standard deviation of the DV for the first group
Prop_N1 is the proportion of total sample allocated to the first group; .50 produces equal sample size
The next ten or so lines perform aspects of the Formula 9.1 calculation

Table 9.12 SPSS Syntax for Group-Based Interaction Tests (*continued*)

```
Compute r1_sq = r1**2.
Compute r2_sq = r2**2.
Compute numer1 = ((n1-1)*r1_sq* sy1_sq)
 + ((n2-1)*r2_sq* sy2_sq).
Compute numer2 = (((n1-1)*r1 * sx1 * sy1)
 + ((n2-1)*r2 * sx2 * sy2))**2.
Compute numer3 = ((n1-1)* sx1_sq)+
 ((n2-1)* sx2_sq).
Compute numer = numer1 - (numer2 / numer3).
Compute denom = ((n1-2)*(1-r1_sq)* sy1_
 sq) + ((n2-2)*(1-r2_sq)* sy2_sq).
Compute f2 = numer/denom.                    Formula 9.1 calculated
Compute df1 = 1.                             here
Compute df2 = n-4.
Compute Lambda = f2 * df2.
Compute F_Table = IDF.F(1-alpha,df1, df2).
Compute Power = 1-NCDF.F(F_table,df1,
 df2, lambda).
```

```
MATRIX.
GET M /VARIABLES=n1 n2 lambda power.
print M/title = "Group Based Regression
 Interaction"/clabels = "n1" "n2"
 "Lambda" "Power"/format f9.3.
End Matrix.
```

Table 9.13 SPSS Output for Group-Based Interaction Tests

Group Based Regression Interaction			
n1	n2	Lambda	Power
60.0	60.0	7.785	.790
61.0	61.0	7.917	.797
62.0	62.0	8.049	.804
63.0	63.0	8.181	.810
64.0	64.0	8.313	.816
65.0	65.0	8.445	.822
66.0	66.0	8.577	.828
67.0	67.0	8.709	.834
68.0	68.0	8.841	.839
69.0	69.0	8.973	.845
70.0	70.0	9.105	.850

MULTIVARIATE ANALYSIS OF COVARIANCE

Multivariate analysis of covariance includes analyses with multiple dependent variables and a covariate. Conceptually, this analysis combines the MANOVA approach discussed in Chapter 7 and the ANCOVA approach presented in this chapter.

Necessary Statistics

Power analyses for MANCOVA require means for each dependent variable broken down by cell, covariate-dependent measure correlations, and standard deviations for all variables.

Factors Affecting Power

As with ANCOVA, larger sample sizes, more liberal Type I error rates, larger differences between means, and smaller standard deviations yield more power. Well-chosen covariates that do not overlap with factors improve power.

Example 9.5 Multivariate ANCOVA

The example in Table 9.14 adds a second dependent variable to the ANCOVA presented in Table 9.1, creating a design with two dependent variables. Recall that the ANCOVA examined support for AA policies based on policy type and justification for the policy while controlling for (covarying) general AA support. Pretest work on the initial study found additional items addressing organizational attractiveness (e.g., "Would you like to work at this company?") that employed the policy of interest provided unique information on policy reactions. These items were related to attitudes toward the policy (e.g., questions such as "Do you agree or disagree with the policy?") but not strongly enough (correlated at .30) to include in a scale with the attitude items. In addition, the items for desire to work showed weaker effects, roughly half the size of those found for attitudes on the effects of interest. Pretest data suggested a small correlation (.20) between desire to work at the organization and the covariate (general AA attitudes). The syntax in Table 9.14 represents the addition of the second dependent variable.

Table 9.15 provides heavily edited output for the MANCOVA. Much of the output that is not useful for the power analysis is included in the table so that readers understand what aspects of the output to ignore as well as where to find the information relevant to power for the testing hypotheses of interest.

The first set of analyses in the output present the "WITHIN CELLS Regression." This refers to tests that address whether our dependent variables have different means. The power analysis for this effect often is not of interest. However, this analysis produces considerable power if means of the dependent measures differ substantially. Similarly, the covariate power analysis (see "Regression analysis for WITHIN CELLS error term") is often not of interest but usually produces high power estimates. Be careful not to confuse these values with the ones relevant to the effects of interest.

The power estimates of interest begin with the interaction (Policy by Justify) that shows power of .73. Compared to the ANCOVA in Table 9.4, which showed power of .801,

Table 9.14 SPSS Syntax for MANCOVA

Syntax	Comments

`MATRIX DATA VARIABLES = Policy`
`Justify ROWTYPE_ Support Workat`
`General`
`  /FACTORS = Policy Justify.`
`BEGIN DATA`
`1 1 N 213 213 213`
`1 2 N 213 213 213`
`2 1 N 213 213 213`
`2 2 N 213 213 213`
`1 1 MEAN 0.85 0.85 2.5`
`1 2 MEAN 0.85 0.85 2.5`
`2 1 MEAN 0.0 0.0 2.5`
`2 2 MEAN 0.6 0.3 2.5`
`. . CORR 1`
`. . CORR .30 1`
`. . CORR .40 .20 1`
`. . STDEV 1.7 1.7 1.0`
`END DATA.`
	Following Rowtype list the DVs then the covariate; recall that order is very important to SPSS
	
	Effect for "Workat" is half the size of the support variable
	Note reorganization of correlation matrix to represent new variable order

`MANOVA Support Workat BY Policy,`
`Justify (1,2) with General`
`  /MATRIX=IN(*)`
`  /POWER exact F (.05)`
`  /CINTERVAL Joint (.95)`
`  /OMEANS = Tables (Policy`
`  Justify)`
`  /PRINT = Parameters (efsize)`
`  /DESIGN.`
	Add the variable Workat after support (can add as many DVs as desired)

the current output shows somewhat less power. This is due to the inclusion of a second dependent measure that has a smaller effect size and a positive correlation with the other dependent measure (see the discussion in Chapter 7 of the effects and patterns of correlations).

ADDITIONAL ISSUES

Reliability for Interactions

Chapter 8 included a discussion of how reliability affects power for regression analyses. Interactions between continuously scaled predictors complicate this problem. In short, with continuously scaled variables, the reliability of the interaction is a product of the reliabilities of

Table 9.15 SPSS Output for MANCOVA

EFFECT .. WITHIN CELLS Regression

Test Name	Value	Exact F Hypoth.	DF	Error DF	Sig. of F
Pillais	.16703	84.82322	2.00	846.00	.000

TEST NAME	Noncent.	Power
(All)	169.646	1.00

Regression analysis for WITHIN CELLS error term

COVARIATE	B	Beta	Std. Err.	t-Value	Sig. of t
General	.68000	.96167	.054	12.702	.000

COVARIATE	Lower -95%	CL- Upper	Noncent.	Power
General	.575	.785	161.333	1.000

EFFECT .. Policy BY Justify

Test Name	Value	Exact F Hypoth.	DF	Error DF	Sig. of F
Pillais	.00971	4.14690	2.00	846.00	.016

TEST NAME	Noncent.	Power
(All)	8.294	.73

EFFECT .. Justify

Test Name	Value	Exact F Hypoth.	DF	Error DF	Sig. of F
Pillais	.00971	4.14690	2.00	846.00	.016

TEST NAME	Noncent.	Power
(All)	8.294	.73

EFFECT .. Policy

Test Name	Value	Exact F Hypoth.	DF	Error DF	Sig. of F
Pillais	.05755	25.83201	2.00	846.00	.000

TEST NAME	Noncent.	Power
(All)	51.664	1.00

the interacting variables. Practically, this means the reliability for the interaction is usually lower than reliability for first-order effects (i.e., main effects). Formula 9.4 details the calculation for the reliability of an interaction. This calculation is accurate only for centered predictors (Aiken & West, 1991). Formula 9.5 calculates the observed effect size for the interaction after adjusting the true effect size for reliability of the measures.

$$\alpha_{1x2} = \frac{\rho_{12}^2 + \alpha_1\alpha_2}{\rho_{12}^2 + 1} \tag{9.4}$$

$$\rho_{obs} = \rho_{true}\sqrt{\alpha_{1x2}\alpha_y} \tag{9.5}$$

The first calculation example reflects a design with two continuously scaled predictors; each demonstrates strong reliability (α_1 and $\alpha_2 = .90$), as does the dependent measure ($\alpha_y = .90$). The relationship between the predictors in the population is small ($\rho_{12} = .20$), and the relationship between the interaction and the dependent measures in the population is $\rho_{true} = .10$. The value α_{1x2} represents reliability for the interaction. Even with measures demonstrating considerable reliability, the interaction reliability is lower than for the first-order effects ($\alpha_{1x2} = .82$).

$$\alpha_{1x2} = \frac{.20^2 + .90 * .90}{.20^2 + 1} = \frac{.85}{1.04} = .82$$

The interaction effect observed, as compared to the relationship in the population, is related to the reliability of both the interaction and the dependent variable. Taking these values to Formula 9.5, the correlation observed in the sample is .086, whereas the population correlation is .100. This may seem like a small reduction (.100 to .086), but it does reflect a 14% drop in effect size.

$$\rho_{obs} = .1\sqrt{.82 * .90} = .086$$

Now, consider a situation in which the reliabilities are more modest (α_1, α_2, and $\alpha_y = .80$). This produces a 28% reduction in the expected observed effect (from .100 in the population to .072 in the sample). Most researchers would not consider $\alpha = .80$ poor reliability; however, when dealing with regression interactions, even moderate departures from perfect reliability produce considerable reductions in observed effect sizes.

$$\alpha_{1x2} = \frac{.20^2 + .80 * .80}{.20^2 + 1} = .65$$

$$\rho_{obs} = .1\sqrt{.65 * .80} = .072$$

SUMMARY

This chapter addressed power analysis for ANCOVA, regression interactions, and MANCOVA. Each analysis requires estimates of correlations between variables and, for ANCOVA and MANCOVA, patterns of mean differences. For the covariate designs, a particular concern is selection of covariates that relate to the dependent measure but are unrelated to the factors. For regression interactions, several approaches exist, with all requiring some estimate of the size of the relationship between the interaction term and the dependent measure.

10

PRECISION ANALYSIS FOR CONFIDENCE INTERVALS

INTRODUCTION

Precision analyses (also known as accuracy in parameter estimation) focus on the width of confidence intervals (CIs). Precision analysis provides information that supplements power analyses and in some cases is more appropriate to research goals. Power analysis determines the likelihood of rejecting a null hypothesis given a particular population effect size, sample size, and Type I error rate. However, rejecting the null hypothesis is only half of the story. Another important issue is what range of values is reasonable to expect for the population given the sample result. A CI provides this information but can be very wide or very narrow. The wider the confidence limits are, the less precise the result is. We can design for more precise (i.e., narrower) CIs around effect sizes or raw values (e.g., mean differences). However, increasing precision requires larger samples or a better design to reduce error variability.

Power analyses and precision analyses often reflect different research goals. For example, if a researcher compared two established HIV risk reduction interventions (e.g., psychoeducational interventions and cognitive–behavioral approaches), the primary question of interest would likely be whether the treatments are differentially effective. This question fits nicely with power analysis. In the design phase, the researcher determines how large differences would have to be to be practically meaningful and then decides on an appropriate sample size using the power analysis techniques discussed in previous chapters.

Now, consider a project addressing how much a cognitive–behavioral intervention reduces HIV risk over no intervention. In this study, it would be hard to imagine that an established intervention based on sound psychological theory would not reduce risk. Instead, a better question is how much the technique reduces risk. For this question, power analysis would address the sample size necessary to support claims of a nonzero effect. More relevant is how large the effect is and what the effect might reasonably look like in the population. For example, if we wanted to estimate the population effect within 0.20 units of standard deviation, precision analyses would establish the sample size necessary to produce this estimate.

NECESSARY INFORMATION

This chapter covers precision analyses for confidence limits around mean differences, correlations, and confidence limits based on noncentral distributions for effect sizes such as Cohen's d for mean differences, R^2 *model*, and R^2 *change*. For all analyses, the primary information is the desired width of the CI (see the section on determining levels of precision). Tests involving mean differences require means (Ms), standard deviations (SDs), and proportional sample sizes (what proportion in Group 1, what proportion in Group 2) for each group. For correlations, only ρ is necessary. Confidence limits on effect sizes such as d or R^2 involve the effect size and, if relevant, degrees of freedom.

CONFIDENCE INTERVALS

Before discussing precision analysis, it is useful to review CIs. Many sources argue that CIs are superior to traditional null hypothesis significance testing procedures (see Finch, Thomason, & Cumming, 2002; Hunter, 1997; and Nickerson, 2000; see also Belia, Fidler, Williams, & Cumming, 2005, and Cumming & Finch, 2005, for a discussion of misunderstandings of CIs). Whereas null hypothesis significance tests yield a simple dichotomy of outcomes (reject or fail to reject), confidence limits provide more information and better quality of information. For instance, CIs indicate a reasonable range of values for a parameter, with values outside the confidence limits relatively implausible. In addition, the distance between the upper and lower limits of the CI indicates the precision of the result. Finally, confidence limits allow for the same decisions of reject/fail to reject the null hypothesis as significance testing procedures. Hypothesized values that fall outside the confidence limits allow for rejection of a null hypothesis at a probability corresponding to the CI (e.g., values falling outside of a 95% CI correspond to $p < .05$; values outside a 90% CI indicate $p < .10$).

One reason CIs are valuable is because CIs provide information not clearly provided by other statistical values. Imagine the following situations:

> Situation 1: Group 1 ($M = 5.0$; $SD = 1.4$) outperformed Group 2 ($M = 3.2$; $SD = 1.5$), $t(10) = 2.23$, $p < .05$, $d = 1.29$.
>
> Situation 2: Group 1 ($M = 5.0$; $SD = 1.4$) outperformed Group 2 ($M = 3.2$; $SD = 1.5$), 95% CI $0.0003 \leq (\mu_1 - \mu_2) \leq 3.700$, $d = 1.29$.

The first situation shows a statistically significant effect and a large effect size. The second situation represents the same differences between the groups and a CI that suggests plausible values for the mean differences in the population are somewhere between large (3.7 points) and miniscule (0.0003 points). Both examples reflect the same data, but the CI presentation clearly suggests limited confidence regarding the size of the differences between the two groups. A narrower CI (e.g., ranging from 1.5 to 2.1) supports a stronger conclusion about how much the groups likely differ in the population. Precision analysis allows for determination of sample size requirements that produce confidence limits of a desired width.

TYPES OF CONFIDENCE INTERVALS

Interval estimates around mean differences are included in most statistical packages. Construct this sort of interval by taking the differences between two sample means plus or minus margin of error. For example, for the CI around the difference between two means, the margin of error involves a t-statistic corresponding to the confidence level multiplied by an index of standard error. Intervals of this type are often termed *central intervals* as their calculation involves the central t-distribution.

Less commonly, interval estimates around effect sizes (e.g., Thompson, 2002) are presented. Use of such values fits nicely with recommendations to present effect sizes and confidence limits (e.g., Wilkinson & Task Force on Statistical Inference, 1999), so I expect presentation of these values to become increasingly common. A CI around an effect size yields information about likely values for the effect size in the population. This concept is appealing as it opens the door to determining what effect sizes are likely or unlikely for the population. For example, a CI of 0.40 to 0.80 drawn around an observed effect size d suggests that it would be unlikely for the standardized difference between means in the population to be smaller than 0.40.

Calculation of CIs around effect sizes requires specialized software or advanced programming in SPSS or other packages because these intervals involve noncentral distributions that require iterative procedures to achieve accurate calculations. That is, there is no simple formula for deriving CIs for noncentral distributions, and most statistical packages do not include built-in functions for direct calculations. A full explanation of the calculation of these intervals is outside the scope of this book. Both Smithson (2003) and Kelley and Rausch (2006) provided calculation details.

CONFIDENCE LIMITS AROUND
DIFFERENCES BETWEEN MEANS

For independent group comparisons, Formula 10.1 presents the 95% CI around the difference between two means. The right-hand side of the formula (following the ± symbol) defines the precision. This is commonly termed the *margin of error*. Sample size exerts considerable influence over the standard error of the differences between means. As sample size rises, the standard error decreases, making for a smaller margin of error. Larger samples therefore give results that are more precise.

Formula 10.1 notes a 95% CI. For other CIs (e.g., 99%), simply replace $t_{.05}$ with the t-value corresponding to the appropriate interval. For example, a 99% CI would use $t_{.01}$, whereas a 90% CI uses $t_{.10}$. Regarding notation, I use $t_{.05,\,2\text{-tailed}}$ to represent the t-value in Formula 10.1. This value corresponds to the two-tailed critical value for t with $\alpha = .05$. Other sources might note this value as $t_{.975}$, indicating the t-value at which or below which 97.5% of the distribution falls.

$$(\bar{x}_1 - \bar{x}_2) \pm t_{.05,2-\text{tailed}} s_{\bar{x}_1 - \bar{x}_2} \qquad (10.1)$$

In Chapter 3, one example examined a study designed to detect a difference between exam score means of 2.0 points (corresponding to $d = 0.40$) when comparing students who completed a computer tutorial to those completing a standard laboratory assignment. In that example, a sample of $n = 99$ per group (198 overall) was necessary to achieve power of .80 to detect a 2.0-point mean differences between the groups. Imagine that for this study, we instead wanted to make particular claims regarding how much improvement could reasonably be expected in the population (i.e., an estimate of the true effect).

The syntax provided in Table 10.1 creates a series of CIs based on the mean difference ($\mu_1 - \mu_2 = 2.0$) shown in the Chapter 3 example. This was the minimum difference between means termed meaningful for that example. For precision analysis, the difference between the means does not impact the precision of the result. Regardless of the difference between means in the sample, given that the expected population standard deviations are accurate, the precision of the interval remains the same.

In thinking about precision, a good place to begin is consideration of the standard deviation. The present example involves a measure with an expected standard deviation of 5.0. Thinking about these values as they relate to the mean difference of 2.0 provides additional context. If our sample mean differed by 2.0, an interval width of 4.0 would correspond to a 95% CI around $\mu_1 - \mu_2$ that ranged from 0.0 to 4.0. An interval width of 2.0 would produce a 95% CI around $\mu_1 - \mu_2$ that ranged from 1.0 to 3.0. If our standard deviation were 20.0, analyses producing these intervals would suggest greater precision. For example, with a standard deviation of 5.0, a width of 4.0 points would be large in comparison to a width of 4.0 when the standard deviation is 20.0.

Before turning to the analysis, it is important to review what power tells us and what confidence limits tell us in the context of this example. In Chapter 3, we determined that if the true population difference was 2.0 points (i.e., the tutorial improved scores by 2.0 points) that 80% of the samples drawn from this population with $n = 99$ per group would allow for rejection of the null hypothesis. Confidence limits drawn around our sample provide different information. Specifically, CIs indicate what sort of population mean differences might reasonably produce the differences observed in the sample. Even with adequate power to detect a 2.0-point difference, we may not be able to conclude that a difference of less than 2.0 points is unlikely in the population. For example, if the sample means differed by 3.5 points (considerably larger than what we termed a "meaningful" difference), a 95% CI with an interval width of 4.0 would range from 1.5 to 5.5. Although the CI clearly rules out conclusions of no difference between the means ($\mu_1 - \mu_2 = 0$), it does not rule out differences that are smaller than meaningful [$1.5 \leq (\mu_1 - \mu_2) < 2.0$].

The syntax in Table 10.1 produces the output in Table 10.2. With 100 participants per group and a mean difference of 2.0 points found in the sample, the CI for the population difference would range from 0.6 to 3.4. That is, reasonable estimates of the actual difference between the population means includes not only some small differences (e.g., 0.6) but also some large ones (e.g., 3.4). The table provides the sample size for each group (N1, N2), the lower limit of the CI (LL in the table), the upper

Table 10.1 Syntax for Confidence Interval Around Mean Differences Precision Analysis

Syntax	Comments
`INPUT PROGRAM.`	
`LOOP n=100 TO 1600 by 100.`	Sets the sample sizes; 10 is the
`END CASE.`	starting point, 1600 is the
`END LOOP.`	endpoint
`END FILE.`	
`END INPUT PROGRAM.`	
`EXECUTE .`	
`Compute Prop_N1 = 0.50.`	Sets the proportional sample size in each group; use 0.50 for equal n
`Compute M1 = 2.`	Use M1 and M2 to establish the
`Compute M2 = 0.`	mean differences (e.g., 2 − 0 =
`Compute S1 = 5.`	2.0 difference)
`Compute S2 = 5.`	SDs for each group; these get pooled later
`Compute Conf = .95.`	This is the CI, 95% in this case
`Compute N1 = N * Prop_N1.`	(Do not change syntax below)
`Compute N2 = N * (1-Prop_N1).`	Calculates sample sizes for each
`Compute df = n1 + n2 -2.`	group
`Compute var1 = s1*s1.`	
`Compute var2 = s2*s2.`	
`Compute nxs1 = (n1-1)*(var1).`	
`Compute nxs2 = (n2-1)*(var2).`	
`Compute s2p = (nxs1+nxs2)/(df).`	
`Compute sp = sqrt(s2p).`	Pooled SD
`Compute d = (M1-M2)/sp.`	Effect size
`Compute MeanDiff = M1-M2.`	
`Compute sx1 = sp/sqrt(n1).`	
`Compute sx2 = sp/sqrt(n2).`	
`Compute sx1x2 = sqrt(sx1**2+sx2**2).`	Standard error of the differences
`Compute fail = ((1-conf)/2)+conf.`	
`Compute t_table = IDF.t(fail,df).`	Tabled t-value calculated
`Compute MOE = sx1x2 * t_table.`	Calculates the margin of error
`Compute LL_MeanDiff = MeanDiff- MOE.`	Lower limit of the CI
`Compute UL_MeanDiff = MeanDiff+ MOE.`	Upper limit of the CI
`Compute Precision_MeanDiff = UL_MeanDiff-LL_MeanDiff.`	Difference between the UL and LL yields the precision or interval width
`Compute alpha = 1-conf.`	
`Compute fail2 = 1-(alpha/2).`	
`Compute tval = meandiff / sx1x2.`	
`Compute t_table = IDF.t(fail2,df).`	

Table 10.1 Syntax for Confidence Interval Around Mean Differences Precision Analysis (continued)

Syntax	Comments
Compute Power = 1-NCDF.t (t_table,df,tval). EXECUTE. MATRIX. GET M /VARIABLES=n1 n2 LL_ MeanDiff UL_MeanDiff Precision_ MeanDiff Power. print M/title = "Precision Analysis for Mean Differences"/ clabels = "N1" "N2" "LL" "UL" "Precise" "Power"/format f10.4. End Matrix.	Section creates output for values of interest; if you want to see other values from the above calculations, you can go to the data file

limit (UL in the table), and the precision of the interval (precise), which is simply the range between the upper limit and the lower. For comparison, the syntax produces power as well. Please note that you cannot accurately convert the CI presented in this table to effect size intervals by dividing the mean values by the pooled standard deviation (discussed in more detail in "Confidence Intervals Around Effect Sizes").

Table 10.2 Output for Precision Around Mean Difference of 2.0 Points

		Precision Analysis for Mean Differences			
N1	N2	LL	UL	Precise	Power
50.0	50.0	.0155	3.9845	3.9689	.5081
100.0	100.0	.6056	3.3944	2.7889	.8036
150.0	150.0	.8638	3.1362	2.2724	.9323
200.0	200.0	1.0170	2.9830	1.9659	.9788
250.0	250.0	1.1213	2.8787	1.7573	.9939
300.0	300.0	1.1982	2.8018	1.6035	.9983
350.0	350.0	1.2579	2.7421	1.4842	.9996
400.0	400.0	1.3060	2.6940	1.3880	.9999
450.0	450.0	1.3458	2.6542	1.3084	1.0000
500.0	500.0	1.3795	2.6205	1.2411	1.0000
550.0	550.0	1.4084	2.5916	1.1832	1.0000
600.0	600.0	1.4336	2.5664	1.1327	1.0000
650.0	650.0	1.4559	2.5441	1.0882	1.0000
700.0	700.0	1.4757	2.5243	1.0486	1.0000
750.0	750.0	1.4935	2.5065	1.0129	1.0000
800.0	800.0	1.5096	2.4904	.9807	1.0000

DETERMINING LEVELS OF PRECISION

Unlike power analysis, for which a power of .80 is often considered a standard, there is no de facto standard for precision analysis. The desired level of precision can be expected to vary widely across applications, but a primary issue to consider for all situations is the consequence of a lack of precision. For example, a study of the absorption of a drug likely requires considerable precision as this information lends itself to dosage decisions. However, for most behavioral science fields, decisions regarding determination of an adequate level of precision are less clear. In the previous example, imagine we designed for a CI width of 2.0, and the sample results indicated that the true difference between the computer tutorial and standard laboratory was between 1.0 and 3.0 points of improvement in the population. In a worst-case scenario, we would find a difference of 1.0 point favoring the computer tutorial. A 1.0-point improvement is less than desirable given that implementation of the tutorial assignment involves several hours of work from instructors.

Now, compare the computer tutorial situation to one involving estimates of drug absorption. Poor precision estimates could lead to absorption that is less than desired. In this case, patients end up with less medicine than intended. Similarly, absorption might be greater than expected, potentially causing overdose. Clearly, considerable precision is required as the cost of an imprecise estimate may have serious health consequences for patients. In this context, the consequences of imprecision in the computer tutorial example are minor.

CONFIDENCE INTERVALS AROUND EFFECT SIZES

An exciting development in the quantitative psychological literature is the specification of techniques to calculate confidence limits on effect size estimates. Confidence limits for effect sizes provide both an index of the likely population value of the effect size and valuable information for comparing standardized values across completed studies.

When I first heard the term *confidence interval around an effect size*, my initial thought was that calculation involved taking a regular CI, such as one around mean differences as described in the previous section, and converting it to an effect size CI by dividing the lower and upper limits of the mean difference by the standard deviation. This approach sometimes provides a reasonable approximation, but an accurate calculation requires far more work. Most sources simply say something to the effect of "let the computer do this." These calculations are outside the scope of the present text, but Steiger and Fouladi (1997) and Kelley (2007a) offered considerable insight on the concepts and calculations.

The sections that follow present computer-based approaches for each analysis.

Precision analysis for d uses the syntax in Table 10.3 and produces an interval around Cohen's d for the example in the mean difference section. This syntax uses, for some calculations, a file from Michael Smithson's *Confidence Intervals* Web page (called NoncT2.sps; see Chapter 11 for more information on this resource, http://psychology3. anu.edu.au/people/smithson/details/CIstuff/CI.html, and Smithson, 2003). The CI for the population effect size shown in Table 10.4 for n = 100 per group ranges from 0.1194 to 0.6795. This lower limit indicates that our CI (if the sample produced d = 0.40) would rule out only very small population effect sizes (i.e., anything less than 0.1194).

As a brief aside, compare the CI around the effect sizes (0.1194, 0.6795) to the interval for the mean differences (0.6056, 3.3944). Taking the mean differences and dividing by the standard deviation of 5.0 does not provide exact confidence limits around the effect size. Dividing the mean difference limits by the standard deviation yields a lower limit of 0.1211 and an upper limit of 0.6789. These values are close to the confidence limits for the effect size but are not exact. CIs around mean differences are constructed using a central t-distribution, whereas the effect size intervals use the noncentral t distribution. As noted in Chapters 2 and 3, with smaller samples, estimates based on the central t diverge considerably from estimates based on noncentral distributions.

Results shown in Table 10.4 provide a great deal of information. For example, an interval that is precise to 0.20 units requires a sample of 750 participants per group. That is a very large sample, but it does provide a particularly narrow range of effect sizes. Note also that the power for that sample size is 1.000, meaning that if the effect size in the population was d = 0.40 that virtually every sample of this size would return a significant result.

Another approach is to design for an interval that excludes a certain effect. For example, Cohen (1988) suggests d = 0.20 as the criterion for a small effect. Despite the reluctance expressed throughout this book to design around small, medium, and large effect size conventions, an attractive strategy for CIs is to find the sample size that yields a CI for which the lower limit exceeds d = 0.20. This strategy allows for claims that, at worst, the effect was small. Of course, whether d = 0.20 is meaningful is another issue. A sample of n = 200 per group corresponds to a result for which the lower limit of the effect size exceeds d = 0.20. This reflects addition of 200 participants (100 per group) over that necessary to obtain power of .80. This increase in sample size achieved a change

Table 10.3 Syntax for Confidence Interval Around Cohen's *d* Precision Analysis

Syntax	Comments
`LOOP n=100 TO 2000 by 100.`	Input desired sample sizes
`END CASE.`	
`END LOOP.`	
`END FILE.`	
`END INPUT PROGRAM.`	
`EXECUTE .`	
`Compute d = .40.`	Effect size for population
`Compute Conf = .95.`	Desired CI
`Compute Prop_N1 = 0.50.`	Proportion in Group 1
`Compute N1 = N * Prop_N1.`	No modifications here or below
`Compute N2 = N *` `(1-Prop_N1).`	
`Compute df = n1 + n2 -2.`	TVAL here also corresponds to the
`Compute TVAL =`	noncentrality value (δ)
`D*SQRT(N1*N2/(N1+N2)).`	Brings in external file for calculations
`EXECUTE.`	Lower limit of the CI
`INCLUDE FILE='d:\Power\`	Upper limit
`NoncT2.sps'.`	Precision is the distance between the
`Compute LL_D = LC2/`	limits
`SQRT(N1*N2/(N1+N2)).`	
`Compute UL_D = UC2/`	
`SQRT(N1*N2/(N1+N2)).`	
`Compute Precision_D = UL_D-`	
`LL_D.`	
`Compute alpha = 1-conf.`	
`Compute fail = 1-(alpha/2).`	
`Compute t_table =`	
`IDF.t(fail,df).`	
`Compute Power = 1-NCDF.t`	
`(t_table,df,tval).`	
`execute.`	
`MATRIX.`	
`GET M /VARIABLES=n1 n2 LL_D UL_D Precision Power .`	
`print M/title = "Precision Analysis for Cohen's d"/`	
`clabels = "N1" "N2" "LL" "UL" "Precise" "Power" /format`	
`f10.4.`	
`End Matrix.`	
`MATRIX.`	

Table 10.4 Output for Precision Around Cohen's *d*

	Precision	Analysis	for	Cohen's d	
N1	**N2**	**LL**	**UL**	**Precise**	**Power**
50.0	50.0	.0031	.7950	.7918	.5081
100.0	100.0	.1194	.6795	.5601	.8036
150.0	150.0	.1710	.6283	.4573	.9323
200.0	200.0	.2018	.5977	.3959	.9788
250.0	250.0	.2228	.5769	.3541	.9939
300.0	300.0	.2382	.5615	.3233	.9983
350.0	350.0	.2502	.5495	.2993	.9996
400.0	400.0	.2600	.5398	.2799	.9999
450.0	450.0	.2680	.5319	.2639	1.0000
500.0	500.0	.2747	.5251	.2504	1.0000
550.0	550.0	.2806	.5193	.2387	1.0000
600.0	600.0	.2856	.5142	.2286	1.0000
650.0	650.0	.2901	.5097	.2196	1.0000
700.0	700.0	.2941	.5057	.2116	1.0000
750.0	750.0	.2978	.5021	.2044	1.0000
800.0	800.0	.3010	.4989	.1979	1.0000
850.0	850.0	.3039	.4960	.1921	1.0000
900.0	900.0	.3066	.4933	.1866	1.0000
950.0	950.0	.3091	.4908	.1816	1.0000
1000.0	1000.0	.3114	.4885	.1771	1.0000

of 0.1642 in precision (0.5601 − 0.3959). Improving the precision by that much again (to roughly .23), requires nearly 600 participants per group, an increase of 800 participants (see sample for N1 and N2 = 600). A rough rule of thumb is that to cut error in half we need to quadruple the sample size.

PRECISION FOR A CORRELATION

Another form of CI around an effect size is the CI around ρ, the population correlation. Formula 10.2 defines this CI. The value z_ρ reflects the Fisher-transformed correlation (see Formula 4.3). This approach uses a central distribution (the normal distribution), so it is possible to calculate the CI by hand. The part of the equation with 1 over the square root of the sample size minus 3 is often termed the *standard deviation of Fisher's z or sd$_z$*. The final step in constructing this interval is to convert values back to correlation units using Formula 10.3. This calculation reverses the Fisher's transformation (see Chapter 4 for examples discussion of the transformations). As before, I present a 95% CI. To produce other intervals, simply replace $z_{.05}$ with the value of interest. For example, a 99% CI would use $z_{.01}$, whereas a 90% CI uses $z_{.10}$.

$$z_\rho \pm z_{.05} \frac{1}{\sqrt{n-3}} \tag{10.2}$$

$$\rho = \frac{e^{2z_\rho} - 1}{e^{2z_\rho} + 1} \tag{10.3}$$

Chapter 4 presented an example examining the correlation between implicit attitudes and aggression for which a meaningful correlation was .30. In that example, a sample of 84 participants produced a power of .80. Extending this example, imagine that we wanted a correlation that was precise to .10 in either direction (precision would be .20 in this case). Table 10.5 includes syntax for completing this calculation. As with the other files, this syntax may also be used for calculation of confidence limits for existing data.

The output in Table 10.6 provides the precision estimates and power. As with the example in the preceding paragraph, even when power is high, CIs remain wide. The desired level of precision of .20 requires a sample of over 300 participants.

An important feature of the correlation CI (as well as any CI based on effect sizes) is that the intervals are not symmetrical. Take, for example, the interval for $n = 80$. The interval, based on a correlation of .30, ranges from .09 to .48. Because of asymmetry of the sampling distribution, the lower limit is .21 units below .30, but the upper limit is .18 above.

PRECISION FOR R^2 CHANGE

In Chapter 8, an example addressed a situation for which R^2 *model* = .467 and R^2 *change* = .307. R^2 *change* reflected the prediction of behavioral intentions relevant to affirmative action policies from internal and external motivations to control prejudice (two variables) after controlling for modern racism (one variable). The R^2 *model* value is the prediction afforded by all three variables. A sample of 24 participants yielded power of .81 for R^2 *change*. The syntax shown in Table 10.7 examines confidence limits on this R^2 *change*, starting with $n = 24$ and including additional values to show a range of limits. The syntax presented here uses a fixed-effects approach. For information on precision for random effects, see the work of Kelley (2008).

Table 10.5 Syntax for Confidence Interval Around Correlation Precision Analysis

Syntax	Comments
`LOOP n=80 TO 400 by 20.`	As before, enter desired range of
`END CASE.`	sample size
`END LOOP.`	
`END FILE.`	
`END INPUT PROGRAM.`	
`EXECUTE .`	
`Compute r = 0.30.`	Enter population correlation
`Compute Conf = .95.`	Enter CI of interest
`Compute prob_1 = ((1-Conf)/2)+Conf.`	No changes necessary here or
`Compute z_tabled =IDF.`	below
` NORMAL(prob_1,0,1).`	
`Compute z_r = 0.5 * (Ln((1 + r) /`	This is the Fisher's
` (1 - r))).`	transformation
`Compute sdz = Sqrt(1 / (n - 3)).`	Standard deviation of the
`Compute LL_Zr = z_r`	correlation
` - (sdz*z_tabled).`	Limits for the CI; this is around
`Compute UL_Zr = z_r +`	the Fisher-transformed
` (sdz*z_tabled).`	correlation using Formula 10.2
`Compute LL_r = (exp(2*LL_Zr)-1) /`	Values converted back to
` (exp(2*LL_Zr)+1).`	correlation units using
`Compute UL_r = (exp(2*UL_Zr)-1) /`	Formula 10.3
` (exp(2*UL_Zr)+1).`	
`Compute Precision = UL_r - LL_r.`	Difference between limits
`Compute t = (r*((n-2)**.5))/`	
` ((1-(r**2))**.5).`	
`Compute d = 2*r/((1-(r**2))**.5).`	
`Compute delta = (d*sqrt(n))/2.`	
`Compute alpha = 1-conf.`	
`Compute alpha_tails = alpha/2.`	
`Compute fail = 1-alpha_tails.`	
`Compute df = n-2.`	
`Compute t_table = IDF.t(fail,df) .`	
`Compute Power = 1-NCDF.t(t_`	
` table,df,delta) .`	
`execute.`	
`MATRIX.`	
`GET M /VARIABLES=n LL_r UL_r Precision Power .`	
`print M/title = "Precision Analysis for Correlation"/`	
` clabels = "N" "LL" "UL" "Precise" "Power"/format f10.4.`	
`End Matrix.`	

Table 10.6 Output for Confidence Interval Around Correlation Precision Analysis

Precision Analysis for Correlation				
N	LL	UL	Precise	Power
80.0	.0859	.4876	.4016	.7933
100.0	.1101	.4688	.3587	.8757
120.0	.1276	.4548	.3272	.9274
140.0	.1411	.4438	.3027	.9586
160.0	.1519	.4349	.2830	.9769
180.0	.1608	.4275	.2667	.9873
200.0	.1683	.4212	.2529	.9932
220.0	.1747	.4158	.2411	.9964
240.0	.1802	.4110	.2308	.9981
260.0	.1851	.4068	.2217	.9990
280.0	.1894	.4030	.2136	.9995
300.0	.1933	.3997	.2063	.9997
320.0	.1968	.3966	.1998	.9999
340.0	.2000	.3938	.1938	.9999
360.0	.2029	.3912	.1883	1.0000
380.0	.2056	.3889	.1833	1.0000
400.0	.2081	.3867	.1786	1.0000

Of particular interest is the result for $n = 24$, shown in Table 10.8. In the example from Chapter 8, a sample of 24 participants gave adequate power to detect a meaningful effect as specified. However, if the R^2 *change* were .307, the confidence limits produced by that sample size range from approximately .03 to .57. This interval is quite wide, and the lower limit is uninspiring. This interval suggests the variance explained by the predictors could be very large or near zero in the population. Doubling the sample size produces a considerably more precise interval (ranging from .13 to .52).

PRECISION FOR R^2 *MODEL*

Precision analysis for R^2 *model* is nearly identical to that for change. In the same example as used for R^2 *change*, R^2 *model* was .467. Table 10.9 presents syntax for precision around R^2 *model*. To save space, this table omits much of the syntax. As with R^2 *change*, the syntax in this table uses a fixed-effects approach.

SUPPORTING NULL HYPOTHESES

Analyses of precision provide a context for discussion of designing to support null hypotheses. Of course, "support the null hypothesis" is usually not a valid statement because the null generally refers to a

Table 10.7 Syntax for Precision Analysis Around R^2 *Change*

Syntax	Comments
| ```
INPUT PROGRAM.
LOOP n=24 TO 80 by 4.
END CASE.
END LOOP.
END FILE.
END INPUT PROGRAM.
EXECUTE .
``` | Sample values as before |
| ```
Compute r2model = .467.
``` | Full model value for $R^2$ |
| ```
Compute r2change = .307.
``` | Value for $R^2$ *change* |
| ```
Compute modelpred = 3.
``` | *df* for the model |
| ```
Compute changepred = 2.
``` | *df* for the change |
| ```
Compute conf = .95.
``` | Desired CI |
| ```
Compute alpha = 1-conf.
``` | No changes here or below (except |
| ```
Compute df_change = changepred.
Compute df_denom = (n - modelpred)
 -1.
Compute k2 = 1 - r2model.
Compute multiplier = df_denom.
Compute f2 = r2change/k2.
Compute lambda = f2*multiplier .
Compute F_Table = IDF.F(conf,df_
change,df_denom) .
Compute power1 = 1 - NCDF.F(F_
Table,df_change,df_denom,Lambda) .
Compute FVAL = f2 *(df_denom/
df_change).
Compute df1=df_change.
Compute df2=df_denom.
``` | for the included statement) |
| ```
INCLUDE FILE='d:\Power\NoncF3.
sps'.
Compute Precision = UR2-LR2.
EXECUTE.
``` | Brings in external file; make sure the directory matches where you placed the file |
| ```
MATRIX.
GET M /VARIABLES=n LR2 UR2 Precision Power1.
print M/title = "Precision Analysis for R2 Change (or
Model)"/clabels = "N" "LL" "UL" "Precise" "Power"/format
f10.4.
End Matrix.
``` | |

Table 10.8 Output for Precision Analysis Around R^2 *Change*

		Precision Analysis for R2 Change		
N	LL	UL	Precise	Power
24.0	.0272	.5656	.5385	.8103
28.0	.0513	.5554	.5041	.8875
32.0	.0719	.5467	.4747	.9356
36.0	.0894	.5391	.4497	.9643
40.0	.1046	.5325	.4279	.9807
44.0	.1179	.5266	.4087	.9898
48.0	.1295	.5213	.3918	.9947
52.0	.1396	.5166	.3770	.9973
56.0	.1488	.5123	.3635	.9987
60.0	.1571	.5083	.3513	.9993
64.0	.1644	.5047	.3403	.9997
68.0	.1711	.5014	.3303	.9998
72.0	.1773	.4983	.3210	.9999
76.0	.1829	.4954	.3125	1.0000
80.0	.1880	.4927	.3046	1.0000

statement that is rarely true (see Loftus, 1996). For example, a typical null hypothesis for a two-group comparison states that the difference between the two groups is exactly zero. In most situations, a difference of exactly zero is not plausible. More importantly, it does not usually matter if the group means are exactly equal, or if they are merely very similar in the population. It is far more important to be able to determine if the means differ by enough to be practically important.

Differing enough to be important or meaningful is the key to testing claims of support for the null hypothesis. For example, if we establish that a reasonable range of estimates (i.e., confidence limits) for the mean differences in the population fall below the criteria set for a meaningful difference, then there is support for the conclusion that the differences between groups are likely not large enough to matter. Practically, this conclusion indicates that the differences between the groups are not deviant enough from zero to suggest a meaningfully important difference in the population.

The first step in this process is to determine a value that reflects the smallest meaningful difference between the groups. This is the same process as for power analyses focusing on differences. The next step is to establish the minimum precision necessary to construct a CI that excludes certain effects. Returning to the example from Chapter 3, we determined that a difference favoring a tutorial assignment over a standard assignment would have to be 2.0 points

Table 10.9 Syntax and Output for R^2 *Model* Precision Analysis

```
Compute r2model = .467.
Compute modelpred = 3.
Compute conf = .95.
(rest of syntax deleted)
```

Precision Analysis for R2 Model

N	LL	UL	Precise	Power
24.0	.0693	.6242	.5549	.9041
28.0	.1066	.6180	.5114	.9570
32.0	.1364	.6124	.4760	.9819
36.0	.1610	.6074	.4464	.9928
40.0	.1815	.6029	.4214	.9972
44.0	.1986	.5989	.4002	.9990
48.0	.2135	.5952	.3817	.9996
52.0	.2265	.5918	.3653	.9999
56.0	.2376	.5887	.3511	1.0000
60.0	.2476	.5858	.3383	1.0000
64.0	.2565	.5832	.3267	1.0000
68.0	.2645	.5807	.3161	1.0000
72.0	.2717	.5784	.3067	1.0000
76.0	.2783	.5762	.2979	1.0000
80.0	.2843	.5742	.2899	1.0000
84.0	.2898	.5722	.2825	1.0000
88.0	.2949	.5704	.2756	1.0000
92.0	.2996	.5687	.2691	1.0000
96.0	.3040	.5671	.2631	1.0000
100.0	.3081	.5655	.2575	1.0000

or more to be meaningful given the investment of instructor time for implementation. An analysis that produces a CI that falls entirely below 2.0 would suggest that the tutorial was not effective enough to improve learning meaningfully.

One approach to this question explores precision for a situation for which the null is true (means exactly equal in the population). This is not a realistic expectation, but it does provide some focus for the analysis. This analysis involves minor modifications to the syntax in Table 10.1, changing it so that the means for both groups are equal. Means and standard deviations for the syntax appear in Table 10.10 (the rest is omitted as it is identical to Table 10.1).

The precision values found in Table 10.10 are particularly useful in helping to determine sample size. First, note that at 50 participants per group, the CI excludes the meaningful difference of 2.0. This result

Table 10.10 Edited Syntax and Output for Mean Difference "Support-the-Null" Analysis

```
(Syntax Modification)
Compute M1 = 0.
Compute M2 = 0.
Compute S1 = 5.
Compute S2 = 5.
```

Precision Analysis for Mean Differences

N1	N2	LL	UL	Precise	Power
50.0	50.0	-1.9845	1.9845	3.9689	.0500
100.0	100.0	-1.3944	1.3944	2.7889	.0500
150.0	150.0	-1.1362	1.1362	2.2724	.0500
200.0	200.0	-.9830	.9830	1.9659	.0500
250.0	250.0	-.8787	.8787	1.7573	.0500
300.0	300.0	-.8018	.8018	1.6035	.0500
350.0	350.0	-.7421	.7421	1.4842	.0500
400.0	400.0	-.6940	.6940	1.3880	.0500
450.0	450.0	-.6542	.6542	1.3084	.0500
500.0	500.0	-.6205	.6205	1.2411	.0500
550.0	550.0	-.5916	.5916	1.1832	.0500
600.0	600.0	-.5664	.5664	1.1327	.0500
650.0	650.0	-.5441	.5441	1.0882	.0500
700.0	700.0	-.5243	.5243	1.0486	.0500
750.0	750.0	-.5065	.5065	1.0129	.0500
800.0	800.0	-.4904	.4904	.9807	.0500
3050.0	3050.0	-.2510	.2510	.5020	.0500
4800.0	4800.0	-.2001	.2001	.4001	.0500
8525.0	8525.0	-.1501	.1501	.3002	.0500
19200.0	19200.0	-.1000	.1000	.2000	.0500

suggests that if differences existed between the groups, they likely were not big enough to be meaningful. However, note that 50 participants per group yield this result only when the sample means are equal. For a study designed to conclude that the groups do not differ, a design with 50 people per group provides enough precision only if the means differ by zero or the relationship is in the opposite direction in the sample.

Of course, this discussion fails to address how much precision we need. The most practical answer when dealing with supporting null results is often how much precision can be afforded. Note that with 200 participants per group, precision would be slightly less than 2.0 points. This level of precision means that sampled differences between means of less than a single point produce a result that supports a claim of no meaningful difference. To double precision (i.e., reducing the width of the CI by half) requires roughly 800 additional participants per group. For reference, the bottom of Table 10.10 shows the sample size necessary for precision of 0.5, 0.4, 0.3, and 0.2.

The basic approach outlined in this section is applicable to any of the precision analyses appearing in this chapter. Simply choose a meaningful effect size and then determine precision.

One final note on the "support-the-null" approach. As the example in this section highlights, ruling out small effects requires large samples. To demonstrate equivalency between groups, be clear on the resources required before beginning.

ADDITIONAL ISSUES

In this section, I address the balance between precision and sample size and designing for certainty of estimates. It is important to note that the present chapter scratches the surface on confidence limits on effect sizes and precision analysis. There are several outstanding resources on this topic. The MBESS package for R provides tools for many CI calculations (see also Kelley, 2007b; Kelley & Maxwell, 2003). In addition, Michael Smithson's Web site and text (2003) provide protocols that were central to many of the analyses in this chapter.

Precision Versus Sample Size

Examining the relationship between precision and sample size is a useful guide to determining reasonable levels of precision. For tests involving mean differences, doubling precision requires quadrupling sample size. For example, in Table 10.1, a sample of 50 participants per group produces a CI with a roughly 4.0-point width (approximately 0 to 4.0). An interval that is twice as precise (i.e., the width is 2.0) requires a sample of 200 per group. To obtain an interval twice as precise as found for $n = 200$ per group requires $n = 800$ per group.

The relationship is similar for precision estimates of d and r. Figure 10.1 presents precision for large effects, but the same general pattern holds for small and medium effects. For d, precision falls below 0.5 at around $n = 275$, falls to 0.4 around $n = 400$, drops to 0.3 near $n = 700$, but does not hit 0.2 until roughly $n = 1,600$. For r, precision is about .20 at $n = 275$, near .15 at $n = 500$, about .10 at $n = 1,100$, and does not reach .05 until around $n = 4500$.

The information in Table 10.1 and Figure 10.1 should inform decisions about designing for greater precision. That is, if you want a more precise result and can afford another 100 participants, it is a great investment when moving from $n = 100$ to $n = 200$. However, a similar

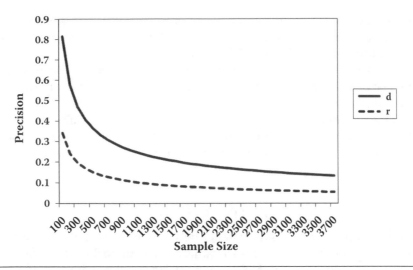

Figure 10.1 Precision and sample size.

investment returns very little added precision when moving from $n = 2,000$ to $n = 2,100$.

Precision and Certainty

Sample size estimates for effect sizes determined through precision analyses may be adjusted to ensure a level of certainty that the CI obtained in a sample is no wider than desired. For example, this approach allows for designs in which we are 99% certain that the interval obtained is no wider than our desired value for a 95% CI around d (see Kelley & Rausch, 2006, for a technical explanation). Table 10.11 presents a rough guide to increasing sample size to achieve various levels of certainty for precision of Cohen's d. For exact values, the MBESS package referenced in Chapter 11 accomplishes these calculations.

The values listed in Table 10.11 may be used in conjunction with sample size estimates drawn from the SPSS approaches presented. The SPSS approaches correspond to the "not specified" values in the table. If you wish to design for increased certainty, take the sample size estimate from SPSS and increase it by the percentage listed in the table. For example, if we wanted to increase certainty to 99% for a 95% CI around an effect size with $d = 0.50$ with a width of 0.8, the first step would be to determine the sample size for a certainty not specified. Using the syntax in Table 10.4, this precision corresponds to a sample size of $n = 100$ ($n = 50$ per group). Next, find the percentage increase listed in Table 10.11 for

Table 10.11 Percentage Sample Size Increase per Group to Achieve 80% and 99% Certainty

CI Width	Not Specified to 80%			Not Specified to 99%		
	$d = 0.2$	$d = 0.5$	$d = 0.8$	$d = 0.2$	$d = 0.5$	$d = 0.8$
0.10	0.13	0.25	0.39	0.36	0.76	1.14
0.20	0.13	0.50	0.84	0.78	1.64	2.41
0.30	0.29	0.85	1.36	1.16	2.55	3.79
0.40	0.52	1.01	1.92	1.55	3.52	5.29
0.50	0.81	1.57	2.26	2.42	4.72	6.77
0.60	1.16	1.12	2.15	3.49	5.62	8.60
0.70	0.00	3.08	2.94	3.13	7.69	10.29
0.80	0.00	2.00	3.85	4.08	10.00	13.46
0.90	0.00	2.50	2.38	5.13	10.00	11.90
1.00	3.23	3.13	2.94	9.68	12.50	14.71

$d = 0.50$. The listed value for moving from an unspecified certainty to 99% certainty is 10.00%. Applied to our sample of $n = 100$, this reflects a total increase of $n = 10$ for a final sample of 110 participants.

Gaining certainty, even at the 99% level, does not involve large proportional increases in sample size. Although there are situations that require 10% or larger increases in sample size, most are those with particularly wide CIs. Situations with large CIs around effect sizes are generally those that deal with relatively small samples (and wide CIs) at the beginning. For example, a CI width (precision) of 1.0 corresponds to a total sample of 60 participants. Although comparatively large percentage increases are listed for an increase to 99% certainty (9.68%, 12.5%, and 14.71%), when applied to $n = 60$, these reflect increases of roughly 6, 8, and 9 participants, respectively. Small increases in sample size therefore produce considerable improvements in the certainty of the result.

SUMMARY

Precision analysis addresses the sample size required to produce a CI with a particular width. Whereas power analysis addresses sample sizes required for detecting a nonzero effect, precision analyses are relevant to questions of accurately estimating population parameters. Designing for considerable precision often requires larger sample sizes than for power analysis. This chapter presented precision analyses for mean differences and effect sizes including r, d, and R^2. For most analyses, the primary information required is the desired level of precision.

11

ADDITIONAL ISSUES AND RESOURCES

INTRODUCTION

This chapter presents a variety of topics, including reporting power analyses, testing assumptions, converting between effect size estimates, the probability of replication (p_{rep}) power, additional resources for power, sources for learning about analyses not covered in this text, a review of power analysis programs, SPSS errors and how to deal with them, and improving power without increasing sample size.

HOW TO REPORT POWER ANALYSES

After conducting a power analysis, it is important to report the analysis accurately and completely. Power analysis is a design issue, so discussions of power go in the "Method" section of a paper based on American Psychiatric Association (APA) style. As Wilkinson and the Task Force for Statistical Inference (1999) noted "[b]ecause power computations are most meaningful when done before data are collected and examined, it is important to show how effect size estimates have been derived from previous research and theory in order to dispel suspicions that they might have been taken from data used in the study or, even worse, constructed to justify a particular sample size" (p. 596). Researchers should report in detail how they arrived at decisions about a meaningfully sized effect and all the statistical values used or assumed in estimation. Some outlets may ask that authors reduce this presentation to save space; however, when submitting work, the inclusion of more information alerts reviewers that you paid attention to power. Finally, always reference the source used to calculate the power analysis.

Example 11.1 Reporting a Power Analysis for a χ^2 Analysis

To determine sample size requirements for the present study, I first estimated a baseline value for rental availability based on the work of Page (1999), who found that renters indicated to 76% of those in the control group that the property was available. Next, I determined that a 20% difference between groups (i.e., the HIV group hearing "available" 56% of the time), constituted a meaningful difference between the two groups. In determining how large a difference would be meaningful, I note that previous work detected larger differences (36%). A 20% difference allows for detection of smaller effects than found in the original study, while allowing for detection of considerable levels of discrimination. These values correspond to $\Phi = .21$. The techniques outlined in the present text found that a sample of 180 participants would yield power of .80 for detecting this effect.

Example 11.2 Reporting a Power Analysis for Within-Subjects Analysis of Variance

To determine sample size requirements for the present study, we examined use of the stereotype negation procedure in other samples. These techniques produced standard deviations of approximately 0.40 with raw score changes of +0.25 to +0.40 (meaning more positive attitudes) for pre-to-post improvement and gradual increases thereafter. Based on this information, we judged +0.25 as the minimum value for a practically important pre–post change, with smaller changes expected from the posttest to 2-h measurement and from the 2-h to 6-h measure. Previous work reported test–retest reliability at .50. However, correlations between measures often decay over time, so we set pre-2-h and 2-h–6-h correlations at .30 and the pre-6-h correlation at .15. We also expected standard deviations to increase slightly over time, so we set the posttest standard deviation at 0.50, the 2-h standard deviation at 0.60, and the 6-h standard deviation at 0.70. Changes to the standard deviations and correlations produce more conservative power estimates than use of the initial estimates across each measurement period. These parameters reflect a multivariate effect size of V = .33. Based on these values, power analyses following the procedures outlined in the present text found that a sample of 30 participants produced adequate power for the omnibus multivariate test (.82).

STATISTICAL TEST ASSUMPTIONS

Throughout, the text mentioned assumptions with regard to specific tests. Regardless of study design, most statistical procedures are most accurate when data meet test assumptions. More often than not, meeting assumptions yields more power for data analyses. This is especially important when dealing with relatively small samples. Pay careful attention to issues such as data cleaning and assumptions prior to analyses as these can impact power considerably.

EFFECT SIZE CONVERSION FORMULAE

Occasionally, it is useful to convert between effect size estimates. Formulae that follow address conversions between several major estimates.

η^2 to d

The values p_1 and p_2 are the proportion of participants in each group. For equal sample sizes ($p_1 = p_2 = .50$), the numerator simplifies to $4\eta^2_{partial}$. Some sources present this conversion formula with $4\eta^2_{partial}$ in the numerator, but that approach is only appropriate for equal sample sizes, whereas the proportional values presented in Formula 11.1 are applicable to equal and unequal samples.

$$d = \sqrt{\frac{\eta^2_{partial} / p_1 p_2}{1 - \eta^2_{partial}}} \tag{11.1}$$

d to η^2

For equal sample sizes, the denominator in Formula 11.2 simplifies to $d^2 + 4$. Some versions of this formula include $d^2 + 4$ in the denominator, but that is appropriate only when sample sizes are equal across groups.

$$\eta^2 = \frac{d^2}{d^2 + \dfrac{1}{p_1 p_2}} \tag{11.2}$$

Correlation to d

The approach of correlation to d applies only to between-group designs. I use ρ to note the population correlation in Formulae 11.3 and 11.4. When dealing with samples simply, substitute r for ρ.

$$d = \sqrt{\frac{\rho^2 / p_1 p_2}{(1 - \rho^2)}} \tag{11.3}$$

d to Correlation

Again, the approach of d to correlation is applicable only to between-group designs.

$$\rho = \sqrt{\frac{d^2}{d^2 + \dfrac{1}{p_1 p_2}}} \tag{11.4}$$

PROBABILITY OF REPLICATION

The probability of replication p_{rep} is a relatively new measure that addresses the probability that future samples find results in the same direction as the sample result rather than the probability that a sample value came from a specified null population (Killeen, 2005; see also Cumming, 2005). At the time of this writing, there is one major outlet (*Psychological Science*) that I know that recommends p_{rep} for research reports.

The p_{rep} value is the probability of obtaining a same-sign result averaged over all populations likely to have given the original. That is, p_{rep} is the likelihood of a similar, albeit not necessarily significant, result in replication studies. For example if a sample result produced $r = -.30$, p_{rep} represents the probability of additional samples showing a negative correlation (regardless of the size of the correlation). This is an attractive measure as it allows for positive claims, such as "this result will replicate about 90% of the time," as opposed to "the sample mean is not likely to come from a population where the null hypothesis is true." When presented alongside an effect size or a confidence interval around an effect size, this can be a strong statement regarding the result. The p_{rep} statistic also moves reporting away from reliance on arbitrary decisions based on traditional null hypothesis significance testing (NHST) criteria such as $p < .05$. Further, p_{rep} provides greater specificity for traditionally significant results. The p_{rep} statistic and traditional p statistics are complementary (as seen in Figure 11.1). As p falls, p_{rep} rises.

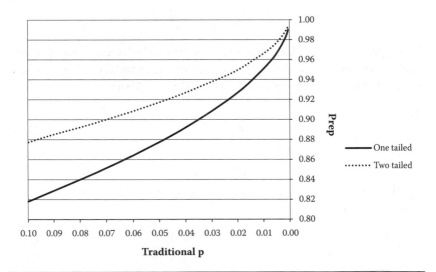

Figure 11.1 Traditional probability and p_{rep}.

Relevant to power, Killeen (2005) provided calculations for required sample sizes to detect particular values of p_{rep}. These tests define power in terms of the proportion of sampled results that will be in the same direction. For reference, I call this replication power. Replication power does not address the proportion of results allowing for rejection of the null hypothesis. This means that sample size estimates based on replication power are often smaller than those for tests designed to reject null hypotheses. This is because replication power focuses on results in a particular direction, not results that are so far in a particular direction that it makes a null result unlikely.

Formula 11.5 calculates the sample size required for obtaining a specific level of p_{rep} for two group comparisons. I modified some values from the original presentation to make them consistent with the notation used in this text. The sample size (n) refers to the entire sample, assuming equal sample sizes for the groups. The population effect size is d. The corresponding value on the standard normal distribution (z) expresses the probability level. This value reflects p_{rep} rather than the desired traditional probability. For example, for $p_{rep} = .99$, we use $z = 2.33$, and for $p_{rep} = .95$, we use $z = 1.645$. Note that p_{rep} values are one tailed as the statistic focuses on results in a specific direction.

The final value is the realization variance (σ_δ^2). This value is analogous to the variance of the effect sizes. Estimating the realization variance is outside the scope of this chapter; however, two general suggestions are useful guides. First, use a value at or near zero if planning exact replications (same method, same population). Second, if possible, find an estimate based on the literature in the area of research. For example, Killeen (2005) reported a median realization variance of 0.08 for social psychology (based on Richard, Bond, & Stokes-Zoota, 2003). In the absence of an estimate, Killeen suggested $\sigma_\delta^2 = 0.08$.

$$n = \frac{8z^2}{d^2 - 2\sigma_\delta^2 z^2} + 4$$

$$(11.5)$$

Presently, several estimation techniques exist for the calculation of p_{rep} (see listing in this chapter for useful Web-based tools). The simplest converts a traditional p statistic to a p_{rep} value. This is the technique used to create Figure 11.1.

Example 11.3 p_{rep} Power Calculation

For a p_{rep} of .95 with an effect size of $d = 0.50$, what sample size is necessary? Using $\sigma_\delta^2 = 0.08$, the following calculation yields $n = 104$, indicating a sample of 52 per group. The value $z = 1.645$ is the one-tailed z with 95% of the distribution falling at or below this value.

$$n = \frac{8z^2}{d^2 - 2\sigma_\delta^2 z^2} + 4 = \frac{8(1.645)^2}{.5^2 - 2(.08)^2(1.645)^2} + 4 = 104$$

A WARNING REGARDING THIS TECHNIQUE

Although the technique is increasingly popular, few outlets encourage the use of p_{rep}. Some outlets may ask authors to omit the p_{rep} value in favor of traditional statistics, others might require presentation of traditional probability values in conjunction with p_{rep}, and still others may set guidelines for acceptable p_{rep} values. Of course, some of these approaches limit the value of the statistic. If designing around p_{rep} rather than a traditional probability, be sure that the outlets targeted are open to the approach.

GENERAL (FREE) RESOURCES FOR POWER AND RELATED TOPICS

Two excellent programs for power analysis are available as freeware. The first is G*Power 3 (see http://www.psycho.uni-duesseldorf.de/abteilungen/aap/gpower3/). The second resource is a set of applets called PiFace (see http://www.math.uiowa.edu/~rlenth/Power/). Both programs are easy to use for simple analyses. The authors of G*Power provide an article that details most of the procedures (Faul, Erdfelder, Lang, & Buchner, 2007). For both programs, users must make sure to understand completely what values the program requires for input. Both programs use language that may be unfamiliar to some users, particularly for complex analyses. When using one of these programs, I strongly recommend checking results against those produced by another program or testing an example for which the correct answer is known. If you misunderstand the required input, power analysis is meaningless.

The Web Interface for Statistics Education (http://wise.cgu.edu) provides an interactive power tutorial that is an outstanding resource for learning about power analysis (note: I cowrote the tutorial). The Web site also provides tutorials on other relevant topics, like the central limit theorem and hypothesis testing, as well as an easy-to-use spreadsheet for calculating distribution probabilities. Another tool useful for hand calculations is the Noncentral Distribution Calculator (see http://www.statpower.net). Finally, there are several excellent SAS protocols for power analysis. See http://www.ats.ucla.edu/stat/stata/dae/ for a summary of these approaches.

RESOURCES FOR ADDITIONAL ANALYSES

There are many analyses not covered in the present text and analyses for which presentation was limited. For these topics, the following listings provide helpful resources and references.

Confidence Intervals Around Effect Sizes

A number of tools exist for confidence intervals around effect sizes. Chapter 10 made extensive use of Michael Smithson's text (2003) on confidence intervals and SPSS syntax from his Web site at http://psychology3.anu.edu.au/people/smithson/details/CIstuff/CI.html. This Web page also includes resources for other programs (SAS, SPlus, and R). For users comfortable with R, Ken Kelley's MBESS Web site contains analysis packages for confidence limits around most parameters (http://nd.edu/~kkelley/site/MBESS.html; see also Kelley, 2007a, 2007b, 2008).

Another outstanding tool is Exploratory Software for Confidence Intervals (ESCI). ESCI provides modules for exploring confidence intervals and noncentral distributions. I used ESCI to create several of the figures in Chapters 1 and 3. See http://www.latrobe.edu.au/psy/esci/ for materials.

Mediation Power

For power of mediated effects, Fritz and MacKinnon (2007) provide an overview and power tables. In addition, there are SAS protocols for calculation of mediation power at http://www.public.asu.edu/~davidpm/ripl/mediate.htm.

Structural Equations Modeling Power

Several approaches are available for power analyses for structural equation modeling. MacCallum, Browne, and Sugawara (1996) present tables for addressing close, not close, and exact fit. Also see Satorra and Saris (1985) and the May 2007 issue of *Personality and Individual Differences,* which is devoted to structural equations modeling.

Hierarchical Linear Modeling Power

An outstanding resource for hierarchical linear modeling (also known as multilevel modeling) is the Optimal Design program and accompanying manual (Spybrook, Raudenbusch, Liu, Congdon, & Martínez, 2008). Both are available from http://sitemaker.umich.edu/group-based/optimal_design_software.

Regression Interaction Power

Aguinis (2004) presents approaches to categorical by continuous interaction power that address issues not covered in this text, such as adjustments for reliability and restriction of range. See http://mypage. iu.edu/~haguinis/mmr/index.html for software associated with these approaches.

Probability of Replication

Peter Killeen provides through his Web page, a packet of useful information on p_{rep}. Particularly useful is a spreadsheet that converts a wide range of values into a corresponding p_{rep}. See http://psychology.clas.asu. edu/killeen/links for materials.

COMPARISON OF POWER PROGRAMS

The generosity of several commercial software companies allowed for construction of Table 11.1, which compares free and commercial software capabilities. In general, the SPSS syntax provided in this text is easier to use for most complex analyses. Before purchasing a commercial program, obtain a trial license to verify that the program fits your needs.

Evaluation and Comments Regarding Software

PiFace provides a dazzling array of procedures for analysis of variance (ANOVA), but program inputs can be confusing. Sparse documentation compounds this problem. It is an outstanding interface after you figure out what to input. However, I found that for some designs it took several hours to understand and estimate required inputs.

G*Power is excellent for basic analyses. When analyses become more complex, the program requests inputs that may not be easily estimated. G*Power does not currently provide a program manual, but the work of Faul et al. (2007) is an essential document for users. The program authors are helpful and responsive to questions.

Commercial programs include PASS (Power Analysis and Sample Size) by NCSS, nQuery Advisor by Statistical Solutions, and SamplePower by SPSS. I rate PASS as the most comprehensive of the three commercial programs. Program information and 7-day trial licenses are available from http://www.ncss.com/pass.html. nQuery's "assistants" are outstanding for determining input values. Program information and demo software are available from http://www.statsol. ie/index.html. SamplePower is also marketed as Power and Precision (Biostat). Program information is available from http://www.spss.com/

Table 11.1 Comparisons of Some Free and Commercial Software Package Capabilities

	PiFace	G*Power 3.0	nQuery	Sample Power	PASS
Mean Comparisons					
t-tests					
One sample	Y	Y	Y	Y	Y
Independent means	Y	Y	Y	Y	Y
Paired samples	Y	Y	Y	Y	Y
Unequal variances	Y	N	Y	N	Y
Unequal *n*	Y	Y	Y	Y	Y
Equivalence	Y	N	Y	Y	Y
ANOVA					
Between subjects	Y	Y	Y	Y	Y
Within subjects	Y	Y	Y	N	Y
Mixed models	Y	Y	N	N	Y
Covariates[a]	N	N	N	Y	N
ε adjustments	N	Y	Y	N	Y
MANOVA	N	Y	N	N	Y
Multiple comparisons	Y	N	Y	N	Y
Nonparametric mean comparisons	N	N	Y	N	Y
Proportions					
χ^2 goodness of fit	Y	Y	Y	N	Y
χ^2 independence	Y	Y	Y	Y	Y
Others (McNemar, proportions, sign, etc.)	Y	Y	Y	Y	Y
Correlation/Regression[b]					
Correlation (any H_0)	Y	Y	Y	Y	Y
MR *R^2 change/β*	Y	Y	Y	Y	Y
MR *R^2 change (df > 1)*	N	N	Y	Y	Y
MR *R^2 model*	Y	Y	Y	Y	Y
Specific tests for moderation	N	N	Y	N	N
Compare two correlations	N	Y	N	Y	Y
Logistic regression	N	N	Y	Y	Y
Precision Analyses for confidence intervals	N	N	Y	Y	Y

[a] With some work, all programs can accomplish this in MRC.

[b] Some programs include procedures for dummy-coded categories, nonlinear relationships, and interactions. Others do not specify this but do calculate each as *R2 change*. Moderation tests include only programs that provide specific approaches (rather than just requesting *R2* for an interaction).

Table 11.2 Linear Dependency Warning

```
*  *  *  *  *  *  *  *  *  *  *  *  *  *  *  *  *  *  *  *  *  *  *  *  *  *  *  *  *
* W  A  R  N  I  N  G * For WITHIN CELLS error matrix, these      *
*                     * covariates appear LINEARLY DEPENDENT on *
*                     * preceding variables ...                 *
*                     * External                                *
*                     * 1 D.F. will be returned to this error term. *
*  *  *  *  *  *  *  *  *  *  *  *  *  *  *  *  *  *  *  *  *  *  *  *  *  *  *  *  *
```

samplepower/. Trial versions of Power and Precision are available from http://www.power-analysis.com/home.htm.

SPSS WARNINGS AND HOW TO DEAL WITH THEM

When running syntax files, errors can produce inaccurate output or prevent analyses from running. Some common errors encountered in writing and using the syntax in this book follow.

Linear Dependency

In some applications, multivariate analysis of variance (MANOVA) procedures using the Matrix command produce the error message found in Table 11.2. Generally, this does not mean that there is a problem with the analysis (although it could if predictors can be predicted perfectly from one another). More often, it results from an SPSS error. SPSS technical staff notes that this is a known error, but there are no plans to fix the problem as the MANOVA program is "no longer in development."

There are a few strategies for fixing this problem. The first involves simply closing SPSS, restarting the program, and running the analysis again. This fixes most problems of this type (and others). Sometimes, however, the issue persists, particularly when running analyses with covariates. Under those conditions, one quick solution is to change your mean values. Means for many analyses are relevant only to tests of the intercept (the constant). Using the same mean for each variable sometimes produces the linear dependency message. Also, when representing means across groups, SPSS sometimes does not perform well when those means sum to zero, so simply adding one to each mean to produce the same mean difference can make an otherwise reluctant syntax run.

Blank Output for Contrasts

In running special contrast comparisons (e.g., orthogonal contrasts), SPSS occasionally produces the output seen in Table 11.3. This is due to

Table 11.3 Blank Output for Contrasts Errors

Parameter	Coeff.	Std. Err.	t-Value	Sig. t	Lower -95%	CL- Upper
2	-6.0000000	.	.	.	.	.
3	-2.0000000	.	.	.	.	.
4	-4.0000000	.	.	.	.	.

Parameter	ETA Sq.	Noncent.	Power
2	.	.	.
3	.	.	.
4	.	.	.

a syntax error in which too many spaces are noted between each weight (i.e., this is a user error). The correct way to list the contrast weights is /CONTRAST (Program) = Special (1 1 1 1 1 1 -1 -1, 1 -1 0 0, 0 0 1 -1).

Order of Entry/Order of Reporting

Order of entry is the most vexing problem discussed in this section. MANOVA syntax requires variables in the same order that they appear in the Matrix syntax. If variables are in a different order, there is no error message, only erroneous output.

Table 11.4 shows an example of this issue. There are two uncorrelated predictors called A and B. Predictor A should have less power than Predictor B because the correlation between B and the dependent measure (Y) is much larger than for Predictor A .50 vs. .05).

Surprisingly, in the first output section of the table, A has more power than B. This results from the order of entry in the MANOVA statement. In the Matrix statement, A comes before B, but in the MANOVA syntax B comes before A. If variables in the MANOVA appear in a different order than expressed in the Matrix, SPSS labels effects incorrectly. The second MANOVA command listed has the variables in the correct order and gives the accurate result.

I cannot stress this enough: Double-check your order of entry. Clearly, results differ greatly if you enter variables in the wrong order.

IMPROVING POWER WITHOUT INCREASING SAMPLE SIZE OR COST

The major focus of this text is statistical approaches to power analysis for which the remedy for low power is usually the addition of more participants. However, several methodological approaches increase power without increasing sample size. These are great options to consider

Table 11.4 Order of Entry Issues

```
MATRIX DATA VARIABLES = ROWTYPE_ y A B.

BEGIN DATA
Mean 1 2 3 4
STDEV 7 1 1 1
N 40 40 40 40
Corr 1
Corr .05 1
Corr .50 .00 1
END DATA.

MANOVA y with b a (THIS IS THE WRONG ORDER)
/MATRIX=IN(*)
/power exact t (.05) F (.05)
/DESIGN.
```

Dependent   y
variable ..

COVARIATE	B	Beta	Std. Err.	t-Value	Sig. of t
b	.35000	.	.995	.352	.727
a	3.50000	.	.995	3.518	.001

COVARIATE	Lower -95%	CL-Upper	Noncent.	Power
b	-2.187	2.887	.124	.064
a	.963	6.037	12.375	.929

```
MANOVA y with a b (NOTE THIS IS THE CORRECT ORDER)
/MATRIX=IN(*)
/power exact t (.05) F (.05)
/DESIGN.
```

COVARIATE	B	Beta	Std. Err.	t-Value	Sig. of t
a	.35000	.	.995	.352	.727
b	3.50000	.	.995	3.518	.001

COVARIATE	Lower-95%	CL-Upper	Noncent.	Power
a	-2.187	2.887	.124	.064
b	.963	6.037	12.375	.929

before adding participants. There are obvious benefits to increasing power without adding costs associated with larger samples. Several of these suggestions received a more thorough consideration in the work of Lipsey (1990).

Stronger experimental manipulations increase effect size. Stronger manipulations result from stronger treatments, weaker controls, or both. As an example of this, a few years ago I conducted a series of studies that manipulated the qualifications and ethnicity of potential job applicants. Manipulations consisted of a cover page attached to a questionnaire that summarized the applicant's qualifications and presented a one-paragraph personal statement that varied ethnicity. Later, I supervised a project in which a student modified the approach by creating files for each applicant that included a resume on nice paper and a photograph of the applicant. The student's study produced a considerably larger effect size than the earlier studies, likely because of the stronger and more engaging manipulation.

Another option is assigning more participants to cheaper conditions and fewer to more expensive conditions or sampling relatively more participants from cheaper or easier-to-obtain groups. When sampling from existing groups, this strategy can be of great use. Chapter 3 presented an example comparing gay men from the community to heterosexual men from campus. The gay men received monetary compensation for their time, but the campus sample participated for course credit. The campus sample could have been increased considerably with minimal cost, resulting in substantial increases in power.

Simplifying research designs reduces sample size requirements as well. Researchers often strive to answer so many questions that the design becomes overwhelming. For example, imagine a $2 \times 2 \times 2$ design in which power analyses suggest 25 participants per cell. Cutting out a factor makes this a 2×2 design and likely reduces total sample size requirements considerably. On a similar note, researchers should always ask whether all factor levels are necessary in designs with more than two levels.

Within-subjects designs usually produce considerably more power than between-subjects approaches. Although within-subjects approaches are not always possible, they are likely underutilized. Researchers with concerns about carryover effects might evaluate carryover by pretesting using within-subjects approaches.

As discussed in Chapter 9, under the right conditions covariate designs increase power. Although experimental paradigms discourage covariates, for studies with larger sample size requirements, covariates help achieve adequate power while saving resources.

Several chapters included discussions of reliability. Poor or even mediocre reliability reduces observed effect sizes considerably. Insist on the most reliable measures possible.

Finally, I want to close with something a colleague once said about power and research design. I consulted briefly on a project and asked my colleague if he had conducted a power analysis. He laughed and said, "That stuff is for people who don't understand research design." I do not agree entirely, but it is clear that good research design substantially improves statistical power.

REFERENCES

Aberson, C. L. (2007). Diversity, merit, fairness, and discrimination beliefs as predictors of support for affirmative action policy actions. *Journal of Applied Social Psychology, 37,* 2451–2474.

Aberson, C. L., Berger, D. E., Healy, M. R., & Romero, V. L. (2002). An interactive tutorial for teaching statistical power. *Journal of Statistics Education, 10,* 3.

Aberson, C. L., & Gaffney, A. M. (2009). An integrated threat model of implicit and explicit attitudes. *European Journal of Social Psychology, 39,* 808–830.

Aberson, C. L., Healy, M. R., & Romero, V. L. (2000). Ingroup bias and self-esteem: A meta-analysis. *Personality and Social Psychology Review, 4,* 157–173.

Aguinis, H. (2004). *Regression analysis for categorical moderators.* New York: Guilford Press.

Aguinis, H., Beaty, J. C., Boik, R. J., & Pierce, C. A. (2005). Effect size and power in assessing moderating effects of categorical variables using multiple regression: A 30-year review. *Journal of Applied Psychology, 90,* 94–107.

Aguinis, H., Petersen, S. A., & Pierce, C. A. (1999). Appraisal of the homogeneity of error variance assumption and alternatives to multiple regression for estimating moderating effects of categorical variables. *Organizational Research Methods, 2,* 315–339.

Aiken, L. S., & West, S. G. (1991). *Multiple regression: Testing and interpreting interactions.* Newbury Park, CA: Sage.

Anderson, C. A., & Bushman, B. J. (2002). Human aggression. *Annual Review of Psychology, 53,* 27–51.

Ayduk, O., Gyurak, A., & Luerssen, A. (2008). Individual differences in the rejection-aggression link in the hot sauce paradigm: The case of rejection sensitivity. *Journal of Experimental Social Psychology, 44,* 775–782.

Belia, S., Fidler, F., Williams, J., & Cumming, G. (2005). Researchers misunderstand confidence intervals and standard error bars. *Psychological Methods, 10,* 389–396.

Brown, J., & Hale, M. S. (1992). The power of statistical studies in consultation-liaison psychiatry. *Psychosomatics: Journal of Consultation Liaison Psychiatry, 33,* 437–443.

Cashen, L. H., & Geiger, S. W. (2004). Statistical power and the testing of null hypotheses: A review of contemporary management research and recommendations for future studies. *Organizational Research Methods, 7,* 151–167.

Cohen, J. (1962). The statistical power of abnormal-social psychological research. *Journal of Abnormal and Social Psychology, 65,* 145–153.

Cohen, J. (1984). The cost of dichotomization. *Applied Psychological Measurement, 7,* 249–253.

Cohen, J. (1988). *Statistical power analysis for the behavioral sciences* (2nd ed.). Hillsdale, NJ: Erlbaum.

Cohen, J. (1992). A power primer. *Psychological Bulletin, 112,* 155–159.

Cohen, J., Cohen, P., West, S., & Aiken, L. (2003). *Applied multiple regression/ correlation analysis for the behavioral sciences* (3rd ed.). Hillsdale, NJ: Erlbaum.

Cole, D. A., Maxwell, S. E., Arvey, R., & Salas, E. (1994). How the power of MANOVA can both increase and decrease as a function of the interrelations among the dependent variables. *Psychological Bulletin, 115,* 465–474.

Cumming, G. (2005). Understanding the average probability of replication. Comment on Killeen (2005). *Psychological Science, 16,* 1002–1004.

Cumming, G., & Finch, S. (2005). Inference by eye. Confidence intervals and how to read pictures of data. *American Psychologist, 60,* 170–180.

D'Amico, E. J., Neilands, T. B., & Zambarano, R. (2001). Power analysis for multivariate and repeated measures designs: A flexible approach using the SPSS MANOVA procedure. *Behavior Research Methods, Instruments, and Computers, 33,* 479–484.

Davis, J. R., & Henry, P. J. (2008, February). *The culture of the lab: Influences of the college setting on social psychology's view of the nature of prejudice.* Poster session presented at the annual meeting of the Society for Personality and Social Psychology, Albuquerque, NM.

Faul, F., Erdfelder, E., Lang, A. L., & Buchner, A. (2007). G*Power 3: A flexible statistical power analysis program for the social, behavioral, and biomedical sciences. *Behavior Research Methods, 39,* 175–191.

Field, A. (1998). A bluffer's guide to … sphericity. *Newsletter of the Mathematical, Statistical and Computing Section of the British Psychological Society, 6,* 13–22.

Finch, S., Thomason, N., & Cumming, G. (2002). Past and future American Psychological Association guidelines for statistical practice. *Theory and Psychology, 12,* 825–853.

Fisher, R. A. (1921). On the "probable error" of a coefficient of correlation deduced from a small sample. *Metron, 1,* 3–32.

Fisher, R. A. (1938). Presidential address, Indian statistical conference. *Sankhyā*, *4*, 14–17.

Fitzsimons, G. (2008). A death to dichotomizing. *Journal of Consumer Research*, *35*, 5–8.

Fritz, M. S., & MacKinnon, D. P. (2007). Required sample size to detect the mediated effect. *Psychological Science*, *18*, 233–239.

Greenwald, A. G., Poehlman, T. A., Uhlmann, E., & Banaji, M. R. (2009). Understanding and using the Implicit Association Test: III. Meta-analysis of predictive validity. *Journal of Personality and Social Psychology*, *97*, 17–41.

Greitemeyer, T. (2009). Effects of songs with prosocial lyrics on prosocial thoughts, affect, and behavior. *Journal of Experimental Social Psychology*, *45*, 186.

Harrison, D. A., Kravitz, D. A., Mayer, D. M., Leslie, L. M., & Lev-Arey, D. (2006). Understanding attitudes toward affirmative action programs in employment: Summary and meta-analysis of 35 years of research. *Journal of Applied Psychology*, *91*, 1013–1036.

Hittner, J. B., May, K., & Silver, N. C. (2003). A Monte Carlo evaluation of tests for comparing dependent correlations. *Journal of General Psychology*, *130*, 149–168.

Hoenig, J. M., & Heisey, D. M. (2001). The abuse of power: The pervasive fallacy of power calculations for data analysis. *American Statistician*, *55*, 19–24.

Hunter, J. E. (1997). Needed: A ban on the significance test. *Psychological Science*, *8*(1), 3–7.

Hunter, J. E., & Schmidt, F. L. (1990). Dichotomization of continuous variables: The implications for meta-analysis. *Journal of Applied Psychology*, *75*, 334–349.

Hunter, J. E., & Schmidt, F. L. (1994). Correcting for sources of artificial variation across studies. In H. Cooper & L. V. Hedges (Eds.), *The handbook of research synthesis* (pp. 323–336). New York: Russell Sage.

Jennions, M. D., & Møller, A. P. (2003). A survey of the statistical power of research in behavioral ecology and animal behavior. *Behavioral Ecology*, *14*, 438–445.

Kawakami, K., Dovidio, J. F., Moll, J., Herrasen, S., & Russin, A. (2000). Just say no (to stereotyping): Effects of training in the *negation* of stereotypic associations on *stereotype* activation. *Journal of Personality and Social Psychology*, *78*, 871–888.

Kelley, K. (2008). Sample size planning for the squared multiple correlation coefficient: Accuracy in parameter estimation via narrow confidence intervals. *Multivariate Behavioral Research*, *43*, 524–555.

Kelley, K. (2007a). Confidence intervals for standardized effect sizes: Theory, application, and implementation. *Journal of Statistical Software*, *20*, 1–24.

Kelley, K. (2007b). Methods for the behavioral, educational, and social science: An R package. *Behavior Research Methods*, *39*, 979–984.

Kelley, K., & Maxwell, S. E. (2003). Sample size for multiple regression: Obtaining regression coefficients that are accurate, not simply significant. *Psychological Methods*, *8*, 305–321.

Kelley, K., & Rausch, J. R. (2006). Sample size planning for the standardized mean difference: Accuracy in parameter estimation via narrow confidence intervals. *Psychological Methods, 11,* 363–385.

Keppel, G. (1991). *Design and analysis: A researcher's handbook* (3rd ed.). Englewood Cliffs, NJ: Prentice-Hall.

Keselman, H. J., Othman, A., Wilcox, R., & Fradette, K. (2004). The new and improved two-sample *t* tests. *Psychological Science, 15,* 47–51.

Killeen, P. R. (2005). An alternative to null hypothesis significance tests. *Psychological Science, 16,* 345–353.

Kirk, R. E. (1995). *Experimental design: Procedures for the behavioral sciences* (3rd ed.). Pacific Grove, CA: Brooks/Cole.

Kosciulek, J. F., & Szymanski, E. M. (1993). Statistical power analysis of rehabilitation counseling research. *Rehabilitation Counseling Bulletin, 36,* 212–219.

Kraemer, H. C., & Thiemann, S. (1987). *How many subjects: Statistical power analysis in research.* Newbury Park, CA: Sage.

Lenth, R. V. (2000, August). *Two sample size practices that I don't recommend.* Paper presented at the Joint Statistical Meeting, Indianapolis, IN.

Lenth, R. V. (2001). Some practical guidelines for effective sample size determination. *American Statistician, 55,* 187–193.

Lipsey, M. W. (1990). *Design sensitivity: Statistical power for experimental research.* Newbury Park, CA: Sage.

Lipsey, M. W., & Wilson, D. B. (2001). *Practical meta-analysis.* Thousand Oaks, CA: Sage.

Loftus, G. R. (1996). Psychology will be a much better science when we change the way we analyze data. *Current Directions in Psychological Science, 5,* 161–171.

MacCallum, R. C., Browne, M. W., & Sugawara, H.M. (1996). Power analysis and determination of sample size for covariance structure modeling. *Psychological Methods, 1,* 130–149.

Maddock, J. E., & Rossi, J. S. (2001). Statistical power of articles published in three health-psychology related journals. *Health Psychology, 20,* 76–78.

Maxwell, S. E. (2004). The persistence of underpowered studies in psychological research: Causes, consequences, and remedies. *Psychological Methods, 9,* 147–163.

Maxwell, S. E., Kelley, K., & Rausch, J. R. (2008). Sample size planning for statistical power and accuracy in parameter estimation. *Annual Review of Psychology, 59,* 537–563.

McCartney, K., & Rosenthal, R. (2000). Effect size, practical importance, and social policy for children. *Child Development, 71,* 173–180.

Mone, M. A., Mueller, G. C., & Mauland, W. (1996). The perceptions and usage of statistical power in applied psychology and management research. *Personnel Psychology, 49,* 103–120.

Nakagawa, S., & Foster, T. M. (2004). The case against retrospective statistical power analyses with and introduction to power analysis. *Acta Ethologica, 7,* 103–108.

Nickerson, R. (2000). Null hypothesis significance testing: A review of an old and continuing controversy. *Psychological Methods, 5,* 241–301.

Onwuegbuzie, A. J., & Leech, N. L. (2004). Post-hoc power: A concept whose time has come. *Understanding Statistics, 3,* 201–230.

Osborn, J. W. (2006). Power analysis for multivariate and repeated measurements designs via SPSS: Correction and extension D'Amico, Neilands, and Zambarano (2001). *Behavior Research Methods, 38,* 353–354.

Page, S. (1999). Accommodating persons with AIDS: Acceptance and rejection in rental situations. *Journal of Applied Social Psychology, 29,* 261–270.

Plant, E. A., & Devine, P. G. (1998). Internal and external motivation to respond without prejudice. *Journal of Personality and Social Psychology, 75,* 811–832.

Preacher, K. J., & Hayes, A. F. (2004). SPSS and SAS procedures for estimating indirect effects in simple mediation models. *Behavior Research Methods, Instruments, and Computers, 36,* 717–731.

Prendergast, M. L., Podus, D., Chang, E., & Urada, D. (2002). The effectiveness of drag abuse treatment: A meta-analysis of comparison group studies. *Drug and Alcohol Dependence, 67,* 53–72.

Richard, F. D., Bond, C. F., Jr., & Stokes-Zoota, J. J. (2003). One hundred years of social psychology quantitatively described. *Review of General Psychology, 7,* 331–363.

Rogers, W. M. (2002). Theoretical and mathematical constraints of interactive regression models. *Organizational Research Methods, 5,* 212–230.

Rosenthal, R. (1979). The "file-drawer problem" and tolerance for null results. *Psychological Bulletin, 86,* 638–641.

Rosenthal, R., & Rubin, D. B. (1982). A simple, general purpose display of magnitude of experimental effect. *Journal of Educational Psychology, 74,* 166–169.

Rossi, J. S. (1990). Statistical power of psychological research: What have we gained in 20 years? *Journal of Consulting and Clinical Psychology, 58,* 646–656.

Satorra, A., & Saris, W. F. (1985). The power of the likelihood ratio test in covariance structure analysis. *Psychometrika, 50,* 83–90.

Sedlmeier, P., & Gigerenzer, G. (1989). Do studies of statistical power have an effect on the power of studies? *Psychological Bulletin, 105,* 309–316.

Siegel, S., & Castellan, J. N. (1988). *Nonparametric statistics for the behavioral sciences* (2nd ed.). New York: McGraw-Hill.

Silver, N. C., & Dunlap, W. P. (1987). Averaging correlation coefficients: Should Fisher's *z* transformation be used. *Journal of Applied Psychology, 72,* 146–148.

Silver, N. C., Hittner, J. B., & May, K. (2004). Testing dependent correlations with nonoverlapping variables: A Monte Carlo simulation. *Journal of Experimental Education, 73,* 53–69.

Smithson, M. J. (2003). *Confidence intervals.* Thousand Oaks, CA: Sage.

Spybrook, J., Raudenbusch, S. W., Liu, X.-F., Congdon, R., & Martínez, A. (2008). Optimal design for longitudinal and multilevel research: Documentation for the "Optimal Design" software. Retrieved June 20, 2008, from http://sitemaker.umich.edu/group-based/optimal_design_software

Steiger, J. H. (1980). Tests for comparing elements of a correlation matrix. *Psychological Bulletin, 87*, 245–251.

Steiger, J. H., & Fouladi, R. T. (1997). Noncentrality interval estimation and the evaluation of statistical models. In L. L. Harlow, S. A. Mulaik, & J. H. Steiger (Eds.). *What if there were no significance tests?* (pp. 221–258). Mahwah, NJ: Erlbaum.

Tabachnick, B. G., & Fidell, L. S. (2007a). *Experimental designs using ANOVA.* Belmont, CA: Duxbury.

Tabachnick, B. G., & Fidell, L. S. (2007b). *Using multivariate statistics* (5th ed.). Boston: Allyn and Bacon.

Thompson, B. (1998). Statistical significance and effect size reporting: Portrait of a possible future. *Research in the Schools, 5*(2), 33–38.

Thompson, B. (2002). What future quantitative social science research could look like: Confidence intervals for effect sizes. *Educational Researcher, 31*, 24–31.

Tropp, L. R., & Pettigrew, T. F. (2005). Differential relationships between intergroup contact and affective and cognitive indicators of prejudice. *Personality and Social Psychology Bulletin, 31*, 1145–1158.

Van Laar, C., Levin, S., Sinclair, S., & Sidanius, J. (2005). The effect of university roommate contact on ethnic attitudes and behavior. *Journal of Experimental Social Psychology, 41*, 329–345.

West, R. F. (1985). A power analytic investigation of research in adult education: 1970–1982. *Adult Education Quarterly, 35*, 131–141.

Wilcox, R. R., & Keselman, H. J. (2003). Modern robust data analysis methods: Measures of central tendency. *Psychological Methods, 8*, 254–274.

Wilcox, R. R., & Tian, T. (2008) Comparing dependent correlations. *Journal of General Psychology, 135*, 105–112.

Wilkinson, L., & Task Force on Statistical Inference. (1999). Statistical methods in psychology journals: Guidelines and explanations. *American Psychologist, 54*, 594–604.

Williams, E. J. (1959). The comparison of regression variables. *Journal of the Royal Statistical Society, Series B, 21*, 396–399.

AUTHOR INDEX

A

Aberson C. L., 6, 103, 110, 143, 182
Aguinis, H., 181, 186, 187, 188, 232
Aiken, L. S., 151, 187, 200
Anderson, C. A., 68
Arvey, R., 141
Ayduk, O., 189, 190, 193

B

Banaji, M. R., 69
Beaty, J. C., 187
Belia, S., 204
Berger, D. E., xiii, 6
Boik, R. J., 187
Bond, C. F., Jr., 229
Brown, J., 9
Browne, M. W., 231
Buchner, A., 230
Bushman, B. J., 68

C

Cashen, L. H., 9
Castellan, J. N., 33
Cohen, J., 2, 9, 21, 29, 41, 69, 92, 110,
        151, 157, 181, 211
Cohen, P., 151
Cole, D. A., 141

C

Congdon, R., 231
Cumming, G., xiii, 204, 228

D

D'Amico, E. J., xii
Davis, J. R., 80
Devine, P. G., 158, 161
Dovidio, J. F., 134
Dunlap, W. P., 76, 80

E

Erdfelder, E., 230

F

Faul, F., 230, 232
Fidell, L. S., 56, 57, 114, 115,
        134, 181
Fidler, F., 204
Field, A., 114
Finch, S., 204
Fisher R. A., 14, 71
Fitzsimons, G., 110
Foster, T. M., 14
Fouladi, R. T., 210
Fradette, K., 62
Fritz, M. S., 231

G

Gaffney, A. M., 143
Geiger, S. W., 9
Gigerenzer, G., 9
Greenwald, A. G., 69
Greitemeyer, T., 69
Gyurak, A., 189

H

Hale, M. S., 9
Harrison, D. A., 103, 161
Haynes, A. F., xii
Healy, M. R., 6, 110
Heisey, D. M., 14
Henry, P. J., 80
Herrasen, S., 134
Hittner, J. B., 76, 85
Hoenig, J. M., 14
Hunter, J. E., 110, 175, 204

J

Jennions, M. D., 9

K

Kawakami, K., 134
Kelley, K., 14, 206, 210, 214, 221, 222, 231
Keppel, G., 93, 114
Keselman, H. J., 62
Killeen, P. R., 228, 229, 232
Kirk, R. E., 93
Kosciulek, J. F., 9
Kraemer, H. C., 21
Kravitz, D. A., 103

L

Lang, A. L., 230
Leech, N. L., 14
Lenth, R. V., 11, 14, 41
Leslie, L. M., 103
Lev-Arey, D., 103
Levin, S., 91
Lipsey, M. W., xii, 10, 59, 237
Liu, X.-F., 231
Loftus, G. R., 218
Luerssen, A., 189

M

MacCallum, R. C., 231
MacKinnon, D. P., 231
Maddock, J. E., 9, 10
Martínez, A., 231
Mauland, W., 9
Maxwell, S. E., 14, 112, 141, 178, 179, 221
May, K., 76, 85
Mayer, D. M., 103
McCartney, K., 12
Moll, J., 134
Møller, A. P., 9
Mone, M. A., 9
Mueller, G. C., 9

N

Nakagawa, S., 14
Neilands, T. B., xii
Nickerson, R., 8, 9, 204

O

Onwuegbuzie, A. J., 14
Osborn, J. W., xii
Othman, A., 62

P

Page, S., 20, 21, 226
Petersen, S. A., 188
Pettigrew, T. F., 143
Pierce, C. A., 187, 188
Plant, E. A., 158, 161
Poehlman, T. A., 69
Preacher, K. J., xii
Prendergast, M. L., 36

R

Raudenbusch, S. W., 231
Rausch, J. R., 14, 206, 222
Richard, F. D., 229
Rogers, W. M., 186
Romero, V. L., 6, 110
Rosenthal, R., 12, 20, 69
Rossi, J. S., 9, 10
Rubin, D. B., 69
Russin, A., 134

S

Salas, E., 141
Saris, W. E., 231
Satorra, A., 231
Schmidt, F. L., 110, 175
Sedlmeier, P., 9
Sidanius, J., 91
Siegel, S., 33
Silver, N. C., 76, 80, 85
Sinclair, S., 91
Smithson, M. J., xiii, 206,
        211, 221, 231
Spybrook, J., 231
Steiger. J. H., 80, 210
Stokes-Zoota, J. J., 229
Sugawara, H. M., 231
Szymanski, E. M., 9

T

Tabachnick, B. G., 56, 57, 114,
        115, 134, 181
Task Force on Statistical Inference, 21,
        42, 205, 225
Thiemann, S., 21

Thomason, N., 204
Thompson, B., 39, 205
Tian, T., 85
Tropp, L. R., 143

U

Uhlmann, E., 69

V

Van Laar, C., 91

W

West, R. F., 9
West, S. G. 151, 187, 200
Wilcox, R., 62, 85
Wilkinson, L., 21, 42, 205, 225
Williams, E. J., 76
Williams, J., 204
Wilson, D. B., xii

Z

Zambarano, R., xii

SUBJECT INDEX

A

Alpha error inflation adjustment, 99,
    101–101, 102
    Bonferonni, 101
    Šidák, 101
Analysis of covariance (ANCOVA)
    calculations, 184, 185
    compared to analysis of variance,
        184–185
    covariate selection, 182
    example, 182–185, 186
    factors affecting power, 181–182
    necessary information, 181
    SPSS syntax, 183, 184, 186
Analysis of covariance, multivariate
    (MANCOVA)
    example, 197–198, 199
    factors affecting power, 197
    necessary information, 197
    SPSS syntax, 198, 199
Analysis of variance, between subjects
    factorial; *see also* Analysis
    of variance, simple effects;
    Multiple effects, power for
    detecting
    calculations, 103–104, 106
    example (omnibus power), 101,
        103–106
    factors affecting power, 87–88
    formulae, 89–90

    necessary information, 87
    power calculation with
        noncentrality parameter, 105
    SPSS syntax, 105–107
Analysis of variance, contrasts/multiple
        comparisons, 88
    calculations, 93–94
    comparing all means, 100–101, 102
    difference contrasts, 97–98
    example, 93–94
    formulae, 89
    Helmert contrasts, 98–99
    necessary information, 87
    noncentrality parameter (δ), 89
    polynomial contrasts, 100
    power calculation with noncentrality
        parameter, 93–94
    repeated contrasts, 100
    simple contrasts, 99
    SPSS syntax, 95, 98, 99, 100
Analysis of variance, mixed model
    example, 134–137
    factors affecting power, 133
    formulae, 115
    necessary information, 133
    SPSS syntax three factors, 139
    SPSS syntax trends, 138
    SPSS syntax two factor mixed
        model, 136
    SPSS syntax three factors, 139

three factors, 137, 140
trend analysis, 135–136, 138
Analysis of variance, multivariate;
    see also Patterns of effects/
    correlations in multivariate
    analysis of variance
    example, 142–145
    factors affecting power, 133–134
    formulae, 115
    necessary information, 133
    SPSS syntax, 144–145
Analysis of variance, one factor
    between subjects; *see*
    also Analysis of variance,
    contrasts/multiple
    comparisons
    calculations, 91–94
    effect size (η^2), 89
    effect size (f^2), 88
    example (omnibus power), 90–93
    factors affecting power, 87–88
    formulae, 88–89
    necessary information, 87
    noncentrality parameter (λ), 89
    omnibus vs. contrast power, 88
    power calculations, approximate, 92
    power calculation with noncentrality
    parameter, 92
    SPSS syntax, 94–97
Analysis of variance, one factor within
    subjects (multivariate tests);
    see also Trend analysis
    calculations, 122
    effect size (η^2), 115
    effect size (f^2), 115
    example, 122
    factors affecting power, 113
    formulae, 114–115
    necessary information, 113
    SPSS syntax, 117–119
Analysis of variance, one factor within
    subjects (univariate tests); *see*
    also Sphericity; Trend analysis
    calculations, 118
    effect size (η^2), 115
    effect size (f^2), 115
    epsilon adjustment
    example, 116–119
    factors affecting power, 113
    formulae, 114–115

necessary information, 113
sphericity, 114, 116, 119–121,
    122–124, 130
SPSS syntax, 117–119
Analysis of variance, simple effects
    calculations, 106
    example, 106–108
    formulae, 90
    SPSS syntax, 107–108
Analysis of variance, two factor within
    subjects
    example, 126, 127–129
    simple effects example, 127, 128, 129
    SPSS syntax, 129
ANCOVA, *see* Analysis of covariance
Analysis of variance, *see* Specific
    designs
Arcsine transformation, 29
Artificial dichotomization, 110–111
Assumptions, 226; *see also* t-test,
    independent samples
    absence of multicollinearity, 151,
    153, 154, 164
    homogeneity of regression
    (covariance), 182
    homogeneity of variance, 51, 56–64
Attenuation of effect size
    artificial dichotomization, 110–111
    reliability, 175, 177
    reliability and interactions, 198–200

B

Bootstrapping, 62

C

Chi-square, 17–28; *see also* Effect size,
    for; Effect size, Φ
    determining effect size based on
    meaningful or practically
    important effect, 20–21
    determining effect size based on
    previous research, 20–21
    effect size (Φ), 19
    expected and observed frequencies,
    18–19
    factors affecting power, 18
    formulae, 18–19
    goodness of fit tests, 28

necessary information, 17–18
noncentrality parameter, 19
overview, 17
power calculation with
    noncentrality parameter,
    22–23
power calculations, approximate
    with z, 23–24
power calculations, with SPSS
    syntax, 24–28
test of independence, more than two
    categories, 28
2 × 2 Test of independence example,
    20–25
Confidence interval correlation (ρ),
    precision, 213–214
formulae, 214
SPSS syntax, 215–216
Confidence interval, R² change
precision, 214, 216
SPSS syntax, 217–218
Confidence interval, R² model
precision, 215
SPSS syntax, 219
Confidence interval, d
calculation issues, 210–211
precision for, 210–211
SPSS syntax, 212–213
Confidence interval, difference
    between means
formulae, 206
precision, 206–207, 209
relationship to power, 207
SPSS syntax, 208–209
Confidence intervals 204–205; see also
    Specific confidence intervals
central vs. noncentral, 205–206
Correlation, comparing two dependent
    no variables in common
calculation, 80–82
effect size (q), 80
example, 80–84
factors affecting power, 67–68
formulae, 79–80
magnitude vs. direction/magnitude
    tests, 83–84
necessary information, 67
power calculation with z, 81
SPSS syntax, 82–84
z test for comparing samples, 84

Correlation, comparing two dependent
    one variable in common
calculation, 77
example, 76–79
factors affecting power, 67–68
formulae, 75–76
magnitude vs. direction/magnitude
    tests, 83–84
necessary information, 67
noncentrality parameter (δ), 76
power calculation with
    noncentrality parameter, 77
SPSS syntax, 77–79
t-test for comparing samples, 79
Correlation, comparing two
    independent
calculation, 73
effect size (q), 72
example, 72–75
factors affecting power, 67–68
Fisher's r to z transformation, 72
formulae, 71–72
magnitude vs. direction/magnitude
    tests, 83–84
necessary information, 67
power calculation with z, 73
SPSS syntax, 73–75
z-test for comparing samples, 75
Correlation, zero-order
calculation, 69
conversion to d, 68
effect size (d), 68
example, 68–71
factors affecting power, 67–68
formulae, 68
necessary information, 67
noncentrality parameter (δ), 68
power calculation with
    noncentrality parameter, 69
SPSS syntax, 70–71
Covariance structure modeling, 231

D

Delta (δ)
analysis of variance, contrasts, 89, 93
correlations, comparing dependent,
    76, 77
correlation, zero-order, 68, 69
graphical representation, 44

multiple regression, coefficients,
155, 160
multiple regression, differences
between dependent
coefficients, 157, 167
multiple regression, differences
between independent
coefficients, 156, 171
multiple regression, differences
between independent R^2,
157, 174
t-tests, 40, 43, 45, 50, 59, 64
Determining effect size for power
analysis; *see also* Specific
analyses
based on previous research,
11–12, 20–21
meaningful or practically important
effects, 12–13, 20–21
pilot work, 13
small, medium, large guidelines,
11, 41–42
standardized vs. unstandardized
measures, 21–22, 41–42
Doubly within ANOVA, *see* Analysis of
variance, two factor within
subjects

E

Effect size conversion
d to η^2, 227
d to ρ (or r), 227
η^2 to d, 227
ρ (or r) to d, 227
Effect size for; *see also* Specific tests
analysis of variance (η^2), 89, 115
analysis of variance (f^2), 88, 115
chi-square (Φ), 19
comparing correlations (q), 72, 80
multiple regression (f^2), 154
multivariate analysis of
variance (η^2), 115
multivariate analysis of
variance (f^2), 115
proportions (h), 29
t-test (d), 40
Effect size; *see also* Specific tests
compared across measures, 3
d, 3, 40

η^2, 3, 89, 115
f, 3
f^2, 3, 88, 115, 154
h, 3, 29
overview, 1
Φ (V or W), 3, 19
q, 3, 72, 80
r, 3
R^2, 3, 153
ESCI software, 16, 65, 231

F

Fisher's transformation, 72–74, 84, 213

G

G*Power (software), 88, 115, 163, 230,
232–233

H

Harmonic n for unequal sample size
comparisons, 29–30
analysis of variance, 89
independent proportions, 29–30, 32–33
independent samples t, 58–59, 62
Hierarchical linear modeling, 231
Homogeneity of variance, *see* Unequal
variances

I

Increasing power, methodological
approaches, 235–237
Influences on power, 3–6; *see also*
Specific tests
α, 3–5
effect size, 3–5
sample size, 3–6

L

Lambda (λ)
analysis of variance, between
subjects, 89, 91, 104
analysis of variance, simple
effects, 106
analysis of variance, within subjects,
115, 118, 122

chi-square, 19, 22
  multiple regression, R^2, 155, 159, 174
Latent variable analysis, 231

M

MANCOVA, *see* Analysis of covariance,
  multivariate
MANOVA, *see* Analysis of variance,
  multivariate
MBESS (R software package),
  221, 222, 232
Mediation, 231
Misconceptions about power, 8–9
Mixed randomized design, *see* Analysis
  of variance, mixed model
Moderated regression, 185; *see also*
  Moderated regression,
  comparing
  correlations/simple slopes;
  Moderated regression,
  regression analogy
  additional resources, 232
  comparing correlations/simple
    slopes, 188–189, 193–196
  determining effect size, 189–192
  effect size conversion d to ρ, 189
  factors affecting power, 186
  interaction effects, size, 187
  regression analogy, 188, 190–192,
    193, 194
  SPSS syntax, 190–191, 193–194, 195–196
Moderated regression, comparing
  correlations/simple slopes,
  188–189, 192–196
  additional resources, 232
  calculations, 195
  formulae, 188
  SPSS syntax, 195–196
Moderated regression, regression
  analogy, 188
  calculations, 192
  formulae, 189
  SPSS syntax, 190–191, 193–194
Multicollinearity, 151, 153, 154, 164
Multicategory chi-square, *see*
  Chi-square
Multiple effects, power for detecting
  analysis of variance, 109–110, 112, 130
  multiple regression, 177–178, 179

Multiple regression, *see* Specific tests
  and statistics
Multiple regression, coefficients,
    see also Multiple effects,
    power for
  calculations, 160
  example, 157–161, 161–166
  factors affecting power, 152–153
  formulae, 154–155
  necessary information, 151
  noncentrality parameter (δ), 160
  power calculation with
    noncentrality parameter
    (δ), 160
  SPSS syntax, 159, 161, 165–166
Multiple regression, comparing
    dependent coefficients, 166
  calculations, 167
  example, 167–169
  factors affecting power, 153
  formulae, 156–157
  necessary information, 151
  noncentrality parameter (δ), 157
  power calculation with
    noncentrality parameter, 167
  SPSS syntax, 168
Multiple regression, comparing
    independent coefficients, 169
  calculations, 170, 171
  example, 169–172
  factors affecting power, 153
  formulae, 155–156
  necessary information, 151
  noncentrality parameter (δ), 156
  power calculation with
    noncentrality parameter
    (δ), 171
  SPSS syntax (comparing
    coefficients), 173–174
  SPSS syntax (shortcut,
    preliminary calculations),
    170, 171, 172
Multiple regression, comparing
    independent R^2s, 172
  calculations, 174
  example, 172–177
  factors affecting power, 153
  formulae, 157
  necessary information, 151
  noncentrality parameter (δ), 157

power calculation with noncentrality parameter, 174–175

SPSS syntax (comparing R^2), 176–177

SPSS syntax (shortcut, preliminary calculations), 174, 175

Multiple regression, R^2 change
effect size (f^2), 154
example, 161–166
factors affecting power, 152–153
formulae, 153–155
necessary information, 151
noncentrality parameter (λ), 155
SPSS syntax, 162, 163–164

Multiple regression, R^2 model
calculations, 158–159
effect size (f^2), 154
example, 157–161
factors affecting power, 152–153
formulae, 153–155
necessary information, 151
noncentrality parameter (λ), 155
power calculation with noncentrality parameter, 159
SPSS syntax, 159–160

Multiple regression, three predictors
effect size (f^2), 154
example, 161–166
factors affecting power, 152–153
formulae, 153–155
necessary information, 151
noncentrality parameter (δ), 160
noncentrality parameter (λ), 155
SPSS syntax (coefficients), 165–166
SPSS syntax (R^2 change), 163–164
SPSS syntax (shortcut, preliminary calculations), 162

Multiple regression, two predictors
calculations, 158–159, 160
effect size (f^2), 154
example, 157–161
factors affecting power, 152–153
formulae, 153–155
necessary information, 151
noncentrality parameter (δ), 160
noncentrality parameter (λ), 155
power calculation with noncentrality parameter (δ), 160

power calculation with noncentrality parameter (λ), 159

SPSS syntax, 159–160, 161

N

Noncentrality parameter; *see also* Delta (δ); Lambda (λ)
overview, 6–8
analysis of variance, between subjects factorial, power calculation for, 105
analysis of variance, contrasts/ multiple comparisons, power calculation for, 93–94
analysis of variance, one factor between subjects, 92
chi-square, 22–23
comparing dependent correlations with no variables in common, power calculation for, 77
comparing dependent regression coefficients, power calculation for, 167
comparing independent regression coefficients, power calculation for, 171
comparing independent R^2, power calculation for, 174–175
multiple regression, coefficient, power calculation for, 160
multiple regression, R^2, power calculation for, 159, 160
zero-order correlation, power calculation for, 69

nQuery (software), 232, 233

Null hypothesis significance testing (NHST)
errors, 1–2
overview, 1

O

Observed power, 13–15

One-way classification, *see* Chi-square

P

PASS (software), 232, 233
Patterns of effects/correlations in multivariate analysis of variance, 140–142
direction of correlations, 144–147
reverse coding, 148–150
PiFace (software), 230, 232–233
Post hoc power, 13–15
Power and Precision (software), 232–234
Power calculations; *see also* SPSS syntax; Non-centrality parameter
approximate with *z*, 23–24, 41, 92
exact with *z*, 73, 81
overview of approaches, xi–xii
value of approximate, xi
Power, desired level, 15–16
Power in published literature, 9–10
Precision analysis, 204–205; *see also* Specific confidence intervals
additional resources, 232
certainty, 222–223
Cohen's *d*, 210–213
correlation (ρ), 213–214, 215–216
determining level of precision, 210
differences between means, 206–209
necessary information, 205
power vs. precision, 207
R^2 *change*, 214, 216, 217, 218
R^2 *model*, 216, 219
sample size impact, 221–222
"supporting" null hypotheses, 216, 218, 219–221
Probability of replication (p_{rep}), 228
additional resources, 232
compared to traditional *p*, 228
example, 229–230
formulae, 229
realization variance, 228
Proportions, single sample
arcsine transformation, 29
calculations, 30–31
effect size (*h*), 29
example, 30–32
factors affecting power, 18

formulae, 29–30
necessary information, 17–18
SPSS syntax, 31–32
Proportions, comparing independent
arcsine transformation, 29
calculations, 32–33
effect size (*h*) 29
example, 32–35
factors affecting power, 18
formulae, 29–30
necessary information, 17–18
SPSS syntax, 34–35

R

R (software), 221, 231
Regression interactions, *see* Moderated regression
Reliability, 175, 177, 198–200; *see also* Attenuation of effect size
Repeated measures, *see* Analysis of variance, one factor within subjects; Analysis of variance, two factor within subjects
Reporting power analyses, 225
chi-square, 226
within subjects analysis of variance, 226
Resampling, 62
Robust data analysis, 62

S

SamplePower (software), 232–234
Sample size-power tradeoff, 15–16
"Shirt size" effects, 11, 41
Software (free) resources, 230
Sphericity, 114; *see also* Analysis of variance, one-factor within subjects
choice of univariate or multivariate approach, 130
comparison of univariate and multivariate approaches, 122–124
epsilon adjustment, 114, 116, 117, 118
example one factor within subjects, 119–121

Greenhouse-Geisser adjustment, 114, 116
Huynh-Feldt adjustment, 114, 116
SPSS syntax sphericity adjusted tests, 120–121
Split plot design, *see* Analysis of variance, mixed model
SPSS syntax power calculations, xii–xiii; *see also* Specific tests
analysis of covariance, 183, 184, 186
analysis of variance, contrasts/ multiple comparisons, 95, 98, 99, 100
analysis of variance, factorial, 105–107
analysis of variance, mixed model, three factors, 139
analysis of variance, mixed model, trends, 138
analysis of variance, mixed model, two factors, 136
analysis of variance, multivariate, 114–145
analysis of variance, one factor between subjects, 94–97
analysis of variance, one factor within subjects (multivariate tests), 117–119
analysis of variance, one factor within subjects (univariate tests), 117–119
analysis of variance, simple effects, 107–108
analysis of variance, two factor within subjects, 129
analysis of variance, within subjects sphericity adjustment, 120–121, 114
chi-square, goodness of fit, 28
chi-square, test of independence, 24–28
confidence interval, correlation (ρ), precision, 215–216
confidence interval, *d*, precision, 212–213
confidence interval, difference between means, precision, 208–209
confidence interval, R^2 *change*, precision, 217–218

confidence interval, R^2 *model*, precision, 219
correlation, comparing two dependent, no variables in common, 82–84
correlation, comparing two dependent, one variable in common, 77–79
correlation, comparing two independent, 73–75
correlation, zero-order, 70–71
moderated regression, comparing correlations/simple slopes, 195–196
moderated regression, regression analogy, 190–191, 193–194
multiple regression, coefficients, 159, 161, 165–166
multiple regression, comparing dependent coefficients, 168
multiple regression, comparing independent coefficients, 173–174
multiple regression, comparing independent R^2s, 176–177
multiple regression, R^2 *change*, 162, 163–164
multiple regression, R^2 *model*, 159–160
multiple regression, shortcuts, 162, 170, 171, 172, 174, 175
multiple regression, three predictors, 162
multiple regression, two predictors, 159–160, 161
proportions, comparing independent, 34–35
proportions, single sample, 31–32
"supporting" null hypothesis, 220
t-test, independent samples, 46–49
t-test, paired samples, 50–55
SPSS warnings and errors, 234
blank contrast output, 234–235
linear dependency, 234
order of entry/order of reporting inconsistency, 235, 236
Structural equations modeling, 231
Supporting null hypothesis, precision analysis, 216, 218, 219–221

T

Transformations
    arcsine, 29
    assumption violations, addressing,
        56–58
    Fisher *r* to *z*, 72–74, 84
    Fisher *z* to *r*, 213
Trend analysis
    analysis of variance, mixed model,
        135–136, 138
    analysis of variance, one factor
        within subjects, 124–126
t-test, correlated mean, *see t*-test, paired
    samples
t-test, independent samples; *see also*
        Unequal sample sizes;
        Unequal variances
    calculations, 43–45
    designing to address violation of
        assumptions, 59–64
    effect size (*d*), 40
    example, 42–49
    factors affecting power, 38–39
    formulae, 39–40
    necessary information, 37–38
    noncentrality parameter (δ), 40
    one vs. two tailed tests, 38–39
    power calculations, approximate, 41
    power calculation with
        noncentrality parameter, 41
    SPSS syntax, 46–49
    unequal sample sizes, 51, 58–59,
        60–64
    unequal variances, 51, 56–58, 59–64

unequal variances/sample size
        example, 59–64
    violation of assumptions, 51, 56–64
t-test, paired samples, 37–41, 47–55
    calculation, 50
    correlation between measures, 38
    effect size (*d*), 40
    example, 47–55
    factors affecting power, 38–39
    formulae, 40
    necessary information, 37–38
    noncentrality parameter (δ), 40
    one vs. two tailed tests, 38–39
    power calculations, approximate, 41
    power calculation with
        noncentrality parameter, 41
    SPSS syntax, 50–55
    Type I error inflation, *see* Alpha
        error inflation adjustment

U

Underpowered studies 9–10
Unequal sample sizes
    analysis of variance, 89
    independent samples *t*, 59–64
    harmonic *n*, 29–30, 32–33, 58–59,
        62, 89
    independent proportions, 29–30, 32–33
    syntax for *t*, 63–64
Unequal variances
    degrees of freedom adjustment, 56
    independent samples *t*, 59–64
    impact on power, 56–58
    SPSS syntax, 63–64*